THE
RISE
OF
CHINA

THE RISE OF CHINA

How Economic Reform is Creating a New Superpower

William H. Overholt

W. W. Norton & Company / New York London

First Edition

The text of this book is composed in 10.5/14 Sabon,
with the display set in Copperplate.
Composition and manufacturing by the Haddon Craftsmen, Inc.
Book design by Chris Welch.

ISBN 0-393-03533-6

W. W. Norton & Company, Inc.
500 Fifth Avenue, New York, N.Y. 10110
W. W. Norton & Company Ltd.
10 Coptic Street, London WC1A 1PU

1 2 3 4 5 6 7 8 9 0

To William Ascher

CONTENTS

7

||||||||||||||||||||||||||||||||||||||||||||||||

ACKNOWLEDGMENTS

During the writing of this book I have received invaluable guidance and criticism from Paul Kreisberg, Robert Scalapino, Frances Lai, Joyce Kallgren, Nicholas Lardy, Paul Bracken, Christopher Gray, Robert Theleen, William Asher, Ezra Vogel, Gage McAfee, Vincent Lo, Zhiling Lin, and many others. Although I have tried to be diligent in footnoting my most substantial intellectual debts, I cannot begin fully to acknowledge all of them. In fact, if there is anyone in Hong Kong whose ideas I have not stolen or abused in some way, I apologize for the oversight. While I have tried to tell the reader my sources, there are occasions on which doing so would have caused embarrassment. I alone am responsible for whatever follies remain, and in fact I have particularly great debts to many people who disagree me with me on important issues, including most notably Christine Loh, the appointed member of the Legislative Council who formally introduced the original Patten legislation, and Gage McAfee, for both of whom I have enormous respect.

I have also benefited from participation in the meetings of several organizations, including Lingnan University, the Young Presidents Organization, the American Chamber of Commerce, the Business and Professionals Federation of

Hong Kong, Vision 2047, and various foundations and professional organizations of economists.

Substantial research assistance in the form of data gathering, fact checking, and devil's advocacy has been provided by Vanessa Chin, who worked for me all too briefly during the summer and fall of 1992. In the later stages of the research, Tom Sung also provided valuable help in collecting and checking key data.

I have not attempted to do a complete survey of the literature in the manner of an academic dissertation, so there will be cases where others have made similar points that I have not noticed. Nicholas Lardy has pionted out to me that Susan Shirk and Sung Yun-Wing have done work on Deng Xiaoping's coalition building and Hong Kong's connection with China analogous to ideas. There may well be other such cases.

The book draws upon the following previously published articles: *Global Political Assessment,* various issues. "Deng, Not Gorbachev, May Get the Laurels," *International Herald Tribune,* June 27, 1990. This is in turn an abridged version of a piece I did for Bankers Trust customers some five months earlier. "Hong Kong and China: The Real Issues," in Frank J. Macchiarola and Robert B Oxnam, eds., *China and East Asia: Implications for American Policy,* proceedings of the Academy of Political Science, 1991. Originally a lecture sponsored by American Chamber of Commerce of Hong Kong, August 30, 1990. "China and MFN," testimony to Asia Pacific Subcommittee of House Foreign Affairs Committee, U.S. House of Representatives, May 29, 1991. "Broken China," *The International Economy* (July–August 1991). "China and British Hong Kong," *Current History* (September 1991). "Les Etats Unis et l'Asie dan les années 90," in Charles Hervouet, ed., *Le Asie-Pacifique: Les Nouveaux Espaces de Cooperation et de Conflit* (Quebec: Presses de l'Université Laval, 1991). "U.S. Economic Policy Toward China," paper for Japanese-

American conference on China sponsored by the Asia Society, New York, December 18–19, 1991. "U.S. Relations with Hong Kong," testimony to Subcommittee on Asian and Pacific Affairs, Foreign Relations Committee, U.S. Senate, on April 2, 1992, regarding S.1731, a bill to establish policy of the United States with respect to Hong Kong after July 1, 1997. And "Tiananmen Square and Objective Possibilities for Hong Kong," *Journal of Politics,* vol. 53, no. 2 (May 1991).

THIS BOOK IS not intended to replace or to compete with the standard basic texts. It provides an interpretive overview rather than new factual knowledge. For those who are not specialists in the field and wish to pursue basic knowledge, I would recommend the following. For Chinese history, the works of John K. Fairbank (inter alia, *China: A New History*) or Jonathan Spence's *The Search for Modern China.* The work of Doak Barnett on the period immediately after the revolution has not been surpassed. On Chinese society, nothing compares with the depth of Ezra Vogel, *One Step Ahead in China: Guangdong Under Reform.* For a more personalized perspective, see Jung Chang, *Wild Swans: Three Daughters of China.* One contemporary Chinese politics, the most interesting work is in articles by Kenneth Lieberthal and Michel Oksenberg. On U.S. relations with China, see Harry Harding, *A Fragile Relationship: The United States and China Since 1972.* For biographies of major leaders, see Harrison E. Salisbury, *The New Emperors: China in the Era of Mao and Deng.* The basic work on modern Hong Kong has yet to be written; in many ways the most useful descriptions of the British colony are not scholarly works but rather the popular fiction of James Clavell, namely, *Taipan* (by far the better of the two for insight into how the colony works) and *Noble House.* Chinese economic reform has moved so fast that scholarship on it has tended to be fragmented. The essays of Nicholas

Lardy and Dwight Perkins have proved particularly insightful. The most comprehensive collection of insights appears in the study papers of the Joint Economic Committee of the U.S. Congress, *China's Economic Dilemmas in the 1990s* (April 1991).

LIST OF CHARTS

LIST OF MAPS

|||||||||||||||||||||||||||||||||||||||||||||||||||||||||||||||||||

INTRODUCTION

Ezra F. Vogel

Henry Ford II Professor of the Social Sciences,
Harvard University

In the Soviet Union and Eastern Europe, communism fell with a bang and the economies were opened with a "big bang." But the economies of these countries stagnated and their reentry into the world economy proceeded at a snail's pace. In China, the Communist Party did not fall at all; the economy has been remade not with a "big bang" but step by step. But its economy grew like wildfire and it has been reintegrated into the world economy with a bang. William Overholt offers an explanation for this paradox.

China's success is staggering. The largest other backward economy thus far to grow for several years at a rate close to double digits is South Korea, with a population of 40 million. China's population is roughly thirty times as large. Overholt boldly sets out some possible consequences of a growth of this size.

As he points out, what makes China's success so striking is the contrast to the economic failures of the European countries that abandoned communism. Many Westerners, and perhaps Americans above all, were thrilled by the overthrow of the communist regimes of Eastern Europe and the Soviet Union, and repulsed by the survival of the Chinese communist regime after the Tiananmen incident. Yet many knowledgeable Chinese familiar with the recent developments in Eastern

Europe are thankful that they live in China. They may not like their Communist Party, but after having seen the results of chaos in their nation over the last two hundred years they are prepared to accept a regime that provides order and allows them to escape poverty and begin to enjoy the benefits of modern industry. Their hope for greater democracy lies in the evolution of totalitarian governments that have undergone economic growth. They have observed the evolution experienced by the South Koreans, but they have been most profoundly influenced by the evolution experienced by their brethren in Taiwan.

In Europe, people overthrew communist parties that had failed to make the transition and provide them with a better style of life. In China and Vietnam, communist parties moved more quickly and boldly to bring about economic reforms that provided economic improvement for their peoples. Their communist parties have therefore been able to survive the changes, by introducing an East Asian pattern of development that Overholt traces so clearly.

An integral part of China's success has come through Hong Kong and been mediated by the development of new markets, markets for capital as well as for agricultural and industrial commodities. These developments Overholt also lays out, with a fresh and vigorous voice. China's success now raises new problems for the world. So much of China's GNP is used up in internal consumption that it does not yet have an economic role in the world comparable to the size of its GNP. But people in China are beginning to think about the political consequences of their new growth and also of what they can do to modernize their military forces with inexpensive purchases from the former Soviet Union.

Other nations know that China's technology is not yet up to world standards, that its infrastructure is far behind modern countries, that its bureaucracy is bloated, with a low degree of efficiency, and that many officials are using their positions for private gain. And yet other countries cannot discount China's rising power. They, too, are beginning to ponder the impact of a stronger China. East Asia remains the most rapidly growing part of the world, and therefore East Asia's role in world affairs is bound to grow larger. And within East Asia, greater China (including Hong Kong and Taiwan) is increasing its influence. Overholt helps us think through these consequences.

WILLIAM OVERHOLT IS uniquely prepared to tell this story. He has the academic training, in social science theory, economics, and a Ph.D. from Yale in political science. For the decade of the 1970s he worked at the Hudson Institute with Herman Kahn, one of the great think tank builders, who looked at the truths from economics, technology, and culture, and dared to face the consequences without regard to how much they challenged conventional thinking. Overholt found a special niche as a strategic planner. Here he worked with Kahn to improve their methods for strategic planning and long-range forecasting. They did not hesitate to attack the big political and psychological issues that could not be quantified. While working with Herman Kahn, Overholt also worked at Columbia University with Professor Zbigniew Brzezinski, later President Carter's national security adviser; together they founded a magazine, *Global Political Assessment.*

Overholt joined Bankers Trust in 1980 to head the global political risk unit, and in 1985 Bankers Trust sent him to Hong Kong, which has been his home base while he travels the world. There has been thinking not only about country risks but corporate strategies. This has given him an excellent vantage point to observe China and its neighbors.

In his private role, Overholt is a political activist for issues of human rights and arms control. He worked with South Koreans to ensure that Kim Dae Jung was not executed and he worked for Cory Aquino when she was fighting for her political existence against Ferdinand Marcos. He has been active in the fighting against the military dictatorship in Burma. But in this study of China, one sees not Overholt as political fighter but Overholt as cool financial and political analyst. He keeps up the Herman Kahn tradition of laying out the facts and thinking the big thoughts. The result is a bold but nuanced pathbreaking study that cracks a lot of the eggs of conventional thinking.

One hopes that many leaders around the world will ponder the significance of the facts. As an American, I can only hope that the Clinton administration will be able to get enough control over America's domestic economy that it can respond to China's new rise. As the sole global military power, the United States must remain engaged in the most dynamic part of the world. In particular, the Clinton administration needs to work with China, Japan, and their neighbors to avoid an arms race and lay the foundations for a regional order that links the region to the world economy and provides Asia a place of honor in the rapidly changing global political structure. We are all indebted to Overholt for laying the issues out so clearly and forcefully.

THE
RISE
OF
CHINA

I

||||||||||||||||||||||||||||||||||||||||

THE RISE
OF CHINA'S
ECONOMY

*Suddenly, with a singlemindedness unprecedented since 1949,
cadres from different party and government departments as well
as ideological schools have been giving their all to making a fast
buck.*

*The Chinese press has reported that 200,000 Party members
have gone into business and become "red capitalists." Army
units all over China, including munitions factories, ports, airports and transportation teams, are signing joint-venture contracts with civilian companies and foreign corporations.*

*Last week, the Party School of Hubei Province, supposedly a
high temple for the purest Marxism, raised eyebrows when it ini-
tialled a co-production agreement with a Hongkong firm to manufacture bamboo art objects. . . .*

*Hongkong businessmen say the offspring of Party elders are
forsaking politics for the safer—and infinitely more lucrative—
arena of trading their guanxi or connections for big bucks. . . .*

*At the same time, a large number of the affiliates of the ultra-
liberal think tanks of ousted part chief Zhao Ziyang have become
taipans in the economic zones and open cities.*

*Heeding the advice of dissident leaders such as astrophysicist
Fang Lizhi, the democracy advocates are apparently building up
an economic base from which to launch another movement several years later.*

Equally significant, ordinary Chinese have caught the get-rich-quick bug. They are living up to the ideal ascribed to Zhao: quanmin jieshang, or everybody in the nation running businesses.

—WILLY WO-LAP LAM, "DENG TAPS A RICH VEIN OF SOCIALIST THOUGHT,"
SOUTH CHINA MORNING POST, AUGUST 5, 1992

F or much of the past two thousand years, China has stood at the pinnacle of world technology and income. Indeed, so strong was China that its people became accustomed to thinking of their country as the Middle Kingdom, the center around which all else revolved. But for the past two centuries the Chinese have experienced weakness abroad and fragmentation at home, and people have lived in unspeakable poverty.

As late as the early 1980s, more than 100 million Chinese had to subsist on an annual income that was less than the cost of a good dinner in New York. Even today about 40 million people live in caves in China's northeast, and the people in 520 of China's 1,903 counties have annual incomes below $35 per person. Such desperate circumstances gave rise to the phenomenon of the one-pants family in many areas of rural China. The one-pants family, so widespread in China it was studied by Chinese sociologists—but never for publication in the West—is a family possessing only enough clothing for one member. Characteristically, the man gets to wear the pants for work in the fields during the day while the woman hides her shame, then the woman gets to wear them in the evening. In another variation, villagers too poor to afford any clothing blackened themselves with charcoal to create the illusion of black clothing.[1]

[1]I was introduced to the concept of the one-pants family by a Chinese professor of sociology, Zhiling Lin, now living in the United States, who said that this phenomenon had been the subject of scholarly studies. The teacher

All this is becoming a thing of the past. The Chinese economic takeoff that began with the implementation of Deng Xiaoping's 1979 economic reform plan is eliminating such poverty at a rate previously limited to South Korea, Taiwan, Hong Kong, and Singapore. In fact, the Chinese phenomenon appears to be unique in history. During the 1980s, China was the world's fastest-growing economy. After a brief late-1980s period of disinflation, it rebounded in 1992 to become once again the world's fastest-growing economy. Previously, this kind of performance appeared to be confined to relatively small countries (Hong Kong with 6 million people, Singapore 2 million, Taiwan 20 million) or to extremely homogeneous countries (South Korea and Japan) or to underpopulated countries experiencing a temporary commodity boom (Saudi Arabia in the 1970s). Before China accomplished this feat, such rapid growth would have been thought impossible for a nation comprising one fifth of the world's population, with an exceedingly diverse economy.

China's economic boom is reshaping the economics of Asia—stimulating, for instance, a corresponding boom for Hong Kong and a rapidly successful adjustment for Taiwan in

---

of a secretary in my office in Hong Kong was aware of a village where charcoal blackening substituted for clothing. Harrison Salisbury, in his book *The New Emperors* (Boston: Little, Brown, 1992) tells of a village in Gruizhou: "A family of ten owned only one pair of pants and wore them serially. Only when the fog was thick did the women emerge from their huts . . ." Lena Sun, Washington correspondent of the *Washington Post,* told me on November 10, 1992, that a colleague had visited villages in Gansu province where people had no clothes at all. On income below $35, see "Economic Clout Overestimated, Official Says," *China Daily,* July 8, 1993, p. 1. On 1985 income and peasant possessions, see He Buochan, *China on the Edge* (Guizhou: People's Press, 1988), p. 68. On families without pants in Ahnei, Jingzhai County, see Chen Yizhi, *China: Ten Years Reform and Democratic Movement* (Taipei: Lainjing Press, 1990).

1991–92 when both the United States and Japan were suffering severe slowdowns. The success and emerging high productivity of coastal China will create severe challenges for countries like Indonesia, the Philippines, and Sri Lanka, which now must either accelerate their own reform programs or lose trade and foreign investment to the more competitive Chinese.

The boom will have other consequences. It is already transforming the politics of China and promises to reshape the politics of Asia and perhaps the world. Economic success has given reformers the initiative and put both bureaucratic and radical factions on the defensive. It has given the coastal areas the initiative over the interior (including Beijing) and has put economics above politics in a country whose central post-revolutionary slogan was "Politics in Command." It has loosened central control over the provinces, the state enterprises, the locus and sectoral thrust of economic activity, and above all over the individual. It has exposed so much of China to the outside world that a cosmopolitan culture has developed along the coast, in many of the major cities, and in virtually all universities and research centers; in these areas, Marxism is dead. It has created striking differences of outlook among at least four generations (the octogenarian leadership, the generation in its mid-sixties, the fifty-year-olds, and those under forty-five), in which each successive generation is determined to press a faster pace of reform.

Internationally, China has muted all its conflicts and geopolitical ambitions in order to pursue economic success. It has ceased to promote revolution abroad, made peace with all its neighbors, reduced military spending to very low levels, contracted its military by nearly a million soldiers, opened trade with virtually all nations (including ideological opponents such as Taiwan), put pressure on North Korea to maintain peace on the Korean peninsula, and established formal or informal diplomatic ties with every one of its old enemies, including South Korea.

ECONOMIC PERFORMANCE

All of these policies have served the goal of economic growth. That goal has now been achieved. After reform began, China's growth climbed rapidly to a 10 percent annual rate.[2] Efforts in 1988 and 1989 to deal with unacceptably high inflation then caused a brief decline to 4 percent, a level all Western countries would still regard as a boom, but re-accelerated to 7 percent in 1991 (the level that in recent years has

[2]Anyone familiar with the Soviet situation, where production and growth numbers turned out to greatly overstate the size of the economy, or with China during the Cultural Revolution, where both local and central government units routinely falsified statistics, must ask whether these growth numbers are accurate. Inevitably in a poor country there are substantial statistical errors just because the statistical collection system has weaknesses; in addition, during the shift to a market economy, certain things get counted that weren't counted properly before, and on the other side the opportunities for a gray market, undercounted economy multiply. Still, there are several reasons for substantial confidence in the rough magnitude of the numbers. First, many of China's numbers can be checked, and those that are checkable turn out to be fundamentally honest, despite statistical uncertainties that are sometimes very substantial, such as the different trade numbers produced by Customs and by MOFERT. Second, as we shall see later, China's GNP seems to be drastically understated rather than overstated. Third, we can now travel widely in China, and the transformations of Chinese society are visible and proportionate to what the statistics indicate. I have personally watched Taiwan, Singapore, and South Korea during the period when they grew at these rates, and have observed coastal China for over a decade, and the evidence of the eyes matches the evidence of the statistics.

characterized the Asian miracle economies as a group), and to
12.8 percent in 1992. In 1992, Beijing set 8–9 percent annual
growth as the goal for the next five years; it remains to be seen
whether this is sustainable without unacceptable inflation,
but China's capacity for growth above 7 percent seems solidly
established.

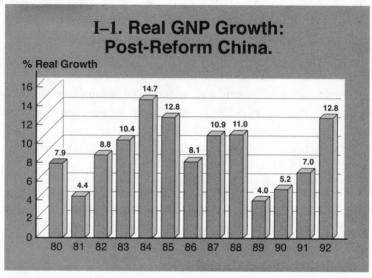

SOURCE: State Statistical Bureau.

The country's economic success has not been confined to
raw economic growth. By 1992, foreign trade had risen to
$166 billion, signifying that China had moved from autarky
to becoming one of the world's major trading powers. Exports climbed from a mere $14.8 billion in 1979 to $85 billion
in 1992.[3] Not only did exports rise, but they also became more

[3]The 1991 figure is from IMF, *Directions of Trade Statistics* (June 1992);
the 1979 figure was provided by Bank of China.

sophisticated; in 1985, manufactured goods comprised only half of China's exports, whereas by 1991 they comprised more than three quarters of all exports.[4] While accomplishing this export growth, China has recently achieved huge trade surpluses.

In its first dozen years of reform China attracted more than $20 billion[5] of foreign investment, including over 30,000 individual ventures, far more than any other Third World country; for comparison, from 1985 to 1989, Brazil, the only Third World country of comparable size, attracted $6.1 billion, while China attracted $9.1 billion.[6] In 1992 alone, foreign investors poured $11.2 billion into China and signed agreements for $57.5 billion of future investments. At the end of 1991, 37,215 foreign-funded enterprises were producing $12.05 billion of exports, or just under 17 percent of the nation's total exports. In 1992 alone, the government approved an additional 47,000 foreign investment projects.[7] Such numbers are well beyond anything that sober economists would have believed possible before they became reality.

Inflation, although periodically a serious problem, peaked at only half the level experienced by South Korea in the late

[4]This point is made by Nicholas Lardy, "Chinese Foreign Trade," *The China Quarterly* 131 (September 1992), p. 697.

[5]Unless otherwise specified, all dollar amounts are in U.S. currency.

[6]IMF, *International Financial Statistics* (June 1992), pp. 120, 154.

[7]The end-1991 figures are from a State Statistical Bureau communiqué of March 18, 1992, republished by BBC Monitoring Service: Far East. Figures on foreign funds actually utilized are generally reliable, although they may miss substantial Taiwanese investment. Significant amounts of contracted future investment fail to materialize because contract negotiations fail. The end-1992 figures are from a widely distributed release by Zhang Zhongji, spokesman of the State Statistical Bureau, on February 18, 1993, reported by Reuters ("China: Reforms Push China Economy to 12.8 Pct 1992"), and in less detail in the *International Herald Tribune,* February 19, 1993, p. 15.

1970s and one hundredth of that seen in Poland and the former Soviet Union.

THE BASIS OF SUCCESS: CHINA VERSUS THE SOVIET UNION

The differences between Chinese and Soviet performance derive from profoundly different economic and political strategies. Much of the West has long believed the myth that China is an impoverished version of the former Soviet Union, which must inexorably follow the latter's failures—because, after all, both were Communist countries. In fact, China has been following a model of development more similar to South Korea than to its formerly Communist bedfellows. Based on analysis of neighboring Asian countries—most notably South Korea, Taiwan, Hong Kong and Singapore—China's strategy has been distinctively Asian. For the Western shopper, there is very straightforward evidence of this. In our major department stores, the shoes, shirts, sweaters, and toys that once said, "Made in Korea," or "Made in Taiwan," now mostly bear labels saying, "Made in China." Virtually none are "Made in Russia."

From the lessons of the neighboring small countries, then, Deng Xiaoping and his colleagues derived superior strategies in four areas: economics, politics, administration, and financial markets.

Economics

Following the examples of the so-called New Industrializing Economies (NIEs), the Chinese gave priority to industries and sectors where limited government investments would produce rapid growth. First, they gave the farms back to the farmers, generating huge increases in productivity, income, and output, with negligible state investment; the state's role was largely limited to issuing a legal ruling and using the existing administrative apparatus to enforce its decisions. Second, China was very encouraging to foreign investment. Although the incentives and rules governing foreign investment have required continual refinement, they were sufficiently generous to attract the huge amounts mentioned above. This produced enormous gains in both output and exports, again at negligible cost to the government. Finally, China gave priority to light and medium industry, where limited initial investment quickly yields a surge of output. Just as Taiwan and Hong Kong had flooded the world market with textiles, garments, shoes, toys, and consumer electronics in the 1960s and 1970s, China quickly became a global force in these same products for the 1980s and 1990s. As in the smaller Asian economic takeoffs, these policies caused an explosion of growth, consumer goods production, personal income, exports, and foreign exchange earnings.

The Soviet Union, by constrast, neglected agriculture, was so ambivalent about foreign investment that it attracted very little, and devoted excessive attention to heavy industry. Mikhail Gorbachev's early programs emphasized massive equipment imports, building more machines, intensified use of machine tools, organization of industry under superministries, improvement of the petroleum industry, and reorganization of the automobile and high-technology sectors. All of these are capital-intensive industries. The later debate over privatization also focused an excessive attention on industries with huge capital requirements and long lead times, rather than on areas of low cost and quick payoff.[8] Such priorities pervade

[8]For a summary of Soviet efforts at reform, see Marshall I. Goldman, *What Went Wrong with Perestroika* (New York & London: W.W. Norton,

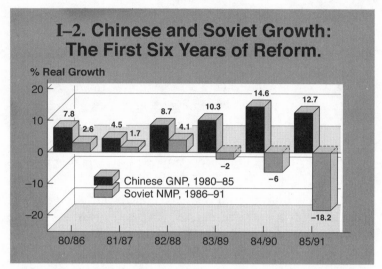

I–2. Chinese and Soviet Growth: The First Six Years of Reform.

SOURCES: IMF; State Statistical Bureau. Net Material Product is the best Soviet approximation of GNP.

Soviet history and Marxist theory; they reflect obsolete views of development based on Marx's analysis of eighteenth-century Britain and the momentum of Soviet overinvestment in military-related heavy industry. But these failed policies also owe much to a premature emphasis on privatizing giant state enterprises which was encouraged by West European and (especially) American professors.

The result of this Soviet strategy—and of some other East European strategies, including most notably Poland's—was a collapse of production coupled with unbearable inflation. One leading scholar argues that Gorbachev achieved a first in

1991). Goldman's valuable book correctly points to the destructive political vacillation of Gorbachev as he shifted among different strategies of reform. I give more emphasis to the point that all of the different strategies pursued by Gorbachev and Yeltsin would have led to disaster even if they hadn't vacillated, and I believe Goldman's faith in spasmodic reform to be misplaced.

economic history: a depression caused by lack of supply rather than inadequate demand.[9] Many of the East Europeans suffered a similar result.

We should not be surprised. The Chinese Revolution, for all its flaws, had deep roots in peasant society, whereas the Soviet Revolution was just a Leninist coup brutally imposed from above. Guiding and relying upon energy from below came naturally to legatees of Mao Zedong, even though Mao would have despised the private enterprise and foreign presence that accompanied this particular energizing of the masses. Not that all was rosy. When reliance on the initiative of the masses went wrong, it resulted in the bloody egalitarianism of China's brutal land reforms and the Cultural Revolution. Channeled into a drive for wealth, however, it results in the clothing, sheltering, and feeding of tens of millions of the world's poorest people. As a result, China's growth curve after reform resembles an airplane taking off, whereas the former Soviet Union's resembles a submarine descending.

An important consequence of the Chinese strategy is the generation of millions of jobs for the very people who need them most. In this strategy, growth and income are focused on ordinary farmers and ordinary workers. Large numbers of workers produce, for instance, cheap shirts, and they generate the income to buy some of those shirts for themselves. The Soviet or Latin American focus on heavy industry, by contrast, creates a much smaller number of higher paid jobs, while leaving a huge fraction of the labor force unemployed; moreover, products such as steel have less immediate impact on people's lives. China's strategy has created a vast new class of consumers who wear modern clothing and use modern amenities. Market research commissioned by Procter & Gamble indicates that many tens of millions of Chinese can now

[9]See Goldman, *What Went Wrong with Perestroika*, p. 28.

afford five dollars to buy a bottle of Rejoice Shampoo. China's Guangdong Province has become second only to the United States as a market for Procter & Gamble's shampoos, and Avon has more than 18,000 Avon ladies successfully selling Western-style cosmetics door-to-door in that province. Motorola, which rates China the best place in the world to manufacture electronic equipment, expects China to become its number-two market in the world for second-generation cordless phones.[10] All of this has revolutionized a society where only a decade ago a billion people dressed in the same frowsy blue outfits and seemed all to have had their hair cut by the same lawn mower.

Politics

Reform is a domestic political process. Great reformers like Turkey's Kemal Ataturk divide reform into manageable phases and in each phase build a politically overwhelming coalition of groups who see reform as serving their interests. Unsuccessful modernizers like the Shah of Iran antagonize so many groups simultaneously that they become overwhelmed by the reaction. Deng Xiaoping was a model reformer in this respect, whereas Mikhail Gorbachev, though a great figure of the twentieth century, was a caricature of failure. It is noteworthy that many Western critics have praised Gorbachev's strategy of doing everything at once, and attacked Deng Xiaoping's strategy of carefully sequencing reforms, whereas

[10]The data on Avon and Procter & Gamble come from remarks made by executives of their companies in Hong Kong. On Motorola's market projections, cf. "China Set to Become CT2 Leader," *South China Morning Post*, February 23, 1993, p. 1 of Technology Post section. The rating of China as a manufacturing center comes from comments by the company's senior economists to a group from the National Association of Business Economists.

historically those reformers—from Joseph II of Austria to
Kuang Hsu of China—who have tackled the whole range of
reforms at once have mobilized opposition and seen their aims
defeated.[11]

Deng's initial farm reforms doubled the incomes of China's
farmers, winning the support of over 800 million people—not
a bad start on a coalition.[12] He then facilitated the rise of a
class of small-scale entrepreneurs and stimulated the takeoff
of light and medium industry, thereby gaining the support of
tens of millions more workers and managers. While there
were losers as well as winners among these groups, most were
winners and—the key political fact—the winners were sufficiently numerous to include almost all of the brightest and
most energetic. Deng revolutionized China's financial system,
and loosened somewhat the restraints on travel and exchange
of ideas by China's intellectuals and students, thereby winning
over these smaller but extremely influential groups. (After
Tiananmen Square, Deng decisively lost the support of intellectuals and students for his personal power and for the power
structure generally, but these groups remained enthusiastic
supporters of economic reform.)

Deng Xiaoping even gained the support of a majority of the
military leadership for economic reform, despite severely con-
stricting military budgets in order to finance his rapid economic advancement. Coincidentally, 1979 was both the year

---

[11]Cf. Samuel P. Huntington, *Political Order in Changing Societies* (New
Haven: Yale University Press, 1968), Chapter 6, for a comparative analysis
of the reform strategies of Ataturk (esp. p. 348) and others. This study has
been a recognized classic, studied by all serious students of political development, for a full generation (it is even a core text in my daughter's high school
class in Hong Kong), but the lessons seem never to be applied to contemporary situations.

[12]See Chapter II for a chart showing the income rises of various groups,
including farmers.

when implementation of reform began and the year when China clashed with Vietnam over the latter's involvement in Cambodia. While China achieved its objectives, its army was unacceptably bloodied by Vietnam. Deng successfully convinced much of the leadership that the army's only salvation lay in access to Western weaponry. This required economic success to finance the trade, accommodation with Western countries to obtain access to weapons, and drastic cuts in the army's budget and manpower in order to fund domestic economic progress. The Chinese military have not in fact had a pleasant time during the reforms. In addition to large personnel and budget cuts, they fell far behind the rest of society in income gains, and they have had to go into business to support themselves; but on balance they have been among the strongest supporters of reform.

Likewise, most government and Communist Party leaders became advocates of reform. After the tragedies of the Great Leap Forward (1958–61) and the Cultural Revolution (1966–76), the radical ideologues were completely discredited and the top Party leaders knew that they had to try something drastically different in order to save both the country and themselves. Chen Yun, the most devoted to central planning of all the octogenarians, actually led the first phase of reform and never advocated reversing the extraordinary successes of his tenure in the early 1980s. Li Peng, a younger devotee of central planning, eventually found himself giving speeches about the virtues of socialist stock markets. Some top leaders (often described as liberals) have strong convictions that the market is the right direction for the country. Others (often described as conservatives, but better characterized as the bureaucratic socialists) have discovered that they can only maintain their constituencies by providing economic benefits, and that the only way they can do that is by increasing efficiency through reform. Meanwhile, the families of both groups, and the families of senior army officers, were bought for reform by the special advantages of their situation: they could use socialist connections to get special advantages at making money in the marketplace. Thus, through a combination of idealism, expedience, and corruption, the nation's power elite was enlisted.

By the end of the 1980s, the extreme socialists were mostly confined to the propaganda organs, and in late 1991 and 1992 Deng began a concerted drive to dislodge them even from those posts. Among prospective leaders in younger generations, there are those who would move forward more slowly and those who would move forward more quickly on market-oriented reforms, but none who would move backward or stand still.

In contrast, Gorbachev quickly lost the support of virtually all important social groups for his economic reform. Farmers remained as neglected and alienated as they had been since Lenin's time. Workers faced stern demands for harder work as their real wages collapsed and their vodka was curtailed. The managerial class found its power and perks curtailed while its real income fell and the overall strategy of industrial revival failed. The Communist Party leadership was told to run for election after three generations of alienating the population. The military, which already had access to high technology, lost much of its budget and access to new technological advance just as all the country's major allies were revolting and aligning with the former enemies to the west. All these groups had reasons to despise the consequences of Gorbachev's reforms and to resist further reform. The principal beneficiaries of his reform were intellectuals and foreigners, the former because freedom of speech was so overwhelmingly important to them, the latter because of Gorbachev's historic statesmanship in ending the Cold War peacefully. Other groups were more affected by economic decline and by shame over the collapse of their country.

In politics as well as economics, China was the beneficiary of successful Asian models whereas the USSR and Eastern Europe were the victims of inexperience and ideology—this time Western democratic capitalist ideology, but ideology nonetheless. The notion that one can have all good things (democracy and all forms of economic liberalization) instantly and simultaneously has proved to be an ideological assumption in the strictest sense: a deeply held belief that has no grounding in practical historical experience. In this case, we Westerners are in fact caricaturing our own ideology: capitalist economics makes an explicit set of assumptions, such as a belief in efficient information flows, which clearly depend on institutional structures that have not been present in Eastern Europe and take time to build. Again, the literature on the prerequisites of democracy dates back to the Greeks, and few of those prerequisites are satisfied by countries in the Third World or Eastern Europe. One cannot build a modern glass-and-steel skyscraper just by putting dynamite under an old brick building and exploding it. Trying to create modern market democracies by blowing up old socialist structures is equally futile.[13]

Administration

China has emphasized gradual, carefully sequenced reform. The former Soviet Union and Eastern Europe have been more

[13]For additional aspects of the politics of economic reform, see Susan L. Shirk, *The Political Logic of Economic Reform in China* (Berkeley: University of California Press, 1993). This excellent book became available just as the present book was going to press.

attracted by spasmodic approaches, notably Poland's "big bang": precipitous liberalization of prices and privatization of enterprises. Sudden liberalization risks unacceptable inflation and currency collapse. Overnight privatization creates economic chaos. For instance, the Shatalin Plan, which received widespread Western approbation in the Gorbachev era, envisaged privatizing much of Soviet industry within five hundred days. The same professors who applauded that plan would have recognized instantly that a plan to change the ownership and management of all the major firms in New York or London within less than two years could only result in chaos and collapse.

China's approach argues that price liberalization must be measured so as to avoid panic that results in hyperinflation, currency collapse, and political disillusionment with economic reform. Sudden liberation of prices in the context of the severe shortages of supply typical of socialism leads directly to hyperinflation. Poland's sudden liberation of prices produced inflation rates in excess of 2,000 percent during the last four months of 1989.[14] The former Soviet Union experienced 91 percent inflation in 1991 and rates around 2,000 percent in 1992. Simultaneously it suffered a potentially catastrophic collapse of its currency.[15]

The social consequences of such developments are severe: for instance, in June 1992, Russian farms were collapsing because "new equipment now costs 70 times what it did a year ago, while the price . . . for milk has gone up only sevenfold.

[14]See Lucja Swiatkowski Cannon, "Aftermath of the Economic Shock Therapy in Poland and Its Implications," paper for Washington Strategy Seminar, Brookings Institution, Washington DC, April 29, 1992.

[15]The estimate of 1991 inflation is from the Institute of International Finance's Country Database for the USSR/CIS, dated February 2, 1992. The 1992 numbers are from press reports.

. . . Animal feed on the free market is priced out of reach."[16] Severe inflation frightens away both domestic and foreign investment, thereby destroying the country's potential for economic growth. Inflation itself can be the cause of widespread unnecessary bankruptcies. Such problems throughout Eastern Europe and the former Soviet Union led to broad-scale political disillusionment (in these cases, with democracy) by early 1992. By mid-1993, starvation was occuring in the Biezcady area of Poland and a majority of voters indicated a preference for communism.[17]

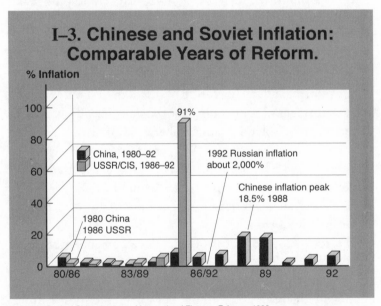

I–3. Chinese and Soviet Inflation: Comparable Years of Reform.

SOURCES: Bank of China; Institute of International Finance, February 1992.

[16]Margaret Shapiro, "In Russia, the End of the Row for Collective Farming," *Washington Post, National Weekly Edition,* June 1–7, 1992, p. 16.

[17]Konstanty Gebert, "Where 'Shock' Too Often Rhymes With 'Crock,' " *Washington Post Weekly,* May 10–16, 1993, p. 25.

China has liberalized prices gradually, and, like other Asian countries such as Indonesia, has been careful to ensure that the price of rice is not allowed to become so volatile as to threaten subsistence-level rural people. During liberalization, China has built up the institutions that will enable it to control inflation, namely, credit controls and bond markets. The result has been rapid growth with a manageable inflation cycle. China's inflation never exceeded 20 percent (less in the countryside where most of the people live, and about double that level in major cities).

China has been particularly cautious about privatization. If one privatizes before price reforms have taken full effect, then many firms are bankrupted not because they were inefficient but because their product prices were set below market levels. For instance, it is not unusual in some socialist countries for prices of a commodity like coal to be set at only 5–10 percent of market levels; having to sell so far below market prices will quickly bankrupt the coal company if it suddenly loses subsidies and has to pay market prices for inputs. This problem is not really solved by "big bang" price liberalization, because an effectively liberalized price system does not just mean instant freeing of prices but also a network of institutions that can receive price signals, analyze trends, and take appropriate action. Such a network takes years to develop. If one privatizes rapidly at a time when inflation is high and growth low, as is typical in the early phases of spasmodic liberalization, then one creates mass unemployment at precisely the time when the economy is least able to absorb extra workers.

Just as important, premature privatization can starve the nation's retirees, because in many of these systems pensions are paid by the enterprises. It can expropriate the rights of long-serving employees, who were entitled to company housing, pensions, medical care, and education under socialism and would have earned a private home under capitalism, but may find themselves suddenly homeless and bereft. Such privatization can cause collapse of a banking system which has been forced for generations to carry loss-making state enterprises by making ever larger "loans" to them.

Finally, an efficient national privatization program requires stock markets, analysts to assess the value of companies, and brokerages to communicate the analysis and to manage stock transactions. Without such a system to assess efficiency, analyze economic trends, communicate the findings widely, and trade efficiently, capitalism cannot function and may produce worse than socialism. Hence China chose to delay privatization until it had successfully liberalized prices, created a national pension system, provided alternative medical and education programs, undertaken major banking reforms, and set up working stock markets. It is characteristic of China's reform that it has moved its currency to near-market levels and opened its stock markets to foreigners in a much earlier phase of reform than either South Korea or Taiwan, but has been much more determined than East Europeans to create the institutions necessary to make markets work properly before undertaking widespread changes of ownership.

No policy has been more criticized in the West than this slowness to privatize. No policy, however, has been more central to China's success than its gradual but steady emplacement of the foundation stones for successful privatization. Spasmodic privatization of major industries followed by collapse of production deters foreign and private investors. In contrast, China has focused on stimulating an explosion of investment and production by foreign and private investors, then using the new production to alleviate its people's poverty and to fund the solution to the problem of the state sector.

The central symbols of China's economic success are the small farmer puttering to market on his new motorbike—the young male worker wearing a shirt with a little crocodile insignia from his own factory, and the female worker trying out her new cosmetics after a day spent assembling Teenage Mutant Ninja Turtles and other pinnacles of Western culture. The central symbol of Russia's economic strategy is a puzzled housewife with a sheaf of vouchers valid for the purchase state enterprises that may constitute a valuable pension or may not be worth the price of a weekend in the countryside.

Financial Markets

China has also created the basic financial markets necessary to manage a market economy. After suffering a severe bout of inflation in 1988–89, the government realized that inflation could be controlled even as prices were being freed if the money supply could be kept under control. Given a reasonably tight fiscal and credit policy, the key to control was a bond market: bonds issued with attractive interest rates could soak up the excess money that threatened to fuel inflation. The government's subsequent encouragement of bond markets, its regulation of them, and its decisive use of high real interest rates proved successful at controlling the 1988–89 inflation. Beijing now has one of the world's more modern computerized bond-trading systems.

The country is also moving quickly to develop its still-diminutive stock markets and futures markets. Stock markets will mobilize savings for productive use and allocate those funds competitively. They will also provide a method for smoothly mixing foreign and local capital, for merging firms, and eventually for privatizing a substantial proportion of state enterprises. They will create a nucleus of trained accountants who can value companies, and will build up a national information network to spread economic and market information efficiently. Futures markets will help to ensure price stability, price predictability, and knowledge of the direction in which the prices of price-controlled commodities should be steered.

In all of this, China's leaders have shown remarkable insight into the institutional requirements of market systems, and have thoughtfully constructed a sequence of steps that build the necessary institutions while avoiding fatal damage to price stability, social welfare, or political support for future economic reform. They have made many mistakes, but so far their analysis has demonstrated the intellectual bankruptcy of the spasmodic strategies favored in the West. Above all, the Chinese experience has shown that a socialist economic system can indeed move to a market system without an intervening social catastrophe—a conclusion that would be very much in doubt if the world had only experienced the Russian and East European approaches.

THE DEGREE OF ECONOMIC REFORM

While China's economic reform has been gradual compared to the "big bang" approach favored in Eastern Europe, it has not been slow or lacking in scope. One indicator of the scope of reform is the fact that by 1992, the vast majority of prices had been liberalized. Throughout the country, by 1990, "only 25.2 per cent of the total agricultural sales and 44.4 per cent of industrial product sales were subject to State-fixed prices, compared with 94 per cent and nearly 100 per cent respectively in 1978." By 1992, "the prices of over 70 percent of consumer goods and production in materials are already determined by the market,"[18] and even many agricultural and industrial input prices (which are sensitive issues) were decontrolled by 1992.

On September 1, 1992, Beijing went further, freeing the prices of all but 111 production materials (out of 737 earlier) and delegating control over 22 of the others to localities.[19] In Guangdong, China's leader in reform and well ahead of the interior provinces, 85–90 percent of prices were at market levels by 1992, and only 32 items remained under price controls.[20] And Beijing has already liberated some of the most sensitive prices. It has freed national sugar prices, and most of the coast has decontrolled grain prices; the political sensitivity of these prices is indicated by the degree to which Washington still manages sugar prices, Tokyo manages rice prices (at eight times world market prices), and France manages many foods. Beijing has adopted a policy that state-controlled prices are gradually adjusted upward until they eventually reach roughly market levels. While price reform still has a long way to go, China has established that such reforms can be successful without causing the catastrophes common in Eastern Europe.

[18]Both of these quotations about price decontrol are from Xie Liangjun, "State to Phase Out Mandatory Prices," *China Daily,* April 23, 1992.

[19]"China Lifts Controls on Prices of 593 Items," *Asian Wall Street Journal,* September 2, 1992, p. 3.

[20]Lee Brundvig (U.S. consul general in Guangzhou), "Guangdong Province: The Economic Explosion," mimeo, 1992, pp. 1, 5. Note that even the United States has a significant number of administered prices, mainly for the purpose of supporting farmers. Sugar, for instance, is supported far above the world price. Most agricultural commodities in Europe have price supports.

A measure of the degree to which socialism has been pushed aside is the share of the economy that goes into the central government coffers. In a truly socialist economy, such as China was at the beginning of reform, the government sequesters a large fraction of gross national product (GNP) for its own purposes. Near the other end of the spectrum, the capitalist, anti-tax U.S. and Hong Kong governments take less than one fifth of GNP. At the time reform was decreed in 1978, Beijing took almost 39 percent. By 1990, the central government's share of the economy was similar to that of Hong Kong.[21]

This number provides both good news and bad. The good

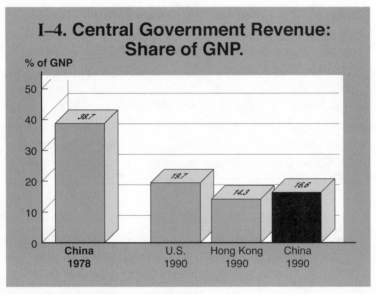

I–4. Central Government Revenue: Share of GNP.

% of GNP

SOURCE: IMF; State Statistical Bureau Yearbook, 1991.

[21]The data in the chart are from China's State Statistical Bureau, *State Statistical Yearbook 1991*, pp. 27, 186, counting all forms of revenue except government borrowing.

news is that a central government committed to reform has been willing to take sweeping measures at great cost to its control over the economy. The bad news is that the measures appear out of control. Had the decline stopped at 20–25 percent of the economy, the good news would have been unalloyed. As it is, the central government delegated so much tax authority to the provinces that the central government is inadequately funded. Moreover, the provinces have so far staved off tax reforms that would revive the central government's revenue base. Thus, Chart I-5 reflects a situation of drastic reform, which creates problems capable of resolution but dangerous if allowed to worsen.

The economy's liberalization is also indicated by the share in the hands of state enterprises. Given that China has done negligible privatization, one would expect this proportion to remain very high. But if one takes the narrowest definition of

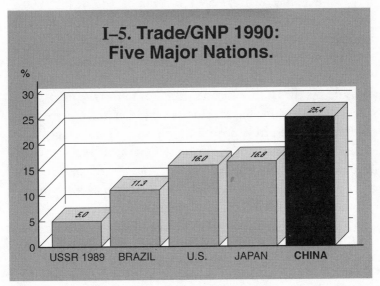

I–5. Trade/GNP 1990:
Five Major Nations.

SOURCE: IMF, IIF Reports.

state enterprises, then China's state enterprises control about one third of the economy, a proportion similar to France or Italy. Taking a broader definition (there are considerable ambiguities because of the many kinds of ownership in China), the state enterprise sector has declined during the reform period from considerably more than half of the total economy to somewhat less than half.

The reasons for this rapid decline are the privatization of most agriculture (which supports the vast majority of the population and therefore sets the tone of society) and the extraordinarily rapid expansion of those enterprises that are owned privately by either Chinese or foreigners. Indeed, foreign enterprises, which already produce a significant share of GNP, are expanding by around 50 percent annually, and independent ownership by 24 percent. While such rates cannot be sustained indefinitely, they have persisted for some time and remained high even in difficult periods (having declined only to 43 percent for foreign-invested enterprises and 24 percent for independent ones in the very bad year of 1989); just a few more years of expansion will make foreign and independent enterprises the predominant force in the economy.

China's foreign trade has also opened wide. At the beginning of reform, China was a largely closed economy, with little trade. As the chart indicates, if one employs the usual measures of GNP, China has far surpassed Japan in the share of its economy devoted to exports and imports. This measure does in fact show that China's previously autarkic economy has become remarkably open; but the degree of openness is greatly exaggerated by the fact that the Chinese have drastically underestimated the size of their own economy.

THE SIZE OF CHINA'S ECONOMY

In fact, the chart showing that Chinese trade is a larger share of its economy than Japan's or America's cannot possibly be accurate. Since the trade figures are known to be reasonably correct (one can compare China's figures on exports to a given country with that country's figures on imports from China, and the figures are generally a reasonable match), there must be something wrong with the GNP figure. Strictly speaking, the measurement of GNP in Third World countries is not comparable with the measurements for developed countries. Whereas the former Soviet Union's economy was vastly overstated by its government, China's GNP is greatly understated by official statistics. If on the contrary one assumes China's per capita GNP to be as high as Thailand's, then the Chinese economy's openness to trade is substantially greater than the former Soviet Union but less than the United States. Many other statistics become reasonable once one recognizes that the Chinese economy is far larger than official statistics portray. Thus the ratio measured in Chart I-5 contains two kinds of good news: first, that China has opened quickly; second, that the economy is probably much larger than has previously been estimated. But we cannot be sure from these statistics what the precise mix of news really is.

The IMF has re-estimated the size of China's economy, ignoring the official estimate of $370 for 1991 and instead pricing all Chinese goods at international prices—so-called Purchasing Power Parity. That study concludes that China's per capita income was $1450 in 1991. An Australian study has shown that Chinese life expectancy of seventy is inconsistent with the average of fifty-six for other countries as poor as China estimates itself to be, and is in fact more comparable to a country like South Korea (average longevity of seventy-one) with a per capita income of $6,000. Food consumption patterns in China are comparable to Taiwan's when its per capita income was about $1,200. The same study showed that the international market value of a few basic materials and goods known to be consumed by the Chinese population adds up to as much as the official statistics show the total size of the economy to be.[22]

While official statistics show similar living standards in China and India, anyone familiar with both countries can confirm that the people of China live so much more comfortably as to be in an entirely different category. Some companies marketing consumer goods in coastal China have noticed that purchasing patterns are typical of people with about four times the income that Chinese statistics claim for these customers. If this is so, a reasonable estimate of per capita GNP would be somewhere about four times what the official statistics show. Based on extensive travel in China and other Pacific Asian countries, I myself have the impression that average Chinese living standards are about as high as Thai living standards, although Thailand's statistics show a per capita income of $1,800. Both have pockets of extreme backwardness and other pockets of extreme progress, but the typical person seems to live at comparable levels. Based on all these data and impressions, Chinese average income is probably $1,500 to $1,800 per year. Such a view of the Chinese economy has become widely accepted by analysts. In fact, this figure is far less than the estimate of $2,500 provided by Lawrence Sum-

---

[22]The Australian computation shows that average food consumption in China is comparable to South Korea. However, people familiar with the rural areas of China know that food is far harder to obtain and more expensive there than anywhere in South Korea. Ezra Vogel says this is true even of Guangdong, which is relatively prosperous. Clearly, China is much poorer than South Korea. In all probability, distribution of food in South Korea is more egalitarian and its use much more efficient.

mers, formerly chief economist of the World Bank.[23]

The divergence between the official statistics on the one hand and the reality of Chinese productive capacity and living standards on the other results from the suppression of prices by the socialist system and from the great disparity between the valuation of various products (rice in China at a fraction of world market prices versus rice in Japan at eight times world market prices) in developing and developed societies. In June 1992, the average urban Chinese paid about $1 per month (7.4 renminbi)[24] for housing; rural people would pay

[23]Albert Keidel, "China's Economic Challenge in the 1980s," paper for conference of the Atlantic Council and the National Committee on U.S.-China Relations, April 7, 1992, estimates that actual GNP is as much as 2.5 times the official figure. Lawrence Summers, ex–chief economist of the World Bank, estimates that China's per capita income on a purchasing power parity basis is one tenth that of the United States; cf. his "The Next Chapter" in *International Economic Insights* (May/June 1992), p. 17. Those who make analogies between China and the former Soviet Union become quite confused on such points, because Soviet statistics systematically overestimated output. Recently a systematic survey of many of these views became available and added invaluable material on longevity and food consumption: Guonan Ma and Ross Garnaut, "How Rich Is China: Evidence from the Food Economy," Working Paper, Economics Department, Research School of Pacific Studies, Australian National University. They conclude that a proper estimate of China's GNP would be two to three times higher than the official statistics. A very systematic survey of different methods of estimating the size of the Chinese economy is the U.S. Central Intelligence Agency's "The Chinese Economy in 1990 and 1991: Uncertain Recovery" (July 1991), Appendix A: Estimates of China's GNP.

[24]The *renminbi,* or people's currency, is China's domestic money, also called *yuan.* The exchange rates of this currency are shown in a chart in Chapter III. China also has a separate currency for foreigners, the FEC or Foreign Exchange Certificate, which has the same official exchange rate as the renminbi but can be used to purchase, in addition to ordinary goods, certain imported luxury goods and hotel and transport services which are not sold for renminbi.

less. While the housing is very sparse, it is certainly worth a large multiple of this for the purpose of any broad international comparison. Again, the average urban Chinese paid about $10 (65.5 RMB) per month for food, $3 (18.1 RMB) for clothes, $2 (11.9 RMB) for household appliances and services), $1 (8 RMB) for education and recreation, 50 cents for medical services, 50 cents for transportation, and $1 for all other goods and services.[25] In addition to the effect of such prices on official statistics, there is a large market economy that eludes the compilers of official data.

These conclusions are vitally important to assessing the nation's future influence over the world economy and world politics. If Summers's calculation is correct, then China's economy would pass the U.S. economy in sheer size within eleven years. If the analogy with Thailand is correct, then it will take a generation. But in global politics, a generation passes quickly. Japan's spectacular rise over the past generation shows that an economic takeoff translates into political respect. These calculations also imply that China's demand and supply for many goods will likely be a major international influence over prices; that China will exert a powerful gravitational force over neighboring economies; and that China's economy will be able to sustain a world-class military in the event of any future conflict.

[25]Cf. Enzio von Pfeil, ed., *Asia Stats: China,* (Smith New Court Far East, June 1992), p. 8.

PROBLEMS OF ECONOMIC REFORM

Any reforming Communist state must face a variety of serious problems. These include potential shortages of foreign exchange as liberalization promotes imports and permits movement of capital out of the country; inflation as prices are freed; budget deficits due to state enterprise losses; unrest stemming from the different impact of reform on different social groups; and reaction by political leaders who are ideologically opposed to reform or fear loss of control. Some of these problems have been important for China while others have proved insignificant. But in each case the leaders' way of managing them reveals essential aspects of their strategy.

Creditworthiness

The process of liberalization creates inherent risks to creditworthiness. Freeing up trade invites a flood of imports, and freeing up capital movements creates the possibility of capital flight. The shock can cause a domino effect of collapsing state industries and banks, which can exhaust a country's financial resources, including its foreign exchange. On the political side, reforms can be both the consequence of political instability and its cause, and under certain conditions political instability can bankrupt a country. The former Soviet Union and much of Eastern Europe have been unable to pay their debts for these reasons.

China on the contrary has proved one of the world's most conservative regimes in managing foreign exchange. For most of their post-1949 history, the leadership simply refused to take on debt. They saw it as potentially endangering the country's independence. Since the reforms of 1979, they have gradually added debt, but in a very conservative way.

China's debt at the end of 1991 was $67 billion, an apparently large number for a Third World country, although Americans accustomed to debts in the hundreds of billions of dollars may be numbed to such figures.[26] Of this, $13.9 billion was trade finance of less than one year's duration: this is just a set of guarantees that traded goods will reach their destination, and it liquidates itself automatically when the goods do arrive. As a result, unless other circumstances lead bankers to believe that the country is in financial trouble, bankers do not count this short-term trade debt when analyzing a country's creditworthiness. That leaves a real debt of $53.1 billion. Against that $53.1 billion, China had $43.7 billion of foreign exchange reserves and $4.5 billion of gold. In short, its net

I–6. Creditworthiness

END–1991		
TOTAL DEBT	**$67.0 billion**	
Short Term	($13.9 billion)	
FX Reserves	($43.7 billion)	
Gold Reserves	($4.5 billion)	
NET DEBT	**$4.9 billion**	
CREDIT MEASURES		**OKAY IF:**
Debt Service Ratio	12%	Less than 20%
Import Cover	9 months	Greater than 3 months
Net Debt/Exports	7.5%	Less than 100%
M/L Term Debt/GNP	14.5%	Less than 100%

SOURCE: IMF, IIF.

[26]This is the highest available estimate of China's debt—the one published by the Institute of International Finance. Most estimates are substantially lower, and if they are correct, the conclusions of this section would be even stronger.

debt was $4.9 billion: a very small number for a fast-growing country of such size.

But the scale of a country's debt—or net debt—is the least sophisticated way to analyze its ability to pay its debts. A more direct measure of ability to pay is how much of its annual export revenues it must pay to service its debt. Most banks consider a country creditworthy if it has not committed more than 20 percent of its export revenues to pay its debt. By this standard (called the debt service ratio), China is extremely creditworthy because it can pay its debt service with only 12.4 percent of its export receipts.

Another key standard asks whether a country has sufficient reserves of foreign exchange and gold to weather a crisis. (The crisis could, for instance, be a downturn in the world economy, economic sanctions, or loss of export markets due to a political crisis at home or abroad.) China's reserves are extraordinarily large. Indeed, only five countries—Taiwan, Japan, Germany, the United States, and Spain—have larger reserves.[27] The general bankers' standard of creditworthiness is that a country's reserves should cover at least three months of average imports; China's cover nine months.

The third and fourth standards have to do with the size of a country's debt and net debt. Bankers get worried if a country's total debt (excluding trade finance) exceeds the size of its

[27]Cf. IMF, *International Financial Statistics* (June 1992), pp. 29, 31. China includes in its reserves both the foreign exchange reserves of People's Bank of China, the central bank, and Bank of China, which was hived off from PBOC to serve as the government's principal international banking arm. International agencies continue to accept China's accounting, both because of the history and because of functions Bank of China performs, but the Chinese are considering the possibility of ceasing to count Bank of China's holdings as official reserves. This would roughly halve the official reserves; interestingly, China's position would still be unusually strong even after such an accounting change.

economy (GNP), or if its net debt exceeds the total size of its export revenues. By these criteria, China's numbers (7.1 percent and 18 percent, respectively) seem diminutive indeed.

The conservative financial practices of Beijing's leadership, like their counterparts in Taiwan, have deep historical roots. China's debt and inflation trauma from the 1930s and 1940s was even worse than Germany's and had an even more intense impact on the mentality of Chinese decision makers; the generation for whom that trauma was a central experience is still in power. Hence the contest has been between liberals who were extremely responsible, moderate reformers who were much more conservative, and firm socialists who want extremely low debt and very high reserves. The radicals—no longer an effective faction—believed that any foreign debt whatsoever was unacceptable. No faction has ever treated foreign debt as anything less than a moral obligation. No foreign financial obligation of central government organs or guarantors has ever been repudiated, although there have been long and expensive court battles in some cases.

Not only do all factions manage the country's finances conservatively, they do so even when under severe political pressure. During and after the Tiananmen Square crisis, Beijing in difficulty never relaxed its anti-inflation austerity program. In most countries, an election is sufficient excuse to abandon sound financial management. In 1989 China, inflation declined and reserves rose throughout the crisis; this is typical of the Asian success stories. (South Korea in 1980, for instance, faced a similar combination of political crisis, high inflation, and determined austerity.) Economic management remained sound throughout the crisis, without the deleterious political games that would have occurred in most countries.

There is a great deal more to be learned by comparing China's situation with the financial disasters of the former Soviet Union and Eastern Europe. The USSR's inability to pay its foreign debts resulted from economic breakdown combined with political fragmentation. In contrast, China severely cut its military budgets and was the first Communist regime other than Hungary to liberalize and at the same time to avoid general political or economic crisis. Nor is fragmentation an issue in China.

China's situation also differs radically from Poland's, where the political opposition deliberately shut down much of the economy as a (successful) political tactic. In China, sabotage of the economy has been an unattractive strategy for opponents of the regime; there is no significant union movement to serve as the foundation for such a strategy. More important, the Polish tactic of economic sabotage derived from a view of the government as a Russian imposition, and for all its political faults the Chinese government is a domestic phenomenon. Finally, the consequences of economic sabotage would be so drastic for those parts of China that are still near subsistence levels, and would provoke such a negative reaction from coastal populations that have just begun to experience prosperity for the first time in generations, that the strategy would be untenable.

Nor is China in the position of Yugoslavia, which could not control cross-border trade and capital flows, and therefore experienced a foreign exchange crisis as a result of financial hemorrhage well before the country's disintegration. China has repeatedly demonstrated the ability to squeeze imports, expand exports, and impose controls on cross-border capital flows. All of these contrasts with Eastern Europe put China in a class by itself compared with other reforming Communist countries.

Inflation

The single most obvious risk of any reforming socialist state is that price decontrol will translate into catastrophic inflation. Indeed, on the surface hyperinflation would seem unavoidable, since most Communist countries have held down the prices of basic goods to a fraction of their market value. In some cases, basic prices have not been adjusted for decades. China has not been immune to this problem, and did not identify the basic mechanism for solution until nearly the end of the first decade of reform. Its initial strategy was simply to liberalize prices very gradually. This is sensible. A typical experience was that of fish in Guangdong. Initially, fish cost 40 fen (i.e., 0.4 renminbi) but was in short supply. After decontrol, the price rose as high as 2 renminbi but there was plenty of fish. The high price stimulated so much production that heavy supply eventually forced the price back down to 80 fen, with a fully adequate supply for everyone. The strategy here was to accept some inflation but to spread it out over a long period of time so that the peaks of the cycles for fish and other commodities do not all coincide.

Still, this strategy proved inadequate. By the late 1980s, price liberalization plus excessive credit (at heavily subsidized interest rates) and other factors had created an excessive demand—and a psychology of inflation. Prices rose 18.6 percent in 1988, 17.8 percent in 1989, and at twice that rate or more in major cities. Anger at this inflation was one prime cause of the Tiananmen Square crisis.

Since that time, the government has sought to borrow Western methods of inflation control. If one can control money supply, the thesis goes, then one can control the overall price level.[28] Inflation requires monetary fuel, and the secret of

[28]China leadership focuses on controlling M2, usually defined as cash plus checking accounts, savings accounts, time deposits, and certificates of

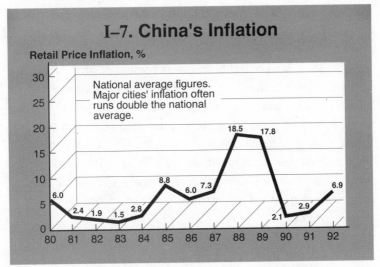

I-7. China's Inflation

Retail Price Inflation, %

National average figures. Major cities' inflation often runs double the national average.

SOURCES: State Statistical Bureau, 1992 Yearbook, p. 207, plus State Statistical Bureau announcements.

defeating it is not to abandon price reform but to take away the fuel. The government therefore moved to curtail its own budget, to control credit growth directly, to change bank loans from grants to Western-style interest-bearing loans, and above all to stimulate the emergence of a bond market. The use of Western-style loans raised the effective price of credit and initiated a system whereby interest rates on loans could be used to control credit growth indirectly. The bond market emerged very quickly and the government used very high interest rates on bonds to soak up the excess money supply. Inflation promptly plummeted.

As any Western central bank governor can testify, having

---

deposit. There are controversies over the connection between M2 and inflation in a socialist economy, and in fact rapid M2 growth in 1991–92 should have led to much higher inflation than actually occurred. But controlling M2 is the most workable standard invented so far, and it seemed to work in 1988–89.

the right theory and the right tools does not mean permanent or easy elimination of inflation. China's tools are still crude, and the country's leaders still lack the experience to know how far they can push their economy without stimulating excessive inflation. In 1992, the central authorities seemed to have lost their ability to control credits issued in the provinces, and money supply grew at a dangerous 30 percent rate, threatening a renewal of serious inflation. So China will continue to have a volatile inflation cycle. It has come through the most dangerous period of price decontrol and now faces more danger from political mismanagement than from the move to market prices.

State Enterprise Deficits

China has been administratively wise to defer widespread privatization. As a result, much of the economy remains under the sway of huge state enterprises—such as steel or coal companies that sometimes have more than 100,000 employees. These are run rather like an American post office, with no incentives for efficiency and almost as little ability to fire lazy or incompetent workers.

One state enterprise is Shanghai Petrochemicals (SPC), a large refinery that plans to seek a listing on the Hong Kong Stock Exchange. SPC makes ethylene, plastic, and synthetic fibers. It employs 60,000 people and has assets worth perhaps $1.3 billion. These numbers make it big but not a behemoth. SPC has been required to provide continued employment for all of its workers regardless of performance. It is responsible for educating the children of SPC workers, so its facilities include a primary school, a high school, and a technical college. It also has responsibility for family medical care, and therefore employs two thousand medical personnel, and it must

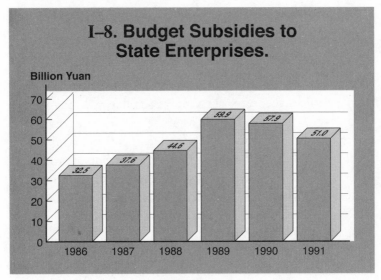

I–8. Budget Subsidies to State Enterprises.

SOURCE: State Statistical Bureau, 1992 Yearbook, p. 192.

pay all of its retirees' pensions. SPC police guard the community, which is largely coterminous with the enterprise, and SPC counselors are supposed to help with marital disputes. A factory Communist Party committee gives mandatory political classes and oversees political correctness. Until recently, SPC had quotas to purchase raw materials at very cheap prices and faced virtually no competition. In the future the company will have to pay market prices for its inputs and will have to compete for its markets. Unlike many state firms, SPC makes a profit and is believed to have sufficient potential to attract Hong Kong investors once it is listed.[29]

The company's social responsibilities make it in some ways

[29]Because of SPC's prospective Hong Kong Stock Exchange listing, the Hong Kong press published many articles on it in early 1993. One of the more comprehensive was "Shanghai Security Blanket," *Window*, February 12, 1993, pp. 50–51.

a Western social reformer's dream, but they also distract the management from the single-minded focus on efficient production that Western competitors have. Social responsibilities hobble the company from firing workers or drastically reorganizing. And they hobble the government from allowing large numbers of such enterprises simply to collapse. Many Americans have vivid, bitter memories of the midwestern towns that effectively collapsed when Japanese competition bankrupted local steel mills or automobile factories. In China, letting such enterprises go under would have much more devastating consequences. Why? Because all the principal social services, which in America are provided by the government, would collapse along with the enterprises.

As Chart I-8 shows, state enterprise deficits are substantial and, more important, they grew fast in the late 1980s. The recent declines should not be taken as a sign that the resolution of the problem is at hand; it isn't. Many of the loss-making enterprises received ever larger "loans" from state-controlled banks, a disguised subsidy that will never be repaid. Moreover, the state enterprise deficits are probably larger than the statistics reveal. It isn't that the government seeks to mislead. Rather, inadequate accounting and control systems, along with an excessive availability of bank credits, enable many state enterprises to hide their losses for long periods.[30] The burden of the deficits takes two forms: first, it enlarges the government budget deficit; second, it gradually accumulates as bad loans on the bank books. China's banks have enough of these "loans" to make the problems of American savings banks appear minor by comparison.

[30]The data for 1990 and 1991 are taken from State Statistical Bureau spokesman Zhang Rongji's presentation on February 28, 1992, published in Reuters News Service for that day. The other figures, and lower numbers for 1990–91, can be found in *State Statistical Bureau Yearbook 1991*, p. 186.

China has been able to defer spasmodic action on the state enterprise deficits because it has one of the world's highest savings rates. Just as Japan can use its high savings rate to mobilize funds to cover a budget deficit that was once proportionately much larger than America's, so China can use its unusual savings rate to cover the state enterprise deficits—for many years, although not forever. Here again the bond market plays a vital role because treasury bonds, bank bonds, and enterprise bonds are the essential mechanism for mobilizing these funds.

Considerable uncertainty and dissension remain over details and timing in handling the state enterprise problem, but the outline of the strategy is becoming clear. Initially, China has done what the United States does when faced with large-scale banking failures: merge failing enterprises with better-

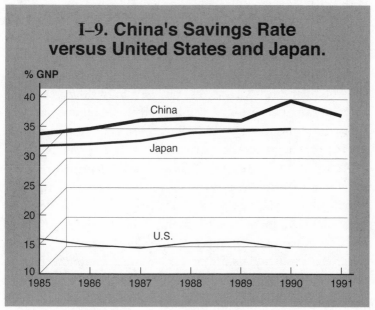

I–9. China's Savings Rate versus United States and Japan.

SOURCES: Bank of China; OECD.

managed ones, giving the latter the responsibility for the debts and employees of the former. The strategy has succeeded in raising the average productivity of state enterprises, but this has only limited the rate of increase of the problem, not solved it. Like the United States, China has shied away from widespread bankruptcy as a solution: a bankruptcy law was passed some years ago, but only about three hundred enterprises have been forced into bankruptcy. Instead, there is a move to force companies which cannot sell their goods to limit further production, coupled with an unannounced cutoff of support for a wide array of money-losing industries. Many of these will be forced by their plight, rather than by explicit government directives, into joint ventures with private enterprises or foreign enterprises. That plight is worsened by their need to compete with rural enterprises, some of which have grown up on a purely market basis from tiny food-processing or brick-making operations into major industrial concerns.

Overwhelming incentives are in place for state enterprises to become partners with foreign firms. Failing state enterprises are being starved of funds so that only a private or foreign partner can rescue them; profit-making ones lose 55 percent of their profits to taxes, but pay only 30 percent and often obtain a generous tax holiday if they go into joint venture with a foreign firm. In such ventures, the trend has been for the private or foreign partner to become dominant.

As an intermediate step, Chinese state enterprises are flocking to transform themselves into stockholding companies. Having done so, they can legally sell off portions of the enterprise to any Chinese "legal person." Initially, the sales tended to be to other state enterprises, but sales to private firms and to Chinese individuals are becoming more common. It is no longer unusual for the public to hold up to 49 percent of a state enterprise, and there are cases where the public holds up to 70 percent. These companies are mostly not listed on the stock exchanges (yet), so for the time being the trades are done privately. This change in the structure of the state sector has not been trumpeted as China's official solution to the privatization problem, and it is unclear how much is planned as opposed to just happenstance. But it is very consistent with the thought of emerging Chinese leaders.

Perhaps the biggest influences on the state enterprises have been indirect. The gradual shift to market prices has forced them to cope with economic forces rather than just lobbying the bureaucracies for a better deal. The opportunity to sell on the open market and to distribute bonuses to employees has created incentives to make profits. Most important of all, the infiltration of their markets and supply chains by town and village enterprises has enhanced competition at all levels. Initially small and devoted almost exclusively to light industry, these enterprises are half-private, half-local government in ownership, but their most important characteristic has little to do with ownership. They are established by entrepreneurial initiative, not by plan, and they have no assured support if they do not meet the test of the marketplace. They are therefore very competitive, and they have seeped into all the nooks and crannies of businesses formerly under the monopoly control of state enterprises, like salt water infiltrating cement and gradually breaking it up.

The result of all these initiatives is that productivity has been rising steadily in the state sector.[31] This does not mean that the problem is solved, or even decisively on the way to solution, or that it can be solved without widespread privatization. But, as in other areas of the economy, China's gradual

[31]Thomas Rawski's work has shown that state enterprise productivity is increasing. Among others, see G. Jefferson, T. Rawski, and Y. Zheng, "Growth, Efficiency and Convergence in China's State and Collective Industry," *Economic Development and Cultural Change* (1992).

approach has created new opportunities and ameliorated old problems. Continued progress of this kind could break the back of the cycle that is fatal to Soviet-style economies: since the government must cover all the losses of state enterprises, and since the government controls most of society's investable funds, the country's resources become channeled ever more exclusively into the least productive firms and sectors—the state enterprises making the worst losses. In China, the government's control of investable funds is declining as private and local sources become more prominent, and it is acting more decisively than in the old Eastern Europe to limit the call of failing enterprises on those resources. Moreover, unlike most socialist economies, China's is not growing just because the government is shoveling more and more resources into industry—a process that has a finite limit. Much of China's growth, even in the state enterprise sector, is due to an increasingly efficient use of capital, labor, and technology.

Virtually all the younger leaders (those in their fifties) believe that China should eventually privatize all small and medium industry. This view is held, among others, by Chen Yuan (now in his late forties), the son of China's most senior socialist opponent of Deng Xiaoping's mid-1980s reforms. Chen Yuan is the most conservative prominent leader of his generation. Such leaders plan to retain effective government control of heavy industry, but many believe that even heavy industry should be partially privatized along the lines of Singapore Airlines, which remains under government control and primary ownership although much of that ownership has been sold to the public.

Beijing has begun restructuring even its largest and most sensitive industries apparently in this direction. The banking system was first divided into a central bank (People's Bank of China), a foreign-oriented bank (Bank of China), and a group of sectorally oriented development banks which do not compete directly with one another but do create a diversity of approaches and ideas. Bank of China spawned a group of highly competitive "sister banks" that compete successfully in the Hong Kong market. Some major non-financial enterprises have acquired capitalist banks and begun to engage in competition with both Western and Chinese banks. And the whole system is being gradually exposed to foreign competition in the special economic zones and elsewhere. This process, though slow and cautious, in some respects is proceeding faster than its counterpart in South Korea did.

While banking competition is still extremely limited, it is beginning to create some competitive instincts. Normally, retail banks are among the world's worst bureaucracies, and so communist banks should be impossible bureaucracies. But now there are exceptions. In June 1992, my family was driving through a grubby, medium-sized city called Shenyang in China's interior, a few hours' drive from the ancient capital of Xian. We were on our way to the airport, having toured Xian and its environs and having nearly exhausted our wallets buying Oriental carpets. At five-fifteen in the evening we decided that we just couldn't live without one more carpet that we had left behind. But we lacked cash, and the carpet dealer only wanted U.S. dollars. Moreover, we had spent more than we had planned, and we were on our way to the deserts of the Silk Road, so I was concerned about running short.

After some quick calculation, we asked our official guide whether there was any way to obtain $3,000 on a few minutes' notice in Shenyang. She said it sounded tough, but we could look for a Bank of China branch and ask. By five-thirty we had located the Shenyang sub-branch of Bank of China, which had theoretically been closed for several hours, but the metal shutters were not down all the way to the ground, so we ducked under and went inside. I explained my problem: I needed $3,000, and I needed it in U.S. dollars cash so I could use it for black market purchases. (Bank of China is of course supposed to be a primary watchdog against the black market.) Could they charge $3,000 to my American Express Gold Card and give me cash?

No, Bank of China had no ties with American Express. But they did take MasterCard. I didn't have a MasterCard but I suggested that my Citibank VISA card should be okay; the bank credit card networks were connected. The manager looked dubious, but he agreed to call Beijing and find out.

He was on the phone for half an hour, after which he hung up with a big smile, unlocked his desk drawer, and counted out thirty hundred-dollar bills. He explained that he would have to charge me the 4 percent service charge ($120) that any establishment pays on a VISA charge. I agreed. The manager allowed me to use his phone to call the gentleman with the black market carpets; he had no transportation, so he rented a Jeep from someone and delivered my carpet to the airport five minutes before the flight boarded.

There was an amusing sequel to all this. When the bill came, Citibank charged me, on top of the $120, a substantial surcharge for a cash advance, a finance charge, and a large fee for changing dollars into renminbi at one rate and renminbi back into dollars at a quite different rate. The overall finance charges on the transaction worked out to an annual rate in excess of 90 percent. When I complained that the entire transaction was in dollars, and no renminbi had been exchanged, Citibank insisted on collecting for the fictitious exchanges but would investigate Bank of China for having charged me 4 percent. I insisted on paying Bank of China, but insisted equally that Citibank had no right to bill me for completely fictitious currency exchanges. After six months of correspondence with Citibank, I gave up and pondered whether perhaps I needed a more customer-oriented institution—perhaps a Chinese bank!

Another sensitive industry is the national airline system. As with the banking system, China's airlines were initially dominated by a single state-owned firm, CAAC, which competed even with Aeroflot in its well-deserved reputation for rickety planes, delays, and surly service. In 1981, one plane got into difficulty when the cabin crew felt hungry and decided to build a fire in the aisle to cook some food. Well into the 1980s, passengers were frequently stranded for many days when a flight was canceled.

In the 1980s, Beijing divided CAAC into six separate regional airlines. Like the sectoral banks, these entities competed only at the margin, and permitted the formation of new airlines not related to the CAAC regionals. Foreign joint ventures in a wide variety of related businesses, such as aircraft maintenance, engineering, catering, airport hotels, airport transportation, and the like, were encouraged. Then Chinese entities acquired major stakes (a total of 22.5 percent by mid-1992) in Cathay Pacific, Hong Kong's privately owned airline, which is one of capitalist Asia's most successful and competitive airlines. This seems to be a prelude to Cathay Pacific's becoming a major international and domestic carrier for China after Hong Kong reverts to Chinese rule. In August 1992, Beijing announced that it was studying plans to sell large chunks of its regional airlines and airports to private and foreign interests, and to engage foreign enterprises in the management of these airlines and airports.[32] China Airlines entered into a 60:40 joint venture with Lufthansa to create Beijing's Aircraft Maintenance and Engineering Corporation, a major maintenance facility.

---

[32]Susan Carey and Julia Leung, "China's Air Plan Raises Hopes, Questions," *Asian Wall Street Journal*, August 11, 1992, p. 1. Other analyses, some of which were less accurate, appeared in the *South China Morning Post* for August 9–10.

Beijing even decided to allow private airlines. Chinese interests set up a foreign-owned but PRC-controlled private airline, Swan International Airlines, to compete in the Chinese market.[33] One day a colleague of mine from New York walked into my office and wanted to know the reputation of a Chinese general and his company, who had asked for Western bank financing to start an airline in Guangdong. In the early 1990s, a twenty-three-year-old Chinese with no particular training started an airline and made himself $2 million. Today, China's principal airlines still could not compete with major Western or (especially) Asian carriers. However, the principal routes now have new Boeing or Airbus or McDonnell Douglas planes, smart stewardesses, decent food, and a punctuality record that is, well, better than it once was.

Throughout Asia, similar logic and evolution have led first to competition among state enterprises, then to privatization of 49 percent so that the government retains majority ownership, and then to privatization of much more because the government can still maintain control by holding a less-than-majority block. South Korea has even managed to retain control of its commercial banks by selling 100 percent to the public, but fragmenting individual shareholdings under a limit of 1 percent per shareholder. It then uses its regulatory authority to retain effective control of the board of directors and, through the board, of high-level personnel and policies.

Having started down this slippery slope, China will find economic and social pressures pushing it to follow its Asian neighbors, and the younger Chinese leaders are outspokenly aware of this. There are significant disagreements on how fast and how far this process should go, but among the serious candidates for future leadership there is little difference as to

---

[33]Kennis Chu, "Swan Flights Won't Lead to Open Skies," *Sunday Morning Post*, Hong Kong, December 13, 1992.

the basic direction. The Asian approach to privatization generates far more political support than the big bang approach common in Eastern Europe because it serves the national interest better. It creates competition and efficiency, and mobilizes domestic and foreign capital; but it also gives local firms time to adapt and become competitive, and avoids selling off the national patrimony at fire-sale prices. Such fire sales are the natural result in Eastern Europe of dumping large numbers of firms on the market when there is already a large supply of firms trying to privatize, a low demand for them, the inevitable poor prospects, and frequently a collapsing currency.

Meanwhile the Chinese economy is being rapidly privatized—not primarily by selling the state firms to the public, but by swamping the state enterprise sector with growth that is occurring in other sectors. Western thought has been dominated by the assumption that the only way to move to a market economy is to sell the state sector—the quicker the better. The Chinese will certainly do considerable selling of the state sector, and when they do so, their stock markets will be ready to handle the process. But the main thrust of their policy, one so successful that its progress is necessarily unsettling as well as exhilarating for old socialists, has been an explosive growth of agriculture, private industry, collective industry, and foreign-invested industry.[34] Not only do these sectors outgrow

[34]Collective industry is an intermediate form which has its Western counterparts in the grain and dairy marketing collectives popular in the midwestern United States and Canada. These forms usually have some village, town, or provincial sponsorship, but operate in competitive markets with little of the bureaucracy that constrains state enterprises, and return profits to the members. One typical township enterprise would be a group of women backed by the town to paint Christmas decorations and export them, with the profits mostly going to the women. Such enterprises are closer to capitalist private firms than to monopolistic state enterprises. They are in some ways the core of China's takeoff.

the state sector, but they seduce it into joint ventures and love it to death. The East European approach is very good at destroying the state sector, but—so far—rather disruptive of the private sector. In military terms, the Polish approach is like the grim trench battles of World War I: your side may win, but at a horrible price. The Chinese strategy has been more like MacArthur's island-hopping in the Pacific during World War II, elegantly bypassing the enemy rather than confronting him head-on.

Western advisers and commentators have praised spasmodic privatization efforts in Eastern Europe and criticized China's cautious approach. But Western European economies burdened by inefficient state enterprises have followed policies closer to the Chinese: liberalize first, privatize later, and even then privatize gradually.

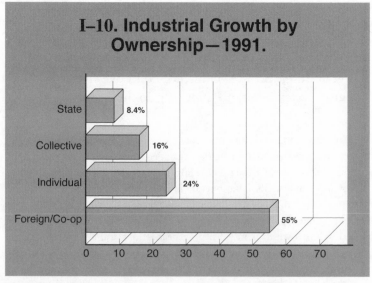

I–10. Industrial Growth by Ownership—1991.

SOURCE: State Statistical Bureau.

Infrastructure

China faces massive infrastructure problems: insufficient telephones, inadequate transport, energy shortages, and so on. Such problems are the almost universal consequence of Asian-speed economic takeoffs. Bangkok, Jakarta, and Taipei are in even worse shape. Singapore, Kuala Lumpur, and Hong Kong have been wiser and luckier, but even Hong Kong occasionally becomes overawed by the scale of infrastructure investment necessary to meet the demands of growth. These infrastructure shortfalls, unlike the inflation and state enterprise problems, are crises of success.

Bottlenecks will persist for the indefinite future, but it is possible to get ahead of the curve. Things are actually far better now than before reform. In 1982, when I was traveling around China, my host in Beijing could not tell me in advance where I would be staying in Chengdu (the capital of Sichuan Province, located in the center of the country), because even the army could not readily get through by telephone to reserve a hotel there. Once in Chengdu, I discovered that the only telex available was an old iron typewriter from the turn of the century that seemed to have been wired up by Rube Goldberg himself to produce telexes—sometimes. Today, businessmen complain if they have to wait a short while before obtaining an open line to the outside world. The lesson of Bangkok, where the traffic has been jammed since 1965 but the national economy has averaged 7 percent annual growth, is that a country can grow through its bottlenecks. It may be difficult to maintain an optimistic perspective while one sits in the line of 18,000 trucks that daily jam the Hong Kong/Guangdong border, but the roads are in fact being built and Guangdong has in fact managed to produce enough power to run its factories. Growth generates the financial resources to pay for the new infrastructure.

Unemployment

No problem is more socially painful or more politically conse-
quential than unemployment. China's unemployment problem is very serious, although no adequate studies have appeared of the problem. Officially, the unemployment rate is a
little over 2 percent, but reports circulate of up to 200 million
people actually unemployed or underemployed—equivalent
to perhaps a 30 percent rate. All these numbers, it should be
stressed, are completely unreliable.

Usually the unemployment problem is formulated in terms
of the loss of jobs created by reform of the state enterprises
and by collapse of businesses that suddenly have to compete
with more efficient foreign firms. But this is not in fact the
problem. The real problem is that a system of socialism and
protectionism ensures the emergence of huge, bloated firms
and bureaucracies that are not serving real market needs and
therefore cannot provide gainful employment for their "employees." And the consequence is a huge buildup of disguised
unemployment. Each firm becomes a miniature welfare system, whose size and costs escalate until eventually they ruin
the firms and the country.

Reform along the lines of the Asian miracle economies begins to resolve this problem by creating millions of net new
jobs. The labor-intensive industries on which these takeoffs
are all initially based are by definition job-intensive: making
shirts, shoes, toys, and cameras requires lots of workers. But
reform rips the veil away from the disguised unemployment.
There is a great political paradox here. Most of the jobs generating China's $80 billion of exports are new jobs, but at the
same time unemployment becomes a source of intense worry.

Important lessons can be learned from the experiences of
the other Asian nations. Even in tiny Singapore, sociologists
of a generation ago counseled that the economy would never

be able to generate enough jobs to overcome unemployment. They added that if the unemployed were educated people, then discontent would lead to organized political dissidence and would destablize the country. The government believed these arguments and hence discouraged large families and limited the availability of higher education. When the predictions proved wrong, Singapore found itself with a severe labor shortage and a worse shortage of highly trained people. Today, it has an urgent program to expand educational opportunities and to persuade Singaporeans to make more babies. (The point here is not that overpopulation is never a problem; in several countries it is. But our techniques are very good at estimating how many jobs will be lost in a competitive situation and very poor at estimating how many will be gained, so they virtually always underestimate the gains in a dynamic economy.)

In South Korea when reform began, unemployment was around 40 percent. After a period of supposedly harmful steps, it declined rapidly to around one tenth of that level. Efficiency created better products at better prices. These reached a broader market, creating more jobs. More people had jobs, so more people bought things, and therefore the market expanded still further.

At the other extreme, the same phenomenon has occurred in particularly dramatic form in Indonesia. In some of the egregiously overpopulated regions, it was the practice to harvest the rice only with fingernail knives, which were so small and inefficient that they assured work for everyone. Modernization, it was argued at the time, would create mass unemployment and even starvation by destroying this egalitarian system. Through the early 1980s, various professors from Cornell and from assorted Australian institutions regularly wrote reports, visited Indonesian villages, and collected statistics purportedly demonstrating that this catastrophe was indeed occurring. On a broader scale, it has been popular even in recent years to tally the number of new entrants to the labor force (very large numbers indeed in Indonesia) and argue that no economy could create that many new jobs. In fact, the villages of central Java today have, on average, more of the population employed in better jobs than ever before. One no longer sees round-bellied babies suffering from kwashiorkor. One no longer sees women wearing inadequate clothing. And everywhere people are riding bicycles, motorbikes, and buses where they used to have to walk. Long before the statistics became available, this writer was issuing reports saying that the evidence of actual living conditions disproved the unemployment thesis so popular in the academic world.

China is experiencing the same phenomenon. The dynamism of its economy is visibly improving living standards virtually everywhere. But the real level of unemployment can no longer be disguised, and therefore it becomes an open social controversy. When people can no longer be prohibited from moving around the country, millions of people who lack jobs, or lack adequate jobs, migrate from one area to another— quite visibly. Not only does invisible employment become visible, but the changes occur more rapidly and therefore more disruptively. The existing unemployment accumulated very gradually; the new shifts of employment and unemployment occur very rapidly as a new firm succeeds and an old firm collapses. This faster shift is far more potent politically.

When the time comes to shut down some giant state enterprises, another phenomenon becomes clear. The employees of giant state enterprises can organize more easily when they become unemployed, so they are politically more dangerous. Even if the net unemployment in an area is decreasing, more often than not disorganized small groups of people are gaining employment and highly organized large groups are losing it. This creates critical problems. The government must be tough enough to face down those who would strike or riot and bring reform to a halt. It must keep the economy growing fast enough to keep the rate of job creation high. And it must act adroitly to implement reform in phases, to spread the pain geographically, and to explain the process so that discontent never reaches a critical mass of anger and organization. In a country as large as China, this is a huge problem—huge enough that there will inevitably be some strikes, riots, and very visible crime. But the examples of the other Asian nations show that it is a manageable one.

CORRUPTION, BUREAUCRACY, AND THE LEGAL SYSTEM

The transition from government ownership and control to market control includes some very messy intermediate phases. Although the Chinese transition works better than Russia's or Poland's, this does not mean that all is smooth. Among the messiest aspects are the intermediate steps in relaxing government control. These create enormous opportunities for corruption, misunderstanding, confusion, and delay. For instance, the first phase of reform allows private companies to form, but leaves most housing, raw materials, credit, and employment firmly in the control of the state and Party bureaucracies. So Mr. Chan can legally start a company, but his workers won't have any housing, his factory won't have any steel, his company won't have any credit from the banks, and his workers may be chosen for him by an organization which has a strong interest in keeping all the able, energetic workers where they are. These problems can be fixed by members of the families of senior Party leaders. If Mr. Chan has access to such people, he will get what he needs—in return for assuring that the Party family shares fully in the proceeds of the new firm.

Then Mr. Chan has to deal with all sorts of state regulations, some published, many unpublished. If he wants to import a machine, he needs a license. If he has to exchange currencies, he needs access to the swap centers. If he wants to build a building, he requires a permit. Such things become major annoyances in America; but most Americans could not imagine how many laws, regulations, and licenses can be created by a bureaucracy thirsty for a stream of capitalist income. On top of that thirst, Mr. Chan often will find that many more government departments will claim to have authority over any given area than actually do. Among those that do, he will discover conflicting policies and power struggles that delay his factory and cost him ever more money. If he has a dispute, Mr. Chan will find that the laws are ambiguous and that the procedures for settlement involve highly personalized, moralistic arbitration procedures rather than Western-style legal procedures. And Mr. Chan will fare much better in this process than Mr. Smith from New Jersey, who would like to create a joint venture with Mr. Chan.

Other Asian countries have gone through this kind of messy transition. South Korea and Taiwan were once known for the outstretched hands of their officials. China is better off than Indonesia in this respect, and infinitely better off than the Philippines. But those who have to negotiate a contract and build a factory for the first time are frequently amazed that the process can work at all. There is an old adage that there are two things one should not watch being made: sausages and laws. The adage needs an addendum to cover Chinese business dealings. The lesson of other Asian countries is that, if the government can maintain control and press through to a largely market economy, then the disciplines of competition take over and businesses that are too corrupt cannot survive.

Government officials come to make better salaries and can eventually prosper without corrupt income. Business necessity and popular demand force the development of a relatively modern legal system. In seeking these goals, however, China faces greater challenges than the smaller countries. Its sheer size creates more opportunities for loss of control. Two generations of socialism have endowed China with more crannies of corruption.

Against these magnified problems, China also has some advantages. In contrast with the Philippines and Indonesia, it has managed so far to avoid giving away whole sectors to corrupt private business groups. If a group becomes dominant in one province, it will likely have to face eventual competition from other provinces. While the offspring of many Chinese leaders are taking full advantage of their parents' positions during the transition, there is as yet no thrust toward creating great family monopolies. The state owns the remaining monopolies, and both the prevailing ethos and the rise of private competition would mitigate against turning over the Chinese economy to analogues of Ferdinand Marcos's friends in the Philippines or Suharto's family in Indonesia. Like Taiwan, South Korea, Singapore, and Hong Kong, China has a ruling elite which, despite other faults, is devoted primarily to building the country rather than to self-enrichment. Nobody has ever accused Mao Zedong or Chen Yun or Deng Xiaoping of being motivated primarily by financial greed. This is a potentially decisive advantage. China faces a critical test in attempting to maintain the patriotic dedication of the next generation of leaders in the face of capitalist temptations. So far, children of top leaders who use influence to become wealthy appear to face serious opposition in acceding to leadership themselves. The fact that the smaller Asian countries were able to pass this test provides encouragement but no absolute assurance that China will do equally well.

THE PATTERN OF ECONOMIC GROWTH

China's spectacular growth has a distinctive structure. The coastal takeoff can be envisaged as four joint ventures and their nearby ramifications. The first and most advanced of these joint ventures is that between Hong Kong and neighboring Guangdong Province. It covers a territory and population the size of France: a region of 66 million people, largely Cantonese-speaking, who have experienced a dozen years of growth that have averaged above 12 percent annually. Hong Kong finances the industry of Guangdong, employs half of the manufacturing workers of the province, provides the technology and the designs, and markets the products. Guangdong provides the workforce and the land. Never in human history has a population the size of France experienced such phenomenal growth. This joint venture is analyzed in greater detail in Chapter IV.

The other three joint ventures link Taiwanese with neighboring Fujian Province; former southern mainlanders on Taiwan with the Shanghai region; and South Koreans, Japanese, and former northern mainlanders on Taiwan, as well as South Korean and Japanese investors, with the Shandong-Tianjin region on the northern coast of China.[35]

The driving force behind this coastal takeoff is a remarkable coincidence of necessity and opportunity. When Taiwan and South Korea democratized at the end of the 1980s, wages rose extremely fast. At the same time, the United States was successfully demanding that these countries appreciate their exchange rates. The result was an increase in labor and other

[35]Income growth in the Shanghai area was limited through 1991 by discriminatory taxation, but Shanghai and adjacent regions are now experiencing explosive growth.

costs that threatened to render the two countries' industries completely uncompetitive. Parallel trends were occurring in Hong Kong and Japan. Hong Kong standards of living had reached higher levels than those of Southern Europe, and wages and other business costs were continuing to rise rapidly. Japan was adjusting to a substantial upward revaluation of its currency on top of normal wage rises. All of these countries needed desperately to move their labor-intensive and land-intensive industries to cheaper areas. It was at this time that the Chinese option became truly attractive: Chinese land and labor costs were a tenth of Hong Kong's.

The combination of these relatively more developed neighbors' needs and China's proffered opportunities was the economic equivalent of a firestorm along the coast of China: over 300 million people, or roughly the population of the European Community, experiencing economic growth at an average rate somewhat above 10 percent annually. This European Community–sized economic takeoff is dragging along with it the remaining 900 million people of China—a population comparable to all of the former Soviet Union plus all of Africa and all of South America. The economy is growing several times faster than Western countries have ever achieved. (Contrary to conventional wisdom, the interior of China is only slightly less dynamic than the coast. The next chapter elaborates on this.) The combined takeoff comprises more than a fifth of the human race growing at rates that economists only a generation ago believed impossible for even a small country to sustain.

China is able to achieve this success because it is becoming an integral part of the Pacific Asian explosion. It has studied and absorbed the principal economic lessons of its smaller neighbors. It takes full advantage of the entrepreneurship, finance, technology, and marketing skills of its smaller neighbors, most notably Hong Kong and Taiwan. It is following the economic and political sequences of its neighbors. And its domestic structure is beginning to replicate the structure of the earlier Pacific Asian takeoff. The New Industrial Economies (NIEs) are playing the role for China that Japan played for the NIEs: As labor markets in the more advanced NIEs become saturated and wages rise, these countries shed their labor-intensive industries by moving them to Guangdong and Fujian. As the economies of those provinces in turn take off and wages rise, the cheap labor industries migrate further into the interior of China. In this analogy, Hong Kong is Japan, Guangdong is South Korea, and Sichuan is Indonesia. By the early 1990s, there were few regions of China that were not feeling the force of the Pacific Asian takeoff.

II

||||||||||||||||||||||||||||||||||||||||||||||||||||||||||||||||

THE POLITICS

OF ECONOMIC

TAKEOFF

"When you open the window, flies and mosquitoes come in."
—DENG XIAOPING, SPEAKING OF THE POLITICAL PROBLEMS
CAUSED BY AN OPEN ECONOMY

While traveling from Beijing across the breadth of China to Kashgar and back to Hangzhou in the summer of 1992, I had the opportunity to speak with dozens of people about China's reforms. I met none who objected to them, although many were impatient for more. In addition, most people—including shopkeepers, tour guides, intellectuals, hotel service people, and many others—could articulate with remarkable clarity why the reforms worked: why competition leads to efficiency; why the "iron rice bowl" of wages that are guaranteed regardless of productivity leads to inefficiency; and why market prices are better than controlled prices. The clarity springs from the direct Chinese experience of both systems, and of a Chinese propaganda machine that drilled into them the theory of the socialist iron rice bowl for three decades, and then the theory of competition and markets for the past decade.

Today, the average Chinese probably grasps the basic justifications of the market economy better than the average American. This knowledge is backed up by a belief in the efficacy of market-oriented reforms on the part of most people outside the government and Party bureaucracies. Moreover, belief in reforms is strengthening, because change has generated continuous improvements in the welfare of the overwhelming majority of the Chinese people—unlike the situation in much of Eastern Europe and the former Soviet Union, where euphoria is giving way to despair. For this, Deng Xiaoping and his reformist colleagues are most grateful.

Chinese leaders are less appreciative of a second development. Ideological commitment to Marxism-Leninism is about as dead among the Chinese as it was in Poland in the early 1980s. My daughter, the captain of her high school basketball team in Hong Kong, goes into China to play basketball against Chinese teams. After a tournament, the local team takes the Americans out for dinner and freewheeling conversation. She has been regaled for hours by the Chinese players with hilarious stories of how silly Marxism classes are. Similarly, American executives visiting Beijing have become accustomed to senior Chinese government officials and business executives telling them after only a few minutes of acquaintance how much they dislike Li Peng or how they hate dealing with the corrupt Chinese police. Leading Party cadres frequently tell tales of socialist economic inefficiencies. Here is one: Complex foreign exchange controls transform a simple sale to Guangdong of raw materials from Hunan into a labyrinthine transaction—Hunan exports the materials to Hong Kong in order to collect the foreign exchange, and Guangdong must in turn pay much higher prices in scarce foreign exchange to import the Hunan materials back from Hong Kong.

Fifteen years ago, the people of China still professed a commitment to the ideas of Marxism. At that time, few voiced anything but praise for socialism, for the Party leadership, and even for the police, lest they lose their jobs or even their lives if they were caught deviating from official lines. Today, China's

leaders still make determined efforts to inculcate Marxist ideology, but for the most part these efforts fail. Today, harsh
punishment still awaits anyone who overtly organizes political dissidence or publishes views that deviate too far from
what is officially acceptable. The range of the acceptable has
widened, however, and the range of what one can get away
with in practice has expanded to a degree that makes the old
totalitarianism seem like a different world.

According to Nicholas Kristof, the Beijing bureau chief for
The New York Times, who won a Pulitzer Prize for his coverage of Tiananmen Square: "Throughout the ideological and
cultural world, Chinese are again testing the limits, and
mostly getting away with it. Bold films, plays and books are
appearing, newspapers are becoming readable, China's fore-
most rock 'n' roll star is back on stage, and sex and democracy
(in that order) are again on the agenda."[1]

The political strategy behind Deng Xiaoping's economic reform has been, first, to use the fruits of economic productivity
to ally with major sectors of the population, those people primarily concerned about income and growth (farmers, workers, bankers, managers, the middle class). Deng hopes, too, to
convince those who are primarily concerned about the future
of the nation (the military, political party leadership, many
intellectuals) that the reform program is the only credible path
to national revitalization, even if it downsizes military budgets, reduces central control of the economy, and implements
ideologically distressing policies. Third, he will use the open
policy with its access to the outside world to gain the commitment of intellectuals and students to the reform program, even
if they oppose the political regime. And, last, Deng will con-
serve central power in order to repress whatever residual op-

[1]Nicholas D. Kristof, "China's Cultural Climate: Warming Trend," *International Herald Tribune,* February 25, 1993, p. 18.

position remains from old radicals, fearful state enterprise workers and managers, and the revolution of rising economic and political expectations. Rapid economic growth is the core of these four strategies, not only to generate rewards for the principal social groups but also to fund the infrastructure, the army, and the government apparatus that must bind the country together during a period of stressful change.

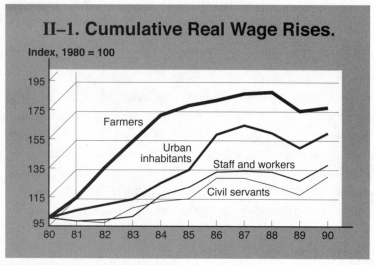

II–1. Cumulative Real Wage Rises.

Index, 1980 = 100

Farmers

Urban inhabitants

Staff and workers

Civil servants

SOURCES: State Statistical Yearbooks,1987, 1991.

The first priority has been to generate income gains for farmers and workers. This has already been achieved, as the chart above indicates. Farmers and urban workers enjoyed a spectacular rise in income, then lost some of it in the inflation and austerity period of the late 1980s, then resumed the climb. (Farmers, however, became victims of local taxes in the early 1990s and began to express discontent.) All social groups appear to have gained real income rises, and at these levels even small increases make an overwhelming difference to quality of life. For instance, the difference between having not quite enough food and just a little bit more than subsistence is one of the greatest gains a human being can make. And the difference between having just enough cloth to cover oneself and having something clean and modern to wear is a huge leap in personal pride. Many tens of millions of people have climbed a ladder that began with hunger, ascended to adequate food but barely enough clothing, then old brown-looking clothing that was once blue, then the universal blue which blotted out all individuality for decades, then a bit of color, and now stylish clothing with a little logo for prestige. This ascent makes the recovery of Western grandparents out of the Depression trivial by comparison. State workers and civil servants fared among the worst, but even they enjoyed substantial raises.

It is particularly important that the greatest gains accrued to groups with relatively low incomes. Farmers and workers had very low incomes, so their disproportionate gains leveled the overall distribution of income—even though a few people managed to become inordinately wealthy. Much has been made of the emergence of inequality within groups as a few farmers and entrepreneurs grew rich, but less note has been taken of the disproportionate income gains of the poorest groups. Socially and politically, the poor are far more important, because the number of rich is still relatively small, whereas the farmers and light industrial workers are the largest groups in the society.[2]

Likewise, as we can see from the income growth map on

---

[2]For professional social scientists, the best measure of social inequality is the Gini Index. The number of rich people is not large enough to shift the Gini Index very much, but the huge relative increase in the incomes of farmers and of workers in light and medium industries would create a major egalitarian shift.

page 107, relatively poor provinces such as Guangdong, Xin-jiang, Qinghai, and Yunnan have been among the greatest beneficiaries of the economic reform program, while the richest region of China—Shanghai and its environs—had the slowest growth prior to 1992. (Shanghai's low growth derived from a hugely disproportionate tax burden, which was alleviated substantially in 1992.) Thus the economic reform has benefited all the major social groups in China, and mostly the groups who most needed improvement. This is typical of Pacific Asian takeoffs, especially those of Japan, South Korea, and Taiwan, which, unlike their Western counterparts, have had relatively egalitarian consequences.

As noted in Chapter I, Deng Xiaoping was more fortunate than his East European counterparts in his ability to gain the support of military leaders for the reform. Intellectuals also

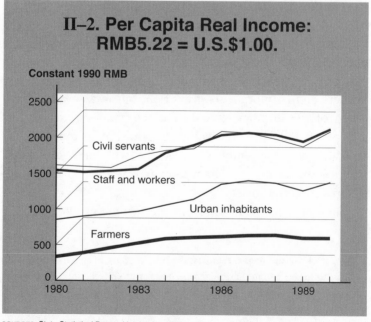

II–2. Per Capita Real Income: RMB5.22 = U.S.$1.00.

Constant 1990 RMB

Civil servants

Staff and workers

Urban inhabitants

Farmers

2500
2000
1500
1000
500
0

1980   1983   1986   1989

SOURCES: State Statistical Bureau Yearbooks, 1987, 1991.

were coopted into the reform coalition. They acquired greater prestige, somewhat greater scope of speech and inquiry, and some ability to travel abroad and to exchange views with their foreign counterparts. Although each of these improvements was severely limited, and still utterly unacceptable by Western standards, there was a great general improvement in the professional lives of a wide range of Chinese intellectuals. Moreover, most intellectuals, hitherto predominantly socialists critical of markets and the greed and disruption associated with them, accepted that the old strategies of development had failed and that the open, market-oriented approach was the only way to success. They demanded much more economic liberalization, and political improvements that were not forthcoming. Tiananmen Square outraged them, and a large proportion of the most dynamic scholars and students opposed the political leadership. Even so, they fully supported further economic reform. Thus Deng Xiaoping put together a very broad coalition to support his reform.

THE POLITICAL PROBLEMS OF ECONOMIC REFORM

The Struggle for Succession

Most discussion of the prospects for the Chinese economy focuses on the interplay of personalities. Will A outmaneuver B, and is C more or less reformist than D? This effort is largely wasted. The future of China will be decided by the political tidal waves of vast group interactions, not by the rivulets of individual personalities. The key to the future is the likely persistence of a broad reformist coalition. The expression of this underlying coalition is the fact that all the potential heirs to

Deng in their fifties and sixties, and virtually all leaders younger than that, support the basic elements of reform. Even Li Peng, a reluctant supporter, now advocates socialist stock markets and socialist bond markets (among other things).

After Deng dies, there will be a power struggle; but power struggles occur throughout the Third World and they rarely lead to catastrophic clashes. While the range of views and depth of division among the current Chinese leaders is substantial, it concerns how fast and how far reform ought to go, not in what direction. Civil wars are made out of disputes over direction.

The Fourteenth Party Congress, held in October 1992, had to face problems of succession at four levels: succession to Deng as top leader; succession to the generation of octogenarians now dominating China; succession to the old form of socialist ideology; and succession to the previous waves of reform. The Congress dealt effectively with the second and third issues but addressed the first and fourth only weakly. This can be put into perspective by comparing the present to the period when Mao Zedong died.

The year 1976 was a pivotal one. A majority of members of the Politburo, including Mao Zedong, died of natural causes in 1976. When Mao went, a group of scholars at Columbia University's Research Institute on International Change began to debate the identity of his true successor and the implications for what these scholars hoped would be the new Carter administration. Zbigniew Brzezinski interrupted the discussion to declare that we were wasting our time. He said that his generation of Kremlinologists had wasted a decade debating whether Stalin's successor would be Molotov, Malenkov, or Bulganin. "When Stalin finally died and Khrushchev rose to power, we got out all the photographs and, sure enough, there was that bald head in all of them, but he was the one who had been smart enough not to be noticed." Few people predicted the rise of Gorbachev or the reemergence after Mao of twice-purged Deng Xiaoping as top leader. Of far greater importance in China in 1976 was a social fact: the Cultural Revolution had so damaged every major group that someone could become a widely respected leader only if he repudiated the radicalism of the Cultural Revolution.

What is important in China now is that every major group has benefited from market-oriented economic reform, and therefore only a leader who epitomizes such successful reform can succeed to top leadership. All the most powerful political groups in China see a stark contrast between the successes of gradual, peaceful, market-oriented reform on the one hand and violent, youth-driven, Cultural Revolution idealism on the other. They also understand the catastrophic upheavals of Eastern Europe and the former Soviet Union, which fragmented several societies and deprived large populations of their livelihoods. Just as economic success in Singapore, Taiwan, Hong Kong, and South Korea narrowed the ideological range by discrediting the communist left, so economic success and radical failure in China has narrowed the range by eliminating Maoist radicalism as a serious political force and fatally crippling advocates of Stalinist bureaucracy.

The Fourteenth Party Congress tended to eliminate risks rather than anoint credible successors. Chen Yen, the second most powerful man in China, manager of the first phase of market-oriented reform, and the great opponent of many subsequent reforms, was persuaded to retire. The family of President Yang Shangkun, which threatened to dominate much of the army and so gain the potential for decisive political influence, was effectively purged from positions of high leadership. And Deng evicted many of the last remnants of leftism from their final bastions in the propaganda departments. (Among the innumerable intriguing parallels between Beijing and Taipei was the retreat of the old Bolshevik types to the propa-

ganda and culture departments, where they survived far longer than those in the rest of the Party and government.) Deng
continued to designate Jiang Zemin as his successor, but Jiang
Zemin seemed to most observers to be a weak transitional
figure—like Hu Yaobang, who briefly succeeded Mao until
the more decisive Deng Xiaoping swept him aside.

Li Peng, the government head, was widely respected as the
man who managed the stabilization of the economy after the
1988–89 inflation and restored China's diplomatic prestige
after Tiananmen Square. But Li Peng had powerful enemies
everywhere—in society, in the Party, and especially in the
army leadership, which felt that he had divided the army from
the people as a result of Tiananmen Square. Zhu Rongji was a
rising star because of his ability to take on the toughest economic problems without being destroyed by them; but his decisiveness also made enemies, and his popularity among foreigners (the Western press occasionally liked to call him
"China's Gorbachev," a phrase that instantly discredits any
Chinese leader) harmed him in Beijing. In short, Brzezinski's
counsel sixteen years earlier remained equally valid.

There was, however, a decisive generational shift. The new
Central Committee members averaged about fifty-five years
in age; about thirty years younger than the octogenarians who
were running China. The Committee consisted overwhelmingly of dedicated reformers who possessed a higher level of
education than their predecessors. They were still heavily
drawn from a Soviet-educated generation, and yet another
vital generational shift would occur when the more cosmopolitan, Western-educated generation matured considerably
later. The younger generation (those under forty-five) are
much more socially open, and trained in markets rather than
engineering.

An ideological transition also occurred. The Congress endorsed the "socialist market economy" as the ideal. This con-

cept, having no precise definition, inspired some jocularity. It did obtain important meaning as a contrast to the previous concept, that of the "planned commodity economy." There, the emphasis was on the continued important role of planning, with major concessions to market forces. In the new concept, the market had center stage but ideology still guided. Prominent scholars, officials, and journalists began ostentatiously referring to the "market economy," without the ideologically correct adjective "socialist." This was an important testimony to the degree of change in China. The media could publicly call attention to their flouting of a concept that had just been endorsed as the core of the Party line.

Such management of the ideological transition is another example of China's successful gradualism under Deng Xiaoping. The nation has lost its way repeatedly over the past two centuries, and the leadership is determined not to sever all ties to its old ideals and heroes. The current transition began with the Party's review of Mao's contributions. It carefully decided that Mao was this percent right and that percent wrong; that he was mostly right in his early years and mostly wrong in his last decade; and made specific judgments about the areas in which he was proved right and the areas in which he was proved wrong. In this way, the nation and the Party could retain Mao as a hero but distance themselves from the terrible sufferings imposed by his radical excesses.

The subsequent ideological path that leads through the planned commodity economy and the socialist market economy, and will inevitably result in a "market economy with Chinese characteristics," seems tortuous to a Western reader. It also seems intellectually arcane; but it does serve a vital political purpose of continuity. And it serves an important intellectual purpose, that of intellectual precision. Confucius emphasized the "rectification of names," or the importance of precise language and definitive conclusions in the search for

right conduct and sound governance. The neo-Confucian societies of today's Asia, including China, however ideologically
ironic that may be, have continued to benefit from his lessons.
If one studies the gradual evolution of Singapore's Lee Kwan
Yew, Taiwan's Chiang Kai Shek and Chiang Ching Kuo, and
South Korea's Park Chung Hee from their original socialist
beliefs to their relatively market-oriented later phases, one
finds a similar evolution. There is a huge contrast between the
gradual evolution and precise thought in some of these societies, and the wild ideological volatility that many Latin American societies have experienced without ever making much
consensual progress. The Party's endorsement of the "socialist market economy" gave legitimacy to the birth of an economic system with markets as the core.

Virtually absent from the Fourteenth Party Congress was
any detailed program for the next phase of reform. In part,
this reflected a consensus on the way forward: more price reforms, fewer subsidies for state enterprises, more trade, more
flexibility in labor markets, and so forth. But, paradoxically,
it also reflected profound disagreements over the sequence
and pacing of reforms, especially for the vital state enterprise
sector.

Radical Upheaval?

The greatest of Western fears has been that the succession
struggle might permit power to revert to Maoist radicals. It is
also the easiest to dismiss. The Maoist radicals no longer possess either a coherent organization or a significant political
base. The Cultural Revolution, the last and greatest outpouring of radicalism, alienated virtually every politically significant group in China. The Cultural Revolution was above all
an attack on the leadership of the Communist Party, and it
decimated that leadership. The experience of Deng Xiaoping's

own son, who was thrown by Red Guards from the upper story of a building and paralyzed for life, is an appropriate metaphor for what happened to the Party leadership. They, and the government bureaucrats, are determined never to let the radicals threaten them again.

Even the army, whose central responsibility is to maintain order, eventually became appalled by the Cultural Revolution, although army chief Lin Piao was a principal perpetrator of the upheaval; in the end the military became the primary instrument for suppressing the radicals. Farmers, workers, and managers found their lives disrupted and their incomes destroyed by the strange alliance of Mao Zedong, the propaganda elite, and rampaging youth. Subsequently the youth, now frequently called the Lost Generation, found that they had been used, and that the loss of their opportunity for education doomed most of them to lifelong poverty. Thus nobody wants another Cultural Revolution.

The remaining factions in Chinese politics bear no resemblance to the old radicalism. The smallest faction, which one might call the Stalinist socialists (e.g., Wang Zhen, China's vice president, and Chen Yun, Deng's great opponent of the mid- to late eighties), accepts and, in Chen Yun's case, led, the first wave of reforms (land to the farmers, incentives in industry, a modest opening to the West), but resents the further reforms of Hu Yaobang and Zhao Ziyang. Significantly, the leaders of this faction, Chen and Wang, agreed in 1992 to support Deng's new wave of reform—not because of any ideological conversion in their late eighties but because of the weakness of their position and their desire to extract some last concessions from Deng.

The second faction, the bureaucratic socialists represented by Premier Li Peng, fully accepts the reforms to date but resists further rapid liberalization. They want to emphasize orderly planning, a strong role for the Communist Party, larger subsidies and advantages for state enterprises as compared with private firms and foreign enterprises, and belief in Marxism. They emphasize the importance of avoiding inflation and any risk of instability—economic, social, or political. Not coincidentally, much of the leadership of this faction was trained in the Soviet Union; in fact, it is often called the Association of Graduates of East European Universities. Led by Li Peng, this group pushed through the acceptance of wholly-owned foreign investments (as opposed to the earlier pressures on foreign investors to form joint ventures with Chinese companies), and a wide range of financial reforms. In 1992, Li and his colleagues eventually—and reluctantly—endorsed Deng Xiaoping's plan for a new wave of reforms, but not until criticism in the National People's Congress had forced Li to make an unprecedented number of amendments to his work report.

The third faction is the authoritarian modernizers. These followers of Zhao Ziyang and Hu Yaobang want very rapid progress, and they are willing to run major risks (of inflation, of social ferment, of ideological heresy) in order to obtain it. Zhu Rongji loads the core of the faction, which is associated with Beijing's elite Qinghua University. The modernizers insist on political stability, but pursue such rapid economic change and jettison so much ideological baggage that they repeatedly stimulate challenges to the Communist order. They were chastened by the experience of inflation and disorder in 1988–89—many of them were temporarily exiled from power because of that disorder—but not greatly chastened.

In 1992, Deng Xiaoping began the revitalization of this faction and propelled many of their policies to the forefront yet again. They pushed for rapid economic growth even at the risk of serious inflation; loosened controls on cultural life and sexual expression; and once again began issuing calls for moderate political liberalization and extension of the rule of law.

A very large proportion of China's younger leaders fit this description. Some would go faster than others, but there are few supporters of Li Peng's very slow pace of economic reforms and even fewer supporters of disruptive political change. Deng has attempted to maintain a balance between the bureaucratic socialists and these modernizers. Neither has a monopoly on correct economic policies. Both Hu Yaobang and Zhao Ziyang pushed reforms at a pace which overheated the economy and stimulated a degree of inflation that could be socially destablizing. Likewise, both opened the political throttle to a speed which led to challenges to the Party's ability to control the system. In early 1992, Deng himself decided to press for high growth; he challenged Li Peng's plan for 6 percent growth and insisted on a goal of 10 percent for the coming Five-Year Plan. In 1992, the economy actually grew 12.8 percent, and it became clear that unacceptable inflation once again threatened; the growth enthusiasts promptly throttled down their aspirations to an 8–9 percent range. (At a comparable stage of development, Taiwan's planners consistently planned for 7 percent in their five-year plans and ended up doing 10 percent. This seems to be the right way to manage. In this case Li Peng was much closer to the mark.)

Finally there are the youthful and intellectual dissidents (Wuerkaixi, Fang Lizhi) who represent innumerable strands of dissent. They want more freedom and faster repudiation of obsolete Marxist dogmas. Like all Asian oppositions, they flaunt the slogans of democracy but often use "democracy" as a blanket term for the right to oppose the evils of inflation, corruption, nepotism, gerontocracy, dogma, national weakness, and specific aspects of personal freedom. (One of the great issues on the students' minds at the time of Tiananmen Square was the government's decision to revoke an earlier policy that would have allowed graduating college students to find their own jobs rather than just accepting what the government assigned them.) The slogans of democracy create an image of greater unity than is warranted by the reality. They also tend to conceal the fact that opposition to these evils actually carries much higher priority than rule by the people. Most individuals prefer change that is peaceful and gradual rather than sudden and violent. Most are infinitely more concerned about enlarging the scope of personal freedom than about electoral democracy. Most are willing to tolerate the regime in practice while noisily opposing it so long as steady progress is made in economic growth and in suppressing the worst of the evils.

This is a central point almost universally misunderstood in the West: These groups are terribly serious about reform, but not necessarily—at this early stage of modern development—about democracy in its Western form. A comparable situation occurred in South Korea in 1960. Students and others demonstrated against Syngman Rhee under the banner of democracy until they succeeded in toppling him. The successor regime of Chang Myon was a true democracy, but the students kept on demonstrating until they toppled him too. The evils most despised by Korean students at the time were corruption and national weakness. When General Park Chung Hee came to power by military coup in 1961, the demonstrations diminished voluntarily for a number of years because the students saw General Park as capable of dealing with the primary evils of corruption and national weakness. (They later resumed, as Korean society changed and Park became more rigid; but Park's economic success ensured him an adequate base of support for eighteen years.) One of the leaders of the demonstrations against Syngman Rhee and Chang Myon was present in Tiananmen Square and said he was amazed at the similarity between the attitudes of Chinese students in 1989 and the Korean students in 1960.

Such oppositions cannot overthrow the regime so long as it continues to progress—at least until that progress creates a vast, educated middle class which believes it can afford economic risks in the search for political dignity. The experience of South Korea, Taiwan, and Singapore has been that opposition can be managed and mollified for a generation or two. When the economy has been built and nationalist fears have been satisfied, the old leadership suddenly finds itself isolated. But by that time the transition can be relatively peaceful—unlike the situation in the former Soviet Union and much of Eastern Europe. Both Taiwan and South Korea achieved peaceful transitions to full democracy in the late 1980s and early 1990s. China is well launched on the same path.

The ultimate kind of civil disturbance is national fragmentation, such as occurred in the former USSR. But China is an ancient nation, not a new creation like the Soviet Union. China's population is 94 percent Han Chinese, whereas the USSR's was less than half Russian. China is growing at over 8 percent, whereas Russia is growing at minus 18 percent, and China is following a Taiwan/Korean model of development that can continue to generate 7 percent growth indefinitely. A strong sense of history, a firm sense of national identity, and a growing economic pie do wonders for unity. Together, these factors have created a Chinese psychology fundamentally different from the former Soviet Union's. Apart from minority regions (notably Tibet, with 2 million Tibetans, and Xinjiang, with 7 million Uyghurs), which harbor only a tiny minority of the population, China's regions, including ones like Guangdong which are always seeking greater *economic* autonomy, would pay some price—for instance, somewhat increased taxes—to maintain national unity if it were threatened. In the former Soviet Union, by contrast, most of the regions were willing to pay a huge price to ensure that the nation disintegrated.

It remains quite common in the West to assume that China is vulnerable to the same kind of fragmentation that occurred in the former Soviet Union and in Eastern Europe. The lesson of modern Asian history is that, so long as the leadership follows the policies required for rapid growth, such fragmentation is extremely unlikely.

Coast vs. Interior

More significant than ethnic strains in China are the differences between the more prosperous coastal regions and the poorer interior provinces. Historically, friction between the coast and the interior has sometimes been serious, and indeed it played a big role in the convulsions of China's civil war. For a while after the post-1979 reform it appeared that tension between the coast and the interior would once again become explosive. Coastal Guangdong reveled in its prosperity, but on the Hunan/Guangdong border there were frequent demonstrations by Hunanese trying to stop the "export" of Hunan's raw materials to fuel the growth of Guangdong, which reaped all the foreign exchange benefits. For a long period, Hunan people demanded that Guangdong's special privileges be taken away. Around 1991, however, a turning point occurred. No longer did they demand repeal of Guangdong's privileges, but rather the right of the interior provinces to enjoy all the same economic liberalization privileges. In the meantime, millions of Hunanese had migrated to Guangdong to work in the factories there and returned to Hunan with money and stories of prosperity. These "remittances" and purchases by Guangdong of materials from Hunan began to lift the poverty of the interior province; in the process, they conveyed an important message about the road to success.

Chart II-3 showing per capita GNP for different provinces (opposite) shows that there are indeed substantial differences

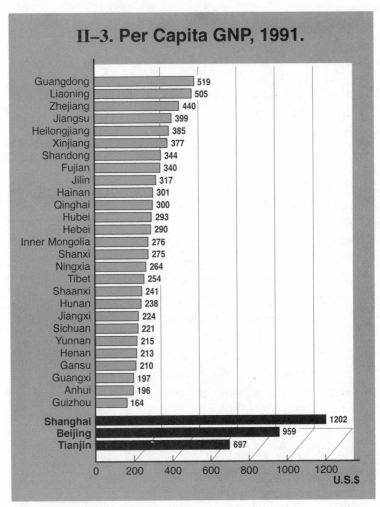

II–3. Per Capita GNP, 1991.

	U.S.$
Guangdong	519
Liaoning	505
Zhejiang	440
Jiangsu	399
Heilongjiang	385
Xinjiang	377
Shandong	344
Fujian	340
Jilin	317
Hainan	301
Qinghai	300
Hubei	293
Hebei	290
Inner Mongolia	276
Shanxi	275
Ningxia	264
Tibet	254
Shaanxi	241
Hunan	238
Jiangxi	224
Sichuan	221
Yunnan	215
Henan	213
Gansu	210
Guangxi	197
Anhui	196
Guizhou	164
Shanghai	1202
Beijing	959
Tianjin	697

SOURCE: State Statistical Yearbook, 1992, pp. 36, 79.

between the incomes of different provinces, and that the interior provinces are indeed generally poorer than the coastal ones. These differences are important but not overwhelming. The biggest are between the major cities (Shanghai, Beijing, Tianjin) and the rural areas; in fact, rural income is about 40 percent of urban income. Taiwan in the 1970s had a similar ratio and, because of the leadership's egalitarian values, worried about it a great deal, but such a ratio is not unusually high and does not provide cause for great political excitement. So there are important inequalities in Chinese society, but they do not now justify political alarm.

In China as elsewhere in successful Pacific Asia, the politically decisive issue has proved to be: Is the local economy moving forward? China's interior provinces have experienced stagnation at subsistence levels for generation after generation. Subsistence has frequently been interrupted by famine—for instance, in the Great Leap Forward of 1958–61 and during the Cultural Revolution of 1966–76. In the context of such extreme poverty, even a little real growth makes for a huge improvement in people's well-being. Few social differences exceed that between people who know they will have enough to eat tomorrow and people who do not. In the context of generations of stagnation, even a little growth provides cause for celebration. Is such growth occurring, or is the image of stagnation accurate?

Many interior provinces are growing more slowly than dynamic Guangdong and Fujian, and from a much lower base, but they are growing faster than any Western country ever managed to grow. People are still very poor, but the issue is no longer whether there is food and clothing but rather the search for more fashionable food and clothing. Travelers in the interior of Hunan and Hupei report that the women working in the rice fields frequently have permanent hair-dos—a small thing but an unimaginable luxury a decade earlier. Dur-

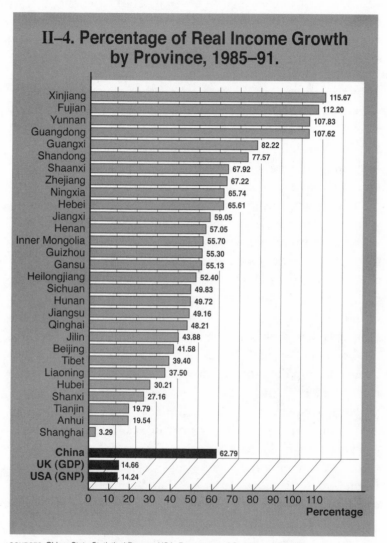

II–4. Percentage of Real Income Growth by Province, 1985–91.

Province	Percentage
Xinjiang	115.67
Fujian	112.20
Yunnan	107.83
Guangdong	107.62
Guangxi	82.22
Shandong	77.57
Shaanxi	67.92
Zhejiang	67.22
Ningxia	65.74
Hebei	65.61
Jiangxi	59.05
Henan	57.05
Inner Mongolia	55.70
Guizhou	55.30
Gansu	55.13
Heilongjiang	52.40
Sichuan	49.83
Hunan	49.72
Jiangsu	49.16
Qinghai	48.21
Jilin	43.88
Beijing	41.58
Tibet	39.40
Liaoning	37.50
Hubei	30.21
Shanxi	27.16
Tianjin	19.79
Anhui	19.54
Shanghai	3.29
China	62.79
UK (GDP)	14.66
USA (GNP)	14.24

SOURCES: China: State Statistical Bureau. USA: Department of Commerce. UK: IMF.

ing my travels across China in 1992, even in the poorest areas people were well fed and had decent housing. Television aerials were nearly omnipresent. Clothing in the cities was colorful and very fashionable; many women riding bicycles to work in interior cities like Xian wear knock-off Hermes silk print skirts and blouses. In the most distant desert outposts of the Silk Road, there are nylons for sale, frequently marked: "Made in France." (Most of these are good copies rather than originals, but it is a revolution to have even copies of any quality available.) The most traditional markets now have, behind the piles of cucumbers and melons, a row of beauty parlors where local women have their hair blow-dried. There is a confident air of progress that is completely absent in, for instance, the much more backward Philippines. So long as there is noticeable progress in the interior, revolts by the interior against the coast will not threaten the stability of China.

In fact, the interior provinces are making a good deal more than minimal progress. The map opposite, which displays total real GNP growth over a six-year period, shows that the image of a rapidly growing coast alongside a stagnating interior is a myth.[3] For the most part, the interior provinces are growing at spectacular rates. Xinjiang, a Uyghur minority area as far from the coast as a province can be, is the fastest-growing. Fujian, the coastal province opposite Taiwan, comes second. Another interior minority area, Yunnan, north of Burma, is third. (One can argue that Yunnan should be set aside because much of its growth derives from the Burmese drug trade.) Guangdong, adjacent to Hong Kong and the best known of China's fast-growing coastal provinces, is fourth.

[3]This time period was chosen because there is a consistent time series starting from 1985. It greatly understates the average effect of the Chinese economic boom, because three of the six years are years of austerity policy and drastically sub-par growth.

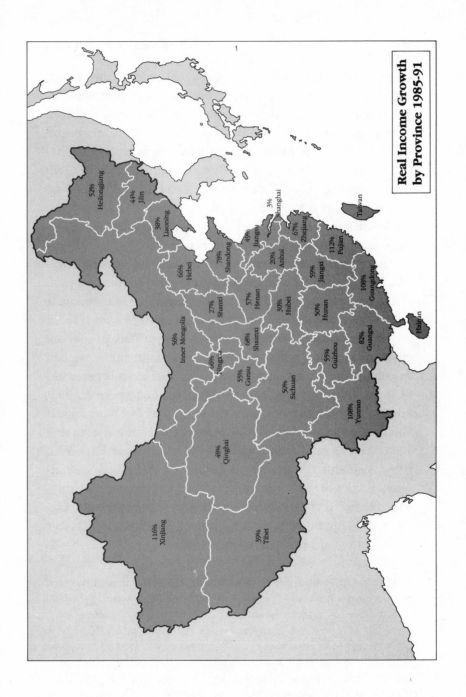

Real Income Growth by Province 1985-91

52% Heilongjiang

44% Jilin

38% Liaoning

116% Xinjiang

56% Inner Mongolia

66% Hebei

78% Shandong

27% Shanxi

66% Ningxia

55% Gansu

68% Shaanxi

57% Henan

49% Jiangsu

3% Shanghai

20% Anhui

67% Zhejiang

112% Fujian

59% Jiangxi

48% Qinghai

50% Sichuan

30% Hubei

50% Hunan

108% Guangdong

39% Tibet

55% Guizhou

82% Guangxi

108% Yunnan

Hainan

Taiwan

Four of the next six are interior provinces; two of the following four are interior provinces; and so forth. The slowest-growing area, Shanghai, is a coastal area. (Shanghai, hobbled during this period by excessive taxes, has subsequently begun its own takeoff.) Sichuan, in many ways the archetypical interior province, with over 100 million people, increased its GNP by half during this difficult period. Even Tibet, plagued by civil unrest, grew three times faster than the United States in the boom years of the end of the Reagan administration and the beginning of the Bush administration.

The growth rates of particularly backward interior provinces show key relationships when compared to the long-term champion, Guangdong. Hunan, just interior to Guangdong, is particularly poor. Sichuan and Hunan rank 17 and 18 in growth rates out of 30 provinces and separately accounted cities. Taking the ratios of long-term growth rates, we can calculate that when Guangdong grows 13.5 percent, as it did on a GNP basis in the not particularly good year of 1991, Hunan and Sichuan would expect to grow 6.2–6.3 percent. If Guangdong slows down to 10 percent, which it has not done since reform began, Hunan and Sichuan would expect to grow 4.6 percent, far above a boom year for the U.S. economy. These are rates unparalleled in China's modern history. The travails of the interior provinces have been greatly exaggerated by pundits who know some history but haven't checked the facts of the current situation.[4]

---

[4]The academic literature on fast-growing Third World countries, and perhaps especially on Asian countries, is filled with arguments that they will be destabilized by growing income "gaps." Many of these arguments work in the following way. Suppose two provinces, or classes, earn $150 per year and $200 per year, respectively. The "gap" between them is $50. Suppose that both of them now grow at spectacular rates and double their incomes in five years, to $300 and $400, respectively. The gap is now $100, and growing gaps are taken to presage impending instability. By this argument, any

Countries like Thailand and Indonesia have dealt with much more serious ethnic and regional problems. (Indonesia, stretched over a larger fraction of the planet, has some 13,000 islands and at independence had distinct groups speaking more than 300 different dialects.) It is the common experience of the successful Asian economies that rapid growth pulls together diverse groups and regions by providing a sense of shared gain. In contrast, countries like Burma and the Philippines, which have failed to grow, disintegrate as different groups grab desperately for shares of a shrinking pie. Burma's initial post–World War II ethnic divisions approximated Thailand's, and the Philippines' are less significant than Thailand's, but Thailand succeeded because it generated steady growth. Indonesia has far more social fragmentation than China, and this was complicated at independence by problems China does not face, most notably lack of a shared history or shared language; Indonesia's difficulties were further complicated by disparities of development and income far more serious than China's. But growth considerably less rapid than China's, together with a firm political hand, overcame such divisions. China has an easier task and greater resources with which to address that task.

An initially more plausible concern is the concentrated plight of factories relocated to the interior for security purposes. During the Maoist era, the leaders were obsessed with the risk of invasion by the United States or, later, by the Soviet Union. To ensure China's economic survival in the event of invasion, Mao Zedong engaged in a vast program of industrial relocation similar to Stalin's World War II relocation of

---

substantial success increases gaps and leads to instability. Thus success comes to be interpreted as failure. In fact, the "gap" is a completely invalid measure. All useful measures, such as the Gini Index or the ratio between the earnings of the top quintile and the bottom quintile, are ratios.

Soviet industry east of the Urals. The result was a concentration of heavy industries in impossible locations like rural Sichuan, where the transport costs would kill them if the inefficiencies of gigantic state enterprises somehow proved inadequate to that task. As Beijing's leadership has grown weary of subsidizing these industries, many have been quietly but relentlessly starved of funds and bureaucratic support. The degree of concentration of such industries (it is politically helpful that Mao's strategy was to disperse them) and the concentration of their political support is impossible to gauge at present. But we know that the only strategies available to such enterprises are desperation moves: support bureaucratic socialist politicians; dissolve into a partnership with a private firm or a state enterprise on the coast; or, best of all, form a joint venture with a foreign firm. (The ultimate irony of Mao's dispersal of these firms in order to hide them from foreigners is the frenetic search by today's managers for foreign partners to save them.)

On balance these industries are probably so dispersed, divided, and demoralized, and so committed to foreign joint ventures as the primary strategy for survival that they cannot organize a rejoinder to the successful strategy of Beijing's current leaders. There will probably be highly publicized strikes and riots as major firms employing many tens of thousands of workers sink; but unless the leadership becomes paralyzed, these are unlikely to coalesce into an upheaval. The process will be messy but not revolutionary.

For related reasons, China is not likely to face upheavals as a result of inequality between rich and poor classes. Even though hundreds of millions of Chinese are still horribly poor, growth on the scale recently experienced creates a Horatio Alger psychology. Such a psychology is a central reason for Hong Kong's stability despite tremendous inequalities. So long as the growth rate continues, the psychology of ambition, and the memory of the privations of the radical years, should limit class conflict. The principal scenario that would put this psychology at risk would be a return of severe privation—caused perhaps by particularly harsh U.S. economic sanctions combined with an unusually severe downturn in the world economy. But even that drastic scenario is not likely to be fatal, since for all its export success China's huge economy grows primarily because of domestic demand; so it can still expand through domestic productivity generated by reform and through investment of its huge domestic savings.

The assumption that China is vulnerable to the same kinds of national disintegration that occurred in Eastern Europe and the Soviet Union has been pervasive in Western thought. Part of the story of President Bush's post–Tiananmen Square cutoff of top-level political contacts was that he believed intelligence reports predicting the overthrow of the leadership. Congressional delegations visiting Hong Kong have persistently expressed the view that China may disintegrate the way the USSR did. Some members of Congress have not only believed this but sought as a matter of policy to accelerate it, as when Representative Nancy Pelosi (Democrat from California) put in early drafts of her 1991 bill to deprive China of most-favored-nation (MFN) status language that treated Tibet as a separate country. One of the arguments for Governor Christopher Patten's political changes in Hong Kong (see Chapter V) was the expectation that instability in China would make it possible to sustain changes that went against what had been agreed with the current leadership. Unless the economic reforms get off track for a lengthy period, such an assumption goes against the central political lesson of the Pacific Asian experience: In the hands of a firmly managed government, rapid economic development provides all the tools necessary to unify even a country dozens of times more fragmented than China.

THE REAL RISK: IMMOBILISM

More broadly, the coalition of groups that supports the reform (farmers, light and medium industrial workers and managers, the financial elite, entrepreneurs, most of the top political leadership, most of the military, and others) is simply too broad to be defeated in any pitched battle or to be diverted for long by any local political explosion. The greatest challenges to China's economic reform derive, rather, from the risk of immobilism.

The political system shares several weaknesses that make possible a scenario where reform just gets bogged down. First, after the Cultural Revolution and Tiananmen Square, Marxist ideology no longer provides much political cement; most people are ideologically cynical. Second, while most of the leadership endorses reform, no consensus has formed on some crucial issues such as the future of state enterprises. China needs a leadership able to cope with opposition and willing to take risks in order to confront such problems. Third, China has depended very heavily for its direction on the unparalleled influence and prestige of Deng Xiaoping, who has demonstrated even in his late eighties the ability to move the nation but obviously cannot live forever. Fourth, Beijing has allowed much initiative to pass to the provinces, and the central government's share of national revenues has shrunk alarmingly; as a result, Beijing might not long be able to impose its policies, including reform policies, on many of the provinces.[5] Finally, although most politically powerful groups support reform, the middle levels of the government and Party

[5]While my formulations are somewhat different from his, my views of China's political weakness are deeply indebted to discussions of the subject with Harry Harding of the Brookings Institution.

bureaucracies (which wield great influence in the implementation of any policy) fear that reform will diminish their power, prestige, and perquisites, and they will take advantage of any weakness at the top to interpret reform in a way that preserves bureaucratic power.

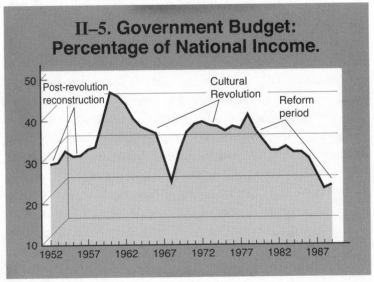

II–5. Government Budget: Percentage of National Income.

SOURCE: State Statistical Bureau, 1990.

These problems are real. The possibility of a combination of factionalism, provincial indiscipline, popular political antipathy, government financial squeeze, and bureaucratic foot-dragging cannot be dismissed. Such a scenario would probably develop from a leadership struggle after Deng's death—not a struggle between reformers and anti-reformers, but rather between powerful factions both of which were committed to reform. If the central government was divided by a prolonged struggle, and each faction competed for the support of various provinces, the government would lack the cohesion to impose a tax reform and raise its share of national revenues. These are already at critically low levels, and failure to mobilize sufficient revenues through tax reform has historically been a key reason for the downfall of China's regimes; it was a fatal flaw of the Qing dynasty.[6]

In such a case, provinces would increasingly follow their own policies, ignoring Beijing. Spending and credit would get out of control and inflation would escalate. Each province would take protectionist measures against neighboring provinces. Cities would vie against cities, villages against villages, in a process that has some tendency to occur anyway. The University of California economist Christine Wong has called such a process "encystation."[7] It would lead to a rapid decline in economic performance and a rapid rise in political confrontations. China would lose its economic dynamism and degenerate into a situation like that of India, or perhaps even worse.

This is the real risk to China's reform, but there are mitigating considerations that limit the risk. Most of the Asian economic takeoffs have occurred in an ambience of ideological disillusionment; the leftism of Lee Kwan Yew in 1959 and the socialism of the early Park Chung Hee quickly gave way to an ideological vacuum in which democratic ideas gradually gathered force—but not overwhelming force until economic development was far advanced. Lack of ideological passion is in fact a prerequisite for the success of the pragmatic, neither

---

[6]Cf. Jonathan Spence, *The Rise of Modern China* (New York: W. W. Norton, 1990), pp. 76–78 and elsewhere on the periodic financial crises and tax reforms of the Qing dynasty.

[7]Christine P. W. Wong, "Central-Local Relations in an Era of Fiscal Decline: The Paradox of Fiscal Decentralization in Post-Mao China," mimeo, Department of Economics, University of California, Santa Cruz, July 1991. This paper is an extremely important contribution to the understanding of an issue that seems very technical but goes to the heart of China's stability.

socialist nor capitalist, Asian mode of development. Since they cannot mobilize support through ideology or internal security fears, leaders must mobilize it by providing concrete benefits. And they can provide concrete benefits only by increasing efficiency through reform. The entrapment of even reluctant reformers like Li Peng in this inexorable political syllogism is one of the keys to long-run success in the Asian strategy of growth.

Diversity among provincial responses, and some degree of willingness to shrug off Beijing's dicta, have been a constant in China's modern political life. So far, the main consequence has been to allow certain coastal provinces, and certain special zones, to charge ahead and experiment with diverse approaches. The government initially described the successful reforms in Guangdong and Fujian as groping, testing, and experimenting.[8] For instance, Guangdong effectively allowed the farmers to get back their land long before Beijing endorsed such a policy; Guangdong has deregulated far more prices than the rest of the country. Shenzhen set up a formal stock exchange before Shanghai did, even though Beijing had decreed that Shanghai would be the first. Guangdong's success has led to emulation by other provinces, and Shenzhen's stock exchange has so far proved far more successful than Shanghai's. Not all of the experiments will succeed, but the ability of different provinces to try different things, and Beijing's conscious use of such experiments, can be a major advantage so long as it does not get out of control.

Finally, the obstructive middle-level bureaucracy faces severe limits on its power. Above its rules a reformist leadership. Below it, farmers and workers have tasted the fruits of the market and are demanding more. All around it is articulate

---

[8] Cf. Ezra Vogel, *One Step Ahead in China: Guangdong Under Reform* (Cambridge, MA: Harvard University Press, 1989), p. 85.

disillusionment with the consequences of the "iron rice bowl" of guaranteed income and employment, and with the results of stifling central control. But the greatest problem for the bureaucratic status quo arises from within the bureaucrats' own families. As the economy liberalizes, enormous opportunities appear for entrepreneurs to satisfy new consumer needs, to compete successfully with the ponderous state enterprises, and to arbitrage irrational prices and financial relationships. Yet it is initially very difficult to exploit these opportunities, because the bureaucracy retains extensive control of access to scarce housing, workers, and raw materials. In the early stages of reform, only those with access to bureaucratic power can quickly acquire the prerequisites of large-scale production. The people with the best access are the bureaucrats themselves, and their families. Usually senior government officials and Party cadres are too set in their ways to become entrepreneurs themselves, but their children do so on a vast scale.

Through this process, China's leading Communist families (and communism, like every other political movement, is heavily a family affair in China) are being transformed during a single generation into China's leading businessmen. As the second in command of China International Trade and Investment Corporation (CITIC), Wang Jun, the son of China's Stalinist socialist vice president, Wang Zhen, has earned a reputation as one of the more colorful buccaneers of business life in Hong Kong and Southern China. Again, as the military budget has been squeezed, China's military units have plunged enthusiastically into every business imaginable. This pattern of reform creates problems of its own, particularly the emergence of innumerable oligopolistic positions from which the sons and daughters of the senior leaders and bureaucrats, now known in China as the "princelings," try to extract a rent for the indefinite future. Along with straightforward businessmen like Wang Jun, who are successful through hard work and business acumen, there are many more who seek their fortunes through corrupt deals. Hence the transformation of socialism turns out to involve a particularly corrupt form of neo-feudalism. But, as we noted in the previous chapter, if the country can maintain the integrity of its top leaders, and if the leadership can retain overall control of the country during transition, this should be a passing phase.

The top leaders require not only integrity but toughness and decisiveness. If immobilism is the principal risk, then the ability to act is vital. The leadership must whip foot-dragging bureaucrats into line. It must defeat groups who seek to block devaluation and price reform. It must root out Party officials and government bureaucrats who seek to retain socialist controls on business. It must suppress unrest among discontented state enterprise managers and workers. It must forthrightly attack great corrupt coalitions of officials' families when their business activities become excessive. Most of the time this requires a fine balance of carrots and sticks; some of the time it requires the very indelicate use of a very big stick. In the previous chapter we saw that the economics of the takeoff, however smooth in theory, can be very messy in practice. So can the politics.

The risk of the reform becoming bogged down, and of this leading to political malaise, is real but in principle manageable. Asian takeoffs tend to reach a point where political consensus on basic direction, together with economic competition, ensure that the flight stays aloft. Uncertainty about the point of definitive takeoff lies behind the intense concern many observers express about whether Deng Xiaoping will have a few more years to consolidate his program. The success of the Asian models shows that China can succeed, but does not prove that it will definitely do so. As it implements more and more of the steps that succeeded in Taiwan and South

Korea, its probability of definitive success will rise. But one must watch for the danger signals of immobilism: prolonged power struggles, failure of tax reforms, inability to tackle new phases of reform decisively, and spreading local protectionism. These problems would be enormously heightened by a situation in which China got into a clash with foreign powers, the foreign powers then created economic problems, and the clash brought to power hard-line advocates of a highly controlled garrison-state economy.

This book is, in addition to an analytic perspective on events from 1979 to 1992, essentially a scenario for continuation of the successful reforms of that period. The author believes this positive scenario to be very likely because the same kind of scenario has been successful elsewhere; success increasingly creates interest groups with an interest in extending reform, and knowledge of successes elsewhere guides them on the road to further success. But success is not inevitable, and the alternative scenario would be a book-length expansion of the above remarks on the dangers of the reforms becoming bogged down.

POLITICAL SEQUENCING

China has also taken an Asian approach to the relationship between politics and economics. Aside from the necessity to build a reformist coalition, the most important lesson drawn from the experience of China's Asian neighbors—one which reinforced the inclinations of its leaders—was that economic reform should precede political reform. The West celebrates countries which undertake political reform first—Mikhail Gorbachev's Soviet Union, Cory Aquino's Philippines, and Alhaji Shebu Shagari's Nigeria, among others. In Chart II-6,

"Paths to Market Democracy," the top arrow represents this path, with a transition from socialist dictatorship (or from traditional Third World dictatorship—the dynamics are the same) to democracy in the absence of any prior transformation of the economy or the institutions of administration. But historically this pattern has virtually always led to economic strains so severe as to cause economic collapse, followed more often than not by a reversion to dictatorship.

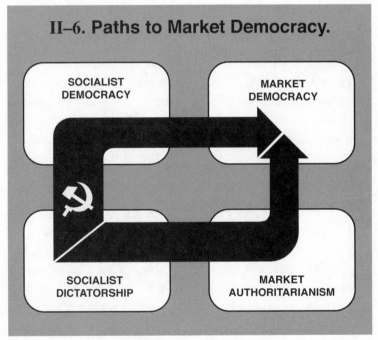

II–6. Paths to Market Democracy.

SOURCE: Harvard Business School Association of Hong Kong, adapted by author.

In this pattern, weak government institutions find themselves set upon by the full force of modern interest groups. Democracy maximizes the power of those interest groups,

particularly elite groups which have the money and education
to resist reform. All groups resist the necessity for austere budgets during a period of transition. The confrontation of powerful interest groups and weak government results in inflation, mismanagement, and disorder. Furthermore, reform
involves so many unpopular decisions that it soon stagnates.
Political leaders who need to control spending, free up prices,
stimulate competition, and privatize state enterprises must
confront voters accustomed to fixed prices, assured incomes,
and lifetime employment. They must seek support from voters
with the prospect that meat prices may triple or worse, their
firms may prove uncompetitive and go bankrupt, and their
jobs may be sacrificed at a time when so many other firms are
collapsing that there is no early prospect for getting new ones.
They must devalue their currencies and mollify voters who
can no longer import foreign fashions or afford vacations
abroad. They must parry the nationalist rhetoric of those who
oppose opening the economy to foreign trade and investment.
Compare these imperatives with the situation of Jimmy
Carter, Ronald Reagan, and George Bush, none of whom
could face the far simpler necessity to tell the voters that services would have to be cut and taxes raised. Moreover, the
disorder, stagnation, and inflation resulting from weak government lead the population to long for the return of dictatorial rule. The general experience (in, for instance, countries as
varied as Brazil, Nigeria, Lithuania, and the Philippines) has
been that politicians in this situation either abandon most reform or lose their jobs.

Three important requirements are lacking to support democracy in most Third World or socialist countries. The first
is strong, modern institutions to govern the country even in
the face of populist pressures for overspending, undertaxa-
tion, patronage at the expense of competence, and special
group deals at the price of national disintegration; the country

cannot function without a strong finance ministry, an efficient central bank, a modern army or police or both, and so forth. Without competent financial management, in the form of a central bank and finance ministry, populist pressures lead to hyperinflation, as has occurred time after time in Argentina. Eventually the public gets fed up and democracy collapses. Or the country just disintegrates in the face of different interest groups or ethnic groups, as has happened in post-Tito Yugoslavia. In such cases, the institutions that are supposed to manage the economy and maintain national cohesion simply collapse in the face of populist pressures.

A second requirement is the overcoming of barriers to the transition to a market economy. In the Philippines under Cory Aquino, the democratic leadership declared its determination to privatize the state firms that had come to dominate much of the economy under the Marcos dictatorship. But powerful pressure groups were able to buy the support of enough members of the legislature to prevent significant implementation of the policy. Again, Aquino tried to make land reform a centerpiece of her administration but was effectively prevented from doing so by powerful landlord pressure groups, since the groups who were dependent on feudal land institutions included most of the civil service which would have had to implement the reform, most of the Congress which would have had to pass the laws, and most of her own major political supporters. Throughout much of the Third World, the penetration of market fluctuations into previously feudal rural areas has led to peasant uprisings. In former communist societies, Party groups, military groups, and coteries of state enterprise managers frequently enjoy a combination of superior cohesion, superior funding, superior access to arms, and superior control of raw materials, technology, transport, and housing that can block essential market reforms.

Third, we have known for centuries that stable democracy

has certain prerequisites. An uneducated population cannot make the intelligent choices necessary to sustain a democracy. In a society without a substantial middle class, either the wealthier elements dominate the parliament and the courts, as has occurred in the Philippines and Thailand, or the society polarizes dangerously. A society that is living on the edge of starvation will shift support to any leader who has a plausible story about avoiding starvation, whether that is a Communist demagogue who promises to get grain from the wealthy, a military dictator who promises to restore order, or an Islamic mullah who promises that restoration of traditional values will bring back a golden age of prosperity. Even Aristotle had a valid analysis of the vagaries of democracy in a pre-modern society.

The history of attempts to create overnight democracies in Asia, Africa, Latin America, and Eastern Europe is a history of failure to overcome these three sets of problems. Cumulatively, I have called these problems the populist barrier, because a suddenly democratized government in a society that does not meet these requirements invariably fails. Virtually all the countries that were decolonized after World War II attempted to create Western-style democracies. Virtually all have failed to achieve stability, and the tiny handful that have sustained democracy either were market democracies from the beginning (Malaysia), or have failed disastrously to cope with major social problems (Colombia with drugs and violence, and Venezuela with economic mismanagement, despite the huge advantages of oil in both cases), or have failed to modernize (India). One searches modern history in vain for successful transitions from Third World or socialist dictatorships to modern market economies by means of democratization followed by economic reform. Yet this failed approach is the only model that receives the approbation of Western scholars and the media, and the only model that consistently receives large amounts of Western financial aid. The aid goes in the front door and right out the back door as capital flight.

By contrast, the pattern of the successful Pacific Asian countries (the bottom arrow in Chart II-6) has been for an authoritarian government to build the institutions, liberalize the economies, and create the educated middle class, and then to experience the emergence of freedom and democracy whether the leaders encourage these political changes or not. And because these systems put the prerequisites of democracy in place, their democracies have favorable prospects.

South Korea, Taiwan, Singapore, and (much more fitfully) Thailand fit this pattern. In South Korea, the basic reforms were done by an authoritarian general trained under the Japanese. Park Chung Hee took over the world's most impoverished society and decided that long-term stability required economic success at any cost. He drastically cut back the military's share of the economy, despite an immediate and apparently overwhelming threat from North Korea; this no civilian government could have done. In the interest of reviving trade and investment, he restored relations with the hated colonial power, Japan. This again would have been overwhelmingly rejected by the voters. He encouraged foreign investment and trade in the face of extremely powerful socialist and xenophobic sentiment. In order to promote exports, he reduced the exchange rate—something that liberal governments in Latin America have generally proved unable to do because of opposition from an economic elite which wants an overvalued currency to facilitate its imports of luxury goods and acquisition of overseas real estate.

Park welcomed foreign investment and increased the competitiveness of Korean industry by reducing tariff barriers on raw materials and machinery, despite opposition from socialist intellectuals and from business groups who insisted on being protected from this foreign competition; in a typical

Third World democracy like the Philippines, elite business groups have such political influence that real tariff reform has been delayed for decades. As in Taiwan and Japan, land reform had been successful in South Korea because it was imposed forcibly by political entities which did not have roots in the local landed elite—as all Third World democracies do. These measures created one of history's greatest economic miracles, catapulting South Korea from an economy worse than even the impoverished African countries to one of the half dozen leading economies of the Third World. That is what has made it a primary model for China.

Because of the enormous wage gains, distributed in an egalitarian fashion, that resulted from Korea's boom, the populace came to accept the market institutions it had once opposed. And the role of the technocratic managers of the economy became entrenched and prestigious.

Second, Park set about to create modern institutions. He built up an army that was better disciplined than the American divisions present in Korea, had fewer drug problems than the Americans, and was more successful in guarding the border against infiltration than the American division that for a long time held the center of the barrier along the demilitarized zone. He purged the ministries and the central bank of corrupt and incompetent personnel, created special think tanks to attract the most highly educated Koreans back from America, and then gradually transferred them into the top levels of the bureaucracy until he had created one of the leanest and most effective governments in the world. In contrast, Cory Aquino, whose intentions were good, was so overwhelmed by patronage pressures that her government expanded by hundreds of thousands of positions while its efficiency deteriorated notably. The brightest ministers were expelled for getting in the way of interest group pressures, and the already huge proportion of the population experiencing absolute poverty and malnutrition grew considerably. South Korean democracy seems vigorous, stable, and prosperous, while Philippine democracy seems fragile and empty of enthusiasm.

The social consequences of South Korea's spectacular growth created the prerequisites of democracy even though Park Chung Hee was not interested in democratization. Economic success created a vast new middle class of government employees, businessmen, highly skilled workers, and others. The requirements of economic success created hundreds of thousands of teaching jobs and enrolled millions of students, who turned out to have strong political feelings. Trade exposed the country to foreigners, and an educated population absorbed ideals of democracy that had previously been alien to their traditional Confucian ways. Prosperity banished the fear of starvation that had pushed concepts of political dignity into the background, and it also paid for a military that could defend the country and reduce the fear of renewed warfare that had justified an anti-democratic garrison state. By 1979, an analysis by the Korean CIA (KCIA) indicated that the government would have to compromise with groups demanding liberalization. When President Park responded instead with plans for assassinating the leaders of student demonstrations, the head of the KCIA assassinated him! It took almost another decade for democracy to triumph; but by the late 1980s, the pressures were insuperable and the prerequisites of successful democracy were clearly in place.

The story is similar in Taiwan, Singapore, and Thailand. These are the Third World countries which can deliver to their citizens the combination of prosperity, security, freedom, and (fitfully in Thailand) democracy that are the common aspirations of mankind.

In Latin America, only Mexico and Chile seem to be making decisive progress toward these goals—though Latin America has been trying for many generations longer than Pacific

Asia. In Chile, many of the economic prerequisites were force-fully installed by the military under Colonel Pinochet. In Mex-ico, reform has been imposed after generations of financially and socially catastrophic failure by a dominant party under the post-emergency leadership of President Salinas. The one Pacific Asian country which has consistently followed Latin American-style democracy interrupted by emergency rule—the Philippines—has had a history of instability, vast poverty and unemployment, and financial failure exactly parallel to the Latin American experience. Africa has yet to provide a single example of achievement of stable security, prosperity, and democracy; the one Asian country that attempted democ-racy in an African-style way—Burma—has had a history of impoverishment, instability, financial insolvency, and ethnic conflict exactly parallel to the typical African experience.

The route to stable democracy in the Third World therefore lies along the bottom arrow in Chart II-6 (page 119), follow-ing the examples of South Korea, Taiwan, Singapore, and Thailand. (Thailand oscillates back and forth more than the others, but achieves steadier progress than its African and Latin American competitors—including Brazil, which once was far ahead and now lies far behind—while ensuring its citi-zens more freedom and a more responsive government than Asian competitors such as Taiwan and South Korea.) Eco-nomic reform precedes freedom, and freedom precedes de-mocracy. But because the West does not understand why this model is ultimately successful, countries like South Korea ex-perience a generation of bitter Western denunciations for not following the instant-democracy models that fail elsewhere. Today's counterpart is the denunciation of China in the same terms that were used for South Korea in the mid-1970s, while Western columnists lavish praise on East European models that are creating widespread hunger, widespread danger of freezing in winter, widespread ethnic conflagrations, and the risk of a vast migration of refugees. Most of these countries are likely to prove unable to sustain their democracies because hungry, frightened people invariably repudiate their governments if they can.

The paradoxical result has been that the Third World's most successful market democracies have been built by leaderships that were initially dictatorial and sometimes even hostile to democracy; by contrast, some of the worst dictatorships, impoverishment, and violence have occurred in countries that have sporadically been ruled by democratic leaders with good intentions.

Supporters of the Gorbachev/Aquino/Shagari model typically argue that durable economic reforms must be built upon a political consensus, and that a political consensus can only be built upon democracy. This strategy does not work because economic failure destroys political consensus. The Asian model addresses people who are desperately poor and in many cases terrified of warfare (South Korea after the Korean War; Singapore after the independence struggle fearful of its neighbors and of civil war; Taiwan and Hong Kong facing Chinese communism; China after a century of bloody upheaval) and uses economic success to build a consensus around economic reform and stability. A generation or two later, when these fears have been alleviated, the regimes are forced to address the need for political dignity for several reasons. First, social changes increase social freedom even in the face of repressive efforts. Second, economic liberalization loosens the regime's most powerful lever, its control over people's jobs. Third, economic growth expands trade and travel and access to foreign information, and thereby exposes the population to democratic ideas. Fourth, demands for some form of democratization from a population that is now educated, self-confident, and able to organize as a political force become overwhelming. Typically democratization leads to a burst of pent-up protest and inflation (as in Taiwan and South Korea in the late 1980s), but by now the institutions and the consensus have sufficient strength to keep their balance.

Western history as it is popularly understood does not adequately comprehend the necessity for sequencing development. Most Western countries did not have to cope with the popular expectations and potentially explosive pressures of a liberalizing socialist country. More important, a country like the United States was historically lucky: it initiated democracy and gradually built up competent institutions at a time when the populace did not expect detailed government management of the economy and, above all, when poor communications and the dispersion of most of the population over a vast area precluded the early emergence of powerful pressure groups. Parties, pressure groups, and factions were anathema to the majority of America's Founding Fathers; they are the common currency of modern Third World development.

The Western pundits' insistence that political and economic reforms must be simultaneous reflects the same analytic fallacies as the insistence that all economic reforms must be carried out simultaneously and spasmodically. Such views derive from an inability to grasp the importance of building up institutions and political support; as soon as one takes such requirements into account, the need for time and a logical sequence of steps becomes apparent. *Moreover in one sense the need for economic reform to precede political reform derives from the need for an extended sequence of gradual economic reforms. Commitment to a generation-long sequence of difficult economic reforms requires a presumption of political stability. Competitive politicians who must run for reelection every two to six years usually cannot escape the moral hazard of giving reelection priority over saving the country's economy.* It is worth recalling that Aristotle believed democracy fatally vulnerable to demagoguery; any Third World politician trying to implement an economic reform would agree. Only an infrastructure of sound economic and administrative institutions can invalidate Aristotle's insight.

In China, an authoritarian regime has imposed successful economic policies, and those policies have so improved public welfare that they have induced widespread public support for reform. In areas such as Guangdong where the policies have been most successful, they are already creating a society where people are more educated, have more contact with foreigners and foreign ideas, have money to spend as they wish, travel more widely than they are officially allowed to do, own illegal radio and television receivers to listen to foreign broadcasts, work for companies not controlled by Communist Party bosses, have a measure (though not a full measure) of the religious freedom previously denied them,[9] and speak relatively freely. But China is still in the phase of South Korea or Taiwan in the late 1960s, when social changes were producing modest initial spots of freedom on a repressive map, but long before social conditions forced the democratization of both polities in the late 1980s. Western commentators have not learned the lessons of Taiwan and South Korea; their denunciations of China in 1992 mimic their denunciations of South Korea in 1976.[10] The Asian model works, whereas the Philippine/

---

[9]See for instance James McGregor, "Returnees to China's Fujian Revive Spirit of the Past," *Asian Wall Street Journal*, June 12–13, 1992, p. 1, which relates how wealthy returnees from Taiwan have been building temples and helping to revive religion. Christian churches have also sent missionaries all over China, sometimes covertly, often using sports and cultural events as a mode of entry.

[10]Reporting by *The New York Times* is a fair proxy for the best of the U.S. press. In 1976, the *Times* gave overwhelming, sometimes almost daily and frequently front-page, coverage to student demonstrations against the South Korean government, accompanied by predictions of imminent political and economic collapse. Reportage of the extraordinary South Korean

Nigerian/Brazilian/Russian model fails both economically and politically.

An important caveat to this argument is that totalitarian systems have sometimes arisen in relatively developed societies. Therefore, economic modernization is a necessary but not sufficient condition of market democracy. Nazi Germany was certainly a totalitarian society, and Germany was one of the more highly developed economies of its day. But totalitarianism in Germany developed in the context of the economic collapse and national humiliation of the Weimar Republic. Such collapse and humiliation breed the frustration and anger that can midwife a totalitarian system at any stage of development. Had Nazi Germany been contained internationally, it probably would have begun to rot and become destabilized internally, just as the Soviet Union did. In today's world, we are dealing primarily with regimes where totalitarianism has failed; that failure has inoculated much of the world—including China and Eastern Europe—against an early return of totalitarianism.

The fallacy of Western ideology is that political reform must always precede or coincide with economic reform. Con-

----

economic growth, which reached its highest peak that year, was negligible. While the coverage of demonstrations and repression was factually accurate, it was wildly overblown in the context of the Third World, and the predictions of collapse were completely wrong because no effort was made to analyze the political implications of economic growth. During this period, liberal commentators reacted with uniform contempt to the view that economic growth would promote pluralism, which would eventually force freedom and democracy—the conclusion that virtually all of Western sociology points toward. Coverage of China from June 1989 through November 1991 followed exactly the same pattern, but in the Chinese case has been followed since December 1991 by excellent economic reporting and increased probing of the social and political consequences of growth. Other publications have been slow to follow.

versely, the fallacy of the Asian authoritarians, including China's octogenarian leaders, is that economic liberalization can proceed indefinitely without political liberalization. The Asian experience is that economic success leads inexorably to political reform, but that political reform lags by a generation in the smaller countries; it may take somewhat longer in a continental-size country.

CHINA'S NEW BRAND OF PACIFIC ASIAN TAKEOFF

In South Korea, Taiwan, and Singapore, development was initiated by radical redistributionist leaders who believed in thorough government control of the economy and dictatorial politics. Park Chung Hee, who came to power in South Korea by military coup in 1961, had strong socialist inclinations. (He was at one point expelled from the army and severely punished for helping out his brother, who was a radical leader.) He believed in thoroughgoing government control of the economy, which he achieved through government ownership of the banks and tight control over a dozen huge conglomerates that were given privileged economic positions and run by politically friendly leaderships. Park was persuaded by his first advisers to permit private ownership and to establish competition among the conglomerates.

Despite such concessions, Park never abandoned much of his radical egalitarianism; to the end of his rule, even though South Korea became the world's leading exporter of color televisions, South Korea banned color television at home because Park did not want social distinctions to develop between those who could afford color and those who could only afford black and white. The land reforms of the Syngman

Rhee era, the leveling of industry by the Korean War, and Park's egalitarian measures (e.g., steep luxury taxes and a ruthlessly egalitarian education policy) produced an egalitarian economic takeoff that served as a broad base for consumer industry.

Taiwan's development began with a variant of egalitarianism: large-scale land reform, egalitarian education and tax policies, and a deliberate effort to spread the ownership of industry as widely as possible. (The emphasis on egalitarian distribution of ownership rather than just income contrasted sharply with South Korea, where the government deliberately concentrated industry to ensure government control and economies of scale.) Through the early 1970s, Taiwan's government publicly emphasized its commitment to socialism. The government owned and controlled the banking system into the late 1980s, and it used the banking and the regulatory systems to control the economy in accordance with a series of one-year, three-year, five-year, ten-year, and even twenty-year plans as it ascended the same ladder of development as South Korea.

Lee Kwan Yew's Singapore began its rapid development after his party's electoral victory in 1959. Lee developed his party as a combined ally and competitor of the Communist Party, espousing a line of radical nationalism and socialist economics that mimicked much of the communists' own platform. Victorious, he suppressed the Communist Party and built a state which sought to control the economy in extraordinary detail, through a combination of state ownership of the principal banks and of major industries, through state financial dominance built on a social security system that controlled a large fraction of every worker's wage, and through regulations that controlled the minute details of business. South Korea, Taiwan, Singapore, and Hong Kong all climbed the same basic route: shoes, textiles, and garments first; toys and other light consumer goods second; then refrigerators and other consumer durables; and later some combination of cars, ships, petrochemicals, computers, and modern service industries.

The three relatively state-controlled economies prospered once they had moved to export-led strategies of development, in part because the economies were very simple. Over time, however, all three were forced by economic reality to make gradually increasing concessions to market forces—concessions which became huge when, by the early 1980s, the economies had grown so pluralistic and complex that they were impossible for the state to manage in detail. Economies that had started by producing rice and T-shirts by then were producing the whole range of modern industrial products, plus a considerable range of modern services. Taiwan and South Korea modified their highly controlled, highly protected economies by creating export processing zones where the controls were relaxed so that foreign companies could use them as export platforms. These in turn became so successful and so influential for the rest of the economy that the broader society appeared more like the export processing zones than like the original semi-socialist economies. (Hong Kong from the start was an export processing zone and in the 1980s became China's principal export processing zone.)

Gradually, political and governmental controls over the major manufacturing and service industries were relaxed. It was a revolution when, for instance, South Korean banks began in the 1980s to give loans based on creditworthiness rather than just government edicts, and to charge interest rates determined by the market rather than by presidential advisers. It was a revolution when the conglomerates no longer had to get a license from the president's office for every major import and every major foreign exchange transaction. Slowly the banking systems were partially privatized. State control over these economies remained far greater than in the West, but by the 1980s the relaxation of the hand of the state had progressed sufficiently that America's Republicans frequently referred to these reformed socialists as prime examples of the success of capitalism. They were in fact neither socialist nor capitalist, but a new amalgam of state leadership, market forces, and state efforts to facilitate market adjustments.

All of the New Industrial Economies (NIEs) were run by relatively authoritarian governments. South Korea was a modified military dictatorship, willing to hold elections so long as they did not interfere with the development program and the power of Park Chung Hee, but not otherwise. Hong Kong was a British colony which had developed a range of mechanisms for consulting various sectors of the community but kept ultimate power to make decisions fully in the hands of the colonial Governor General. Singapore was a state in which Lee Kwan Yew and his People's Action Party so dominated political life that elections which yielded one or two opposition legislators were treated as a risk to the nation—and the opposition legislators were isolated and hounded accordingly. Taiwan was initially a repressive authoritarian state with a structure virtually identical to that of communist Beijing: a single party, headed by an overwhelmingly powerful figure and structured on the Bolshevik model under the guidance of Soviet communist Mikhail Borodin, with the full panoply of Central Committee, a legislature guided from above, deep roots down to the village level, and near-totalitarian methods of control exercised through an alliance of Party, army, and intelligence services.

All of the NIEs found that development eventually brought pressures for greater political freedom and representation. When the economy became too complex for the chief of state to control it personally, the ensuing decentralization cost the government one of its most powerful political levers. As the number, concentration, and education levels of workers rose, they formed powerful pressure groups regardless of government wishes; by the late 1980s, South Korea and Taiwan both had organized mass labor unions, and even Hong Kong's government was being pushed around by its civil service. As trade and education brought more and more contact with foreigners, the population increasingly demanded the democratic rights they heard articulated. As fear of starvation and war diminished, governments could no longer play on those fears to justify authoritarian control, so the priority for individual rights and political dignity rose. Park Chung Hee found it useful to have a tame opposition organized into a political party. Taiwan's one-party state first suppressed (and sometimes executed) opposition leaders; later it tolerated an officially illegal opposition. By the mid-1980s, Kuomintang leaders briefed visitors on a long list of reasons why they had found it useful to have an organized opposition to articulate problems and negotiate solutions. By the late eighties both Taiwan and South Korea were forced to convert from authoritarian rule to democracy; Singapore had to tolerate an organized opposition and the presence in parliament of opposition figures; and Hong Kong had an emergent—but much weaker—democratic movement.

The Asian economic powers have not abandoned socialist and dictatorial controls willingly. Park Chung Hee of South Korea, his successor, Chun Doo Hwan, and Chiang Kai Shek of Tiawan were no democrats. They were forced by security fears to emphasize economic growth, by the demands of economic efficiency to accept market economic practices, and by the social consequences of economic success to liberalize their politics.

China began its post-revolutionary development in a way that could have led in the same direction as the smaller Asian success stories. Its land reform, urban egalitarian measures, ruthless emphasis on national unity and stability after the civil war, and its early technocratic efforts to restore and enhance production (1949–52 for restoration, 1952–57 for relatively technocratic efforts at development) were analogous to events in South Korea and Taiwan. But it diverged in crucial ways. It ruthlessly crushed small business. It emphasized monopolies rather than competition. It imposed autarky rather than internationalization. It gave priority to heavy industry over light and medium industry. It failed to provide adequate mass education. Its priority for politics over economics caricatured the worst early mistakes of the smaller countries. Unlike the smaller countries, China failed to recognize and correct these errors. In the Great Leap Forward, Mao Zedong disrupted China's development through inappropriate and unsettling economic policies, and during the Cultural Revolution he simply ripped China's social structure apart, destroying its institutions of governance, its cadre of leaders, its educational system, and its intellectual elite.

Taiwan and South Korea made many of the same early mistakes as China. They tried import substitution (the small country's version of autarky), but under U.S. pressure rectified their errors. South Korea's Syngman Rhee tried emphasizing politics and military strength at the expense of the economy and failed miserably, as did his democratic successor Chang Myon, whose priority for politics fatally neglected economic imperatives. Gradually, as the result of failures and pressure from the United States, the smaller countries moved to systems where patriotic elites used their dominant position to impose economic efficiency as the country's supreme priority; they learned from U.S. and IMF pressure, and from watching one another, which policies worked, then imposed those policies ruthlessly. Those countries which took other routes—such as the Philippines' patronage democracy, which emphasized political values at the neglect of the economy;

Burma's Buddhist and military regimes, which emphasized cultural and security values at the expense of the economy; or Sukarno's Indonesia, which emphasized international influence and domestic political gamesmanship at the expense of the economy—all experienced domestic fragmentation and international vulnerability. Those countries which emphasized economic priorities, on the other hand, gradually acquired the resources to calm domestic political quarrels and to defend themselves from foreign aggression or subversion.

China has learned the same lessons more slowly and painfully. Politics in command has given way to economics in command. Import substitution has given way to export-led growth. Autarky has given way to a welcome of foreign trade and investment much warmer than in, for instance, the Philippines or even Indonesia. Socialist commands have given way to market forces—but very gradually, with light and medium industry first and the banks a distant last. Capital grants are giving way to interest-bearing loans. Monopoly is giving way grudgingly to competition. Priority for heavy industry has given way to priority for light industry. A closed society has given way to a still repressive but much more open one. Intellectuals have reluctantly been granted more (albeit still very limited) leeway to debate and to disagree with the leadership than would ever have been tolerated before. Economic and political liberalization were allowed to progress only to the extent that they did not interfere with institutional stability and expert management of the economy. There were significant differences of emphasis and pattern among these Asian takeoffs, but most of them shared most of these common features.

China's political liberalization has just begun. Most of it has not come about as a result of changes in government policies, but rather from changes in social structure over which the government has very little control. Twenty years ago

China was a caricature of totalitarianism, worse than Hitler's Germany in the degree of control over individuals. Everyone wore the same blue clothes; everyone wore nondescript haircuts; the women looked like the men. Political indoctrination classes constituted a major aspect of life. It was not just that wrong thoughts were penalized, but that everyone was constantly forced to speak out and make his or her thoughts available for public scrutiny. "Struggle" sessions brutally imposed political correct thoughts and behavior. Children were taught to spy on parents. Neighborhood committees kept everyone under constant surveillance. Living in China was far worse than living in any Latin American country and worse than living in virtually any African country.

Vogel describes the emotional aftermath of the political struggles that immediately preceded the era of reform: "Some liberated cadres were too old to return to work, and many of those still of working age were so debilitated emotionally that they found it hard to follow routines. It took years for many people to take a real interest in their work, and fears had not fully dissipated a decade later."[11]

Today, China remains an authoritarian country with widespread political controls and extensive abuses of human rights. But the cloud has just begun to lift. People speak relatively freely; even government officials in Beijing bitterly criticize their top leaders in front of near strangers, whereas this would have been a death sentence before. The totalitarian aspects are fading; more time is devoted to production and less to political classes. Efficiency and expertise are valued more and political correctness less. Millions of foreigners and Taiwanese wander around China, spreading new ideas. Foreign magazines and newspapers are widely available; anyone who reads English can buy the Asian Wall Street Journal or the

[11]Vogel, One Step Ahead in China, p. 32.

International Herald Tribune at a hotel newsstand. While CNN television is confined to major hotels, when Chinese wanted to follow something like the Gulf War of 1991, they rented a hotel room and used it like a movie theater to watch the Americans bombing Saddam Hussein. An entire nation was immediately aware of the details of the electoral defeat of George Bush, whereas it was long kept in the dark about the fate of Richard Nixon.

Politicians and Communist Party institutions are no longer sacrosanct. Some have come forward to sue Party institutions, for example, the official newspaper *People's Daily,* and some courts have been willing to hear the lawsuits. Recently, the carefully selected Party candidates for local office have been losing elections in droves.

Controversies over government policy have also thrown the window open. Previously, the government tried to maintain a facade of unity and to suppress public knowledge even of which issues were being debated. Now, policy debates are open and often highly personal. During the Fourteenth Party Congress, Li Peng's work report was severely criticized in public debates and he was forced to amend it many dozens of times. In another famous debate, Vice Premier Tian Jiyun ridiculed the leftists and suggested setting up a special region for them where prices would be kept very low but no goods would be available. While the debate still falls far short of the British House of Commons, the public now knows what the issues are and which politicians take which positions. Increasingly, the politicians are being forced into open efforts to mobilize public support.

Lifestyles (as we saw) have been transformed. People wear clothing as colorful as anywhere in the world. Chinese students avidly watch videos of American movies. Abstract art and nudes are acceptable once again. Art and movies, while still subject to censorship, are no longer relentlessly politicized, and the censor's touch has become relatively light; instead of socialist realism and politics, art and movies celebrate natural scenery and beauty of all kinds and increasingly examine such themes on multiple levels which include critiques of the authorities and their views.[12] Religion has become open; traditional Confucian temples are being built or refurbished, and Christianity is spreading everywhere in China. Karaoke bars are omnipresent and unavoidable—to the great pain of this non-singer and anyone who has to listen to him. Each bar carries a wide range of Chinese, Japanese, and Western songs; if you want to sing an old Frank Sinatra or Elvis Presley or Beatles hit, there will be no problem finding the tape at any of dozens of karaoke bars in any major city of China. In this once-prudish society, the Guangdong-based factory that makes Victoria's Secret lingerie decided in 1991 to have its first fashion show—with Hong Kong models, of course, so that the local girls would not besmirch their reputations. (I related this to a visiting ardent feminist who worked for a congressional committee in Washington, D.C., and she angrily rebutted, "That's not progress!" But Chinese women, after a generation of unisex blue rags, are just as enthusiastic about this form of liberalization as the men.)

As Dai Qing, a leading dissident journalist, recently told the *Asian Wall Street Journal,* "The media are more lively than they have been for several years. It is the result of economic reform, not of political reform. Now the party says as long as you don't curse us, and as long as you don't demand that we step down, you can say anything you want. . . ."[13] This is not Western freedom. But it is a different world from the

---

[12]See for instance Geoffrey O'Brien, "Blazing Passions," *New York Review of Books,* September 24, 1992, especially pp. 38–39.

[13]Catherine Sampson, "China's Media Go to Market," *Asian Wall Street Journal,* February 26–27, 1993, p. 9.

effort at total control of people's thought which used to be the defining characteristic of Chinese communism.

The greatest progress has come in Guangdong Province, where the economy is furthest advanced and contact with foreigners is most intense. There, life is coming to resemble the Hong Kong of ten to twenty-five years ago. People wear Hong Kong fashions, listen to Hong Kong radio, and watch Hong Kong television via illegal satellite dishes that are installed by the local military units; members of the army technical units make most of their annual income by installing and maintaining these illegal dishes that pour subversive ideas into every household.

As in countries like South Korea, the universities create a major dilemma for an authoritarian government. On one hand, the government wants to keep the students under control and has resorted to sending them off to a period of required military training. At Beijing University, in some ways China's most prestigious university, this form of repression threatened to cripple the institution for several years after Tiananmen Square. (By 1993 things were returning to normal.) Organized dissidence or published criticism of the leadership of the Communist Party brings immediate repression. On the other hand, the same government knows that it desperately needs creative intellectuals, and creativity requires intellectual space. As the stature of intellectuals rises, the long-term trend is for intellectual space to increase despite the regime's repressive intentions. In its better moments, even the Party leadership knows it has to come to terms with the necessity to give the intellectuals room for debate and critical thought. Over lunch with a graduate student in Beijing recently, I chose a list of very sensitive issues and asked her whether it was possible to discuss them seriously. She said, "Oh, yes. We divide into teams and debate them." Many intellectuals are openly critical of the regime in a way they could not have been before the beginning of reforms, and they have access to foreigners—and foreign media—to a degree that was once unthinkable. The media presence highlights the high degree of repression that remains, but simultaneously creates a wedge that over time tends very gradually to increase freedom of maneuver.

Economic progress requires the separation of politics from management. Hitherto, the Party secretary was the real boss of most firms. Pushing these potentates of political indoctrination aside has been gradual and difficult in the largest state factories, but steady progress has been made. More important, the proliferation of private, foreign, village and town enterprises has meant that the Party secretaries have simply been bypassed in all the most dynamic sectors of the economy. Large foreign joint ventures frequently still have Party secretaries, but in much of the country they have been given the job of making sure that corporate policies are fully implemented. The ironic fate of the Communist Party boss in the modern Chinese enterprise is to ensure that foreign capitalist policies are faithfully followed by obedient workers.

There are efforts, also, to separate government administration from Party politics. These efforts have only just begun, but the widespread acknowledgment that the separation must occur is a major breakthrough.

One of the more amusing problems of economic reform has been coping with the excessively high wages paid by foreign firms. Traditional ideology held that multinational corporations must be expelled to avoid exploitation of the workers. As it happens, the multinationals pay so much more than the state enterprises and the Chinese government that everyone wants to work for them. Beijing responded by putting limits on the wages foreign firms could pay—so as to avoid "theft" of workers from the government and the state enterprises. The multinationals responded by providing workers with a wide range of benefits. Beijing in turn demanded that the multi-nationals collect heavy taxes on the benefits. As a group, the multinationals refused. Away from Beijing, most authorities refused to fight this battle. The whole exercise has been profoundly damaging to traditional Marxist ideology. Now only America's AFL-CIO unions are left to continue the tradition of denouncing the multinationals for running awful Asian sweatshops.

Another clash between economic progress and arbitrary government comes in the realm of the law. Foreign companies insist on contracts, and on reasonably familiar judicial or arbitration measures to enforce them. The result has been a revolution in China's legal system: the desire to do long-term, large-scale business with foreigners has forced Beijing to begin creating a legal system that is not just one more arm of arbitrary state policy. The rule of law is still largely confined to commercial contracts, and local courts still treat criminal and political law as pretty much an arm of the Party. But this too is beginning to change; there are some independent lawyers and there are occasional cases of citizens trying to sue the state. During 1991–92 citizens of Sichuan Province sued the government on over three thousand occasions.[14] In Beijing the formerly sacrosanct *People's Daily* has been sued for libel.

China is still a very repressive country, with widespread abuses of basic human rights. It is still a worse place to live than most South American countries, but better than either El Salvador or Guatemala. It has a very long way to go, but no other country has progressed more rapidly in improving people's lives during the past decade. Westerners who take the

[14]See "Notable and Quotable," *Asian Wall Street Journal*, Editorial Page, May 10, 1993, quoting an article by Guo Luoji from *China Rights Forum*, Spring 1993.

full range of freedoms for granted usually have difficulty distinguishing one authoritarian Third World regime from another. Or their images are based on one vivid televised incident like Tiananmen Square in June 1989. China's situation today is comparable to South Korea's a generation ago: the repression is real, but the success and stability and glimmerings of freedom are real, too.

In this, the role of the Communist Party is ambivalent. There are the octogenarian leaders and Tiananmen Square. Yet it is worth recalling that two successive heads of the Communist Party, Hu Yaobang and Zhao Ziyang, lost their jobs for excessive enthusiasm for political reform. The tree of reform has high branches in the leadership and deep roots in the people. None of the major aspects of economic reform is reversible, and few of the major political reforms are reversible.

Characterizing China as one more liberalizing communist country leads one into the trap of believing that it will inevitably follow the Soviet or Eastern European models of collapse. Perceiving it as a country that is painfully but avidly learning and applying the lessons of its successful smaller Asian neighbors provides a more valid view. As Robert Scalapino has argued:

> The probability is that this society will move into a phase I have labelled that of authoritarian-pluralism. Politics will still be authoritarian, with various restraints and controls, although not operating under the same degree of rigidity as that of the classic Leninist state. Social institutions including those relating to education, religion and the family will have a certain degree of autonomy, varying with conditions. And in the economy, the market will play a prominent role, albeit, with the state still a vital force. Such a system bears consid-

erable resemblance to that of South Korea and Taiwan in earlier times, and permits intercourse across political boundaries with greater ease than is possible in hard authoritarian systems.[15]

Contemporary China is not another Soviet Union, nor is it the totalitarian Chinese state of 1966, but rather a gigantic, vintage 1972 South Korea.

[15]Robert Scalapino, "China and Its Neighbors—Old and New Trends," paper for the Asia Society Conference on "China and East Asia: Implications for American Policy," Wingspread (January 1991), subsequently reprinted in Scalapino, "China's Relations with Its Neighbors," *The China Challenge: American Policies in East Asia* (New York: Academy of Political Science and the Asia Society, 1991).

III

||||||||||||||||||||||||||||||||||||||||||||||||||||||||||||||||||||||||||||

THE EMERGENCE

OF CAPITAL

MARKETS

Police with cattle prods and batons battled to keep order last night as thousands of Chinese thronged to Shenzhen for the chance to buy shares in a wave of get-rich-quick fever.

China's capitalist revolution went mad with a deluge of people hoping for the chance to buy shares in the city's Stock Exchange.

Queues formed outside more than 300 locations, sparking disturbances and surprising the authorities who were preparing for a potentially explosive situation when doors opened this morning. . . .

So great was the demand for stocks and so small the number of shares that the announcement of new issues caused mayhem.

—KENNIS CHU AND GARY CHAN,
"SHENZHEN SHARES FRENZY: THOUSANDS QUEUE FOR CAPITALISM,"
SOUTH CHINA MORNING POST, FRONT-PAGE LEAD ARTICLE, AUGUST 9, 1992

In September 1982, on a visit to Chengdu, the capital of China's Sichuan Province, I told my host that I wanted to see a village. After much consideration, I was taken by car more than two hours outside Chengdu to view a village deemed prosperous enough to be observed by a foreigner. The 200-odd families of this experimental village had been allowed to choose their own occupations and market their products on the free market. They had virtually abandoned agriculture and in its place had established over thirty rural industrial enterprises such as brick making. They were exceedingly prosperous compared with their neighbors, as demonstrated by a proliferation of new, two-story, 3,000-renminbi ($1,700) houses. Since the average income in the province was around $50 per year, these were fabulously luxurious compared to anything else I seen.

But these villagers had a problem: their experience gave them no basis for distributing the profits of their numerous overlapping enterprises. Therefore they had invented what they described at length as the socialist concept of share ownership: villagers could buy shares in whatever enterprises they liked and would receive profits proportionate to the number of shares they owned. After listening for two hours to the elaboration of the socialist concept of share ownership, I joked that I would return in a few years and find them explaining the socialist concept of a stock exchange. Both my host and the "peasants" found my joke distinctly unfunny. They knew the stock market to be the arch symbol of capitalism, and they knew that any association of their socialist shares with a share market could be fatal.

Nine years later, on August 15, 1990, I was sitting in the Beijing conference room of Chen Yuan, deputy governor of China's central bank and son of Chen Yun, China's most famous opponent of Deng Xiaoping's market-oriented reforms. Mr. Chen explained the latest stage of China's economic development, which would emphasize the expansion of China's bond markets, the development of a widespread secondary market in bonds, the expansion of foreign exchange markets, the use of market-oriented monetary policy to control inflation, the forthcoming experiment with futures markets to stabilize grain prices, the improvement of China's system of shareholding, and, quite notably, the further development of China's stock markets.

Such was the condition of Chinese socialism in 1990, under the rule of China's orthodox post-Tiananmen leadership, as articulated by the son of China's most orthodox socialist economic leader. The continued expansion of stock markets was taken for granted, and the leadership was fully committed to building China's economic management around precisely those market tools that are the central symbols of modern capitalism. Economists from the Hong Kong Stock Exchange and two of Hong Kong's major stockbrokers even endeavored to provide China with a rationalization for the role of a stock exchange in a socialist system.[1]

THE DEVELOPMENT OF MARKETS

The emergence of financial markets in China is a somewhat technical but vitally important theme of the post-1979 economic reforms. These markets' development responds to the central problems of China's reform, and the debate over them pulls together all the central ideological struggles: command vs. market, central control vs. efficiency, state vs. private ownership, egalitarianism vs. growth, and Party vs. government control. Barring national disintegration, the expansion of

---

[1]Cf. Christopher Chong, Iris Cheung, and C. K. Law, "Does China Need a Stockmarket?", *Securities Journal,* Hong Kong (January 1991), Their essay was originally written for a research trip organized by my deputy, C. K. Law, of fifteen Hong Kong financial economists who went to Guangzhou and Beijing to analyze Chinese financial markets. I have benefited greatly from that trip and from the ideas of the other economists on it.

these financial markets is destined to be one of the dominant trends of the 1990s. And China's economic success or failure will depend on whether these great tools of capitalism can be employed to mold its future socialist reforms.

The way China has handled the development of capital markets illustrates its broader strategy of reform. The authorities responded to concrete needs of the economy rather than to a master ideological blueprint. And early and late they made great efforts to explore alternative ways of achieving their goals and projecting a coherent sequence of reform. They permitted and encouraged extensive local initiatives, even at times ratifying decisions which, as with the premature opening of the Shenzhen Stock Exchange, explicitly contravened central directives. They let institutions like the bond market develop organically—and somewhat chaotically—then stepped in to regulate them when they felt they understood the needs of the economy and the options for regulation. They exhibited a remarkable grasp of the institutional requirements of Western-style financial markets. They understood the need for institutions to grow gradually, and to mature before being asked to bear the full weight of national reform.

In all this, China's reform constituted the sharpest possible contrast to some of the East European countries, where institutions were frequently expected to appear magically overnight. Apparently much of Western academia has spent so much time focusing on the mathematical manipulation of market models that it has forgotten the institutional assumptions behind the market models: a Western legal system; Western accounting techniques; "perfect information" provided to accountants by firms and by accountants to a financial communications network that embraces much of society; a population that has been educated to receive and understand such information; and many others. One Soviet proposal (alluded to in Chapter I) was to allocate equal amounts of vouchers to all citizens and then suddenly sell the nation's industries to the voucher holders; somehow the citizenry was expected to make rational decisions without any experience in valuing companies and without any systematic information to guide their decisions.

Financial reforms are never easy, but they are far easier than most other kinds of reform, so financial reform has raced ahead, creating stock markets, bond markets, futures markets, and currency reforms even in the Li Peng years immediately following Tiananmen Square. The pace of financial reform made an enormous contribution to the rational allocation of China's economic assets. At the same time, it ran the risk that financial reform would so far outpace every other kind of reform, and that the ideology of the market in the financial sector would so far outpace ideological change elsewhere, that a crisis could conceivably occur.

The emergence of capital markets was a response to specific problems. Without a share system, enterprises could not distribute their profits equitably. Without a bond market, price reforms led to massive inflation. Without treasury bonds, the government could not finance vital infrastructure programs (and socialist subsidies). Without stocks and enterprise bonds, successful enterprises could not raise adequate capital to sustain their growth. Without a system of bank loans, rather than socialist grants, the government could not control its capital expenditures and allocate them efficiently.

GOVERNMENT BONDS

Government bonds were first issued in 1981. By 1989, the state's need to raise funds for development projects, to finance its rising deficits, and to soak up inflation-causing excess liquidity had stimulated the issuance of 54 billion renminbi worth of government bonds. They were sold both to institutions and to individuals. Initially, bonds had uniformly long maturities and low interest rates; but by the latter 1980s a differentiated market was emerging, and interest rates were responding to market forces. Instead of ten-year bonds, the market was increasingly dominated by three- and five-year maturities. Interest rates were made responsive to inflation and rose from 8 to 14 percent per annum in 1988.

By the end of the decade, the forms of state-issued bonds had proliferated: they included government bonds, treasury bonds, special project bonds, and value-guaranteed bonds with interest rates indexed to inflation.

Primary sales of bonds were such an obvious way to raise money they created few ideological problems. But financial and economic changes led the holders of bonds to need to trade them—and to trade them at prices reflecting market conditions as well as the face value of the bonds. In a free market, when interest rates rise, the principal value of old bonds falls, and vice versa when interest rates decline. Beginning in 1988, Chinese authorities decided to allow the emergence of such secondary market trading in seven big cities. By June 1988, they expanded this to fifty-four cities, of which eight were in fast-growing Guangdong. But they restricted trading to government bonds, negotiable certificates of deposit, and other instruments approved by People's Bank of China (PBOC). And they allowed trading only by securities companies, trust and investment companies, and others specially approved by the government.

In April 1988, the State Council (central government) set up secondary markets for bonds in sixty-one cities. PBOC in Beijing reported that it had authorized thirty-four securities companies and four hundred trust and investment companies

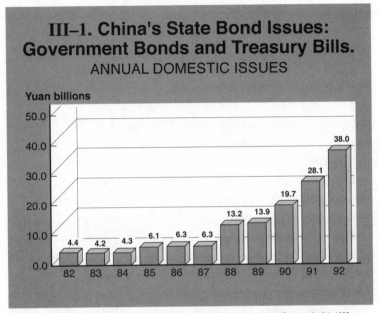

III–1. China's State Bond Issues: Government Bonds and Treasury Bills.
ANNUAL DOMESTIC ISSUES

SOURCES: State Statistical Yearbook, 1992, p. 200; "China Starts 31 Billion Yuan Issue," Reuters, April 1, 1992.

nationwide to deal in securities;[2] Guangdong officials said their province had about one hundred approved companies.[3]

Government bonds were followed by enterprise bonds. Then a 1984 explosion of credit and inflation led to tight government controls that cut off many enterprises from their traditional sources of capital. Thus, starting in 1985, many enterprises began issuing their own bonds to the public. Guangdong officials presented this as a relatively spontaneous response to new conditions.

But the widespread issuing of bonds created serious prob-

[2]Discussion with Jin Jian Dong, Director of Financial Administration, People's Bank of China, August 13, 1990.

[3]Interview with Jin Wei Chang, President, PBOC Guangdong Branch, August 9, 1990.

lems. People confused bonds and shares; the instruments were
not standardized and were therefore illiquid; and the state objected that they were being used to finance fixed-asset investments that were not approved by the state plan and therefore
undermined the plan. In response, Guangdong promulgated
in 1986 the "Temporary Regulation to Control Bonds and
Shares in Guangdong Province," followed in 1987 by the
State Council's "Temporary Regulation of Enterprise Shares
and Bonds."

There is even an emergent credit-rating process for enterprise bonds. In Shanghai, all bonds must obtain third-party
assessment of their creditworthiness. Guangdong has the
Credit Department of the People's Bank of China do this, but
is experimenting with a third-party system. Such assessments
seem destined to displace the current simplistic system
whereby the government simply requires a firm to show that
the total value of its bonds does not exceed its net asset value.

While these developments began to regulate the market,
they also legitimized it. By beginning to standardize the forms
of bonds, the regulations set the stage for the later emergence
of national bond markets. Officials emphasize that regulations are still amended frequently and controls are quite imperfect. The government is still overregulating the market: it
prohibits bonds that pay interest above levels set by the state,
bonds that would finance fixed assets not approved as part of
the national plan, and trading that would result in a secondary market yield in excess of 15 percent. But the process of
forming bond markets is well under way.

The 1984–85 experience of a credit squeeze and need to
rely on enterprise bonds repeated itself with a vengeance in
1989–90. By this time, the government was more comfortable
with the idea and, led as always by Guangdong, encouraged
the proliferation of new instruments. Bonds issued by commercial entities to the public now include two kinds of state

enterprise bonds: bank financial bonds and negotiable certificates of deposit; and enterprise bonds with short-, medium-, and long-term maturities. In addition, some enterprises issue bonds to their own workers. (These are distinct from the IOUs forcibly distributed in lieu of wages by some enterprises during the credit squeeze.)

By 1990, the total value of securities issued in China since 1981 reached about 100 billion renminbi ($16.5 billion), of which stocks constituted only 4 percent. By the end of 1992, stocks alone were worth more than that. Growth of both stock and bond markets is exponential. In December 1990, China opened a world-class, nationwide, computerized bond-trading network, the Securities Trading Automated Quotations System (STAQS), which can expand to include stocks as well as bonds.

Beijing has also been modernizing China's bond-issuing mechanisms. In the 1980s, an extremely common practice—called "administrative flotation"—imposed bonds on workers by docking their pay.[4] An executive of China's Stock Exchange Executive Council tells the story of "one university professor who stubbornly refused to buy the 100 renminbi worth of treasury bonds allocated to him by the university, while buying 3,000 renminbi worth of the same bonds through his own bank. He explained his action by saying that it was not that he disliked treasury bonds as such, but that he could not accept the method of 'administrative flotation.'"

Beginning in 1991, the central bank began using securities companies as underwriters; each securities company committed itself to sell a certain amount of bonds and to buy any unsold remainder of its allocation. The underwriting system avoided the resentment created by forced allocation, and it

[4]Xie Simin, "China's Stock Market—Problems and Future Development," *China Newsletter* 89 (November–December 1990), p. 21.

also soaked up pools of money that otherwise could have suddenly flooded into purchases of goods and caused serious inflation.[5] In this system, government bureaucrats usually set the price. Typically, they set interest rates high enough that there was excessive demand for the bonds; underwriters eagerly grabbed as many as they could, and for issues to which private individuals could subscribe, people queued up before dawn.[6] Later, Beijing began allocating some by auction, as the U.S. government does with its Treasury bonds, with the price or interest rate set by the resulting market. This system faltered in early 1993, when officials refused to allow interest rates to rise proportionately to accelerating inflation.

Also in 1991, China began large-scale issuance of yen bonds, and in 1992 it started issuing U.S. dollar and Hong Kong dollar bonds, both through the Bank of China and through large enterprises that required foreign exchange. By doing so it raised foreign currency from its own people as well as from foreigners, thereby reducing any potential future problems in raising foreign exchange. In February 1992, *Standard and Poor's* began rating China's foreign debts by Western standards.[7]

[5]Jim McGregor, "China Is to Use Underwriters for Bond Issue," *Asian Wall Street Journal*, April 19, 1991.

[6]Lincoln Kaye, "Debt Without Tears," *Far Eastern Economic Review*, April 16, 1992.

[7]"S&P Assigns Ratings to China Debt Issues," *Asian Wall Street Journal*, February 21–22, 1992.

MANAGEMENT OF AGGREGATE DEMAND

The shift to financing investment through bank loans rather than state grants, and the emergence of securities markets, raised the possibility of using market controls on money supply (rather than imposed prices) to manage the overall price level of the economy. By 1988, the total bank loans for capital construction were 30 billion renminbi, out of total capital construction investments of 150 billion, and the bank loan portion was growing very fast. In addition, the banks' voice in economic management was rising, and planners' familiarity with market concepts was improving.

This led China's central bankers to a firm conviction that inflation could be managed through control of overall money supply (with a focus on M2),[8] even during a process of price decontrol. And it was this idea that provided the foundation for the post-1989 wave of Chinese economic reform. The 1980s wave was aborted temporarily by excessive inflation. A combination of price liberalization, low interest rates, excessive credit, excessive investment, and an explosion of consumer demand caused that inflation, and central authorities tried ineffectually to manage it through price controls. Eventually, they panicked and temporarily rescinded some of the price liberalization. But China's bankers and planners now believe that controlling money supply through interest rates and fiscal policy can stabilize the overall level of prices during a new wave of decontrol of individual prices.

It remains to be seen whether China's decision makers will have the discipline to implement a reasonably tight fiscal policy and to use interest rates responsibly. In 1991–92, policy

---

[8]M2 is the total amount of cash, checking accounts, savings accounts, certificates of deposit, and time deposits in the economy.

makers began to have great difficulty controlling their banks'
allocation of credit, with the result that the money supply
rocketed upward dangerously. The problem occurs in an intermediate phase. Under full socialism, the central bank can
dictate everything; under full capitalism, banks that lend irre-
sponsibly will go bankrupt. In the intermediate phase, the central government has delegated a great deal of authority to
local banks, but these banks are still giving large numbers of
grants rather than loans and still know they will not be allowed to fail, so they can provide volumes of irresponsible
credit and get away with it. Yet the conceptual breakthrough
certainly shows the path to a successful price reform without
disastrous inflation. And the monetary tools work: so effective were Chinese bonds and banks at soaking up liquidity
that the 1990 marginal propensity to save reached 30 percent
in the rural areas. Bank deposits rose from 68 billion renminbi
in 1988 to 1.2 trillion in 1992. Success was achieved through
market-oriented interest rates; at the height of inflation, nominal interest rates on government bonds rose to 25–28 percent
and real rates to 5–6 percent. A few years earlier, such rates
would have been unthinkable.

FOREIGN EXCHANGE MARKETS

China's foreign exchange transactions are also evolving from
a highly controlled, artificially priced system toward a modern, national, market-priced system. Early transactions
focused on importing technology and capital equipment in return for commodity exports; an artificial, wildly overvalued
renminbi was perceived as useful for making imports cheap. If
this stimulated an excess of imports, the command system
could be used to block them.

Similarly, foreign investment consisted largely of participation in joint ventures; the artificially high renminbi overvalued the Chinese partner's contribution and thereby seemed to give China the better deal. With a few exceptions for high technology, infrastructure, and other high-priority projects, all joint ventures have been required to balance their foreign exchange earnings by exporting enough to pay for their imports of raw materials and technology.

China did not participate in international bond markets before the mid-1980s. In 1986, however, it began to issue bonds in the Tokyo market. After the June 4, 1989, tragedy in Tiananmen Square, China was briefly shut out of foreign bond markets, but it reentered yen markets on a large scale by 1991 and dollar markets by 1992. Another form of participation came through management of the country's massive foreign exchange reserves (over $40 billion by the end of 1991, earned—as we saw in Chapter I—by running trade surpluses). Most of the reserves were invested in foreign government bonds. Bank of China officials told me in 1990 that they were adjusting their foreign reserve portfolio by doing foreign exchange swaps on a daily basis. This makes China a significant player in international bond markets—and increasingly a sophisticated one.

As development accelerated, direct borrowing increased, and by the end of 1992 the foreign debt reached U.S. $69 billion. To keep this debt under control, China needed to encourage exports and discourage imports. But an overvalued renminbi did the opposite. Managing through direct controls on imports ended up blocking many needed imports or creating lengthy delays in getting them approved. It also encouraged vast corruption and caused trade conflicts with Western countries, notably the United States, which in 1992 threatened multi-billion-dollar sanctions unless China reduced the use of administrative measures to block imports.

In this situation, China began to learn the same lessons that most other countries in Northeast and Southeast Asia had learned in the previous three decades: To encourage development, one needs to promote exports and discourage imports through a cheaper currency. Hence China devalued the renminbi twice by over 20 percent each time, in 1989 and again in early 1990, moving it much closer to the market rate.[9] Afterward, it moved to a system of mini-devaluations designed to move the currency in the direction of its market rate.

In 1992, responding to U.S. trade pressures and to its own

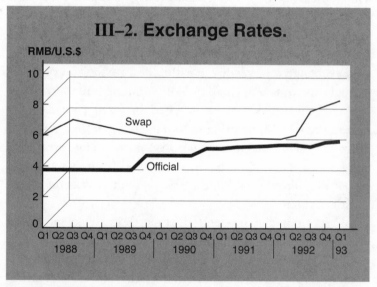

III–2. Exchange Rates.

SOURCES: State Administration of Exchange Control; IMF; U.S. Treasury Department; and various press reports.

[9] The promotion of exports through devaluation works differently, but nonetheless with great effectiveness, in China compared to free markets. Most trade is denominated in dollars, so devaluation does not make exports cheaper. But it increases the number of renminbi the exporter receives and therefore greatly increases his incentive to export.

success in exporting and accumulating foreign reserves, Beijing greatly liberalized its import policy. The ensuing surge of imports raised demand for foreign currencies and depressed the value of the renminbi so that official and market rates came to diverge by over 20 percent.[10] During that same year the Chinese people discovered that they could gain access to foreign currencies and began to hoard them in very large amounts. This caused the value of the renminbi to fall sharply, taking the Chinese authorities by surprise. They failed to adjust the official rate quickly; in fact, they moved slightly in the other direction, probably in a misguided effort to slow the decline. This took them in the wrong direction if they wanted to move toward a freely convertible currency, as they said they were determined to do.

While this was happening, they were debating whether to move quickly to a fully convertible currency or to do it in measured steps. One of the proposals under consideration in 1992 was to create a fully convertible currency along the coast but continue to work with a non-convertible currency in the interior. The idea seemed to me unworkable, but Chinese authorities were profoundly concerned to avoid currency collapses such as those that had occurred in Eastern Europe and were determined to veto any sudden move that carried even a small risk of such collapse. The principal threat of a sudden currency decline probably did not derive from moves toward convertibility, but rather from public fears that China's proliferating money supply portended high inflation and therefore a less valuable renminbi.

Faced with an apparent scarcity of foreign exchange during the austerity programs, the government sought to make more efficient use of existing foreign exchange. It began allowing

---

[10]On December 27, 1992, the official rate was 5.57374 and the market rate ranged as high as 7.3, a discrepancy of 27 percent.

enterprises to retain a portion of their own foreign exchange earnings instead of turning all of them over to the state. In 1986, it introduced small foreign exchange markets that were completely free to find their own levels. Termed "foreign exchange adjustment centers," or swap centers for short, these markets in each major city allowed ventures with surplus foreign exchange to trade with ventures that needed additional foreign exchange—at whatever rate the parties found acceptable. Although the rate of exchange was a market rate, the trades occurred under government scrutiny; the acquisition of funds was restricted to enterprises needing them for high-priority projects; and the selling of foreign exchange was restricted to U.S. dollars (not other foreign currencies) acquired through legal retention by enterprises. Banks were prohibited from engaging in these trades, which were a monopoly of the State Administration of Foreign Exchange Control.

The government has gradually extended the swap centers throughout China and has now also made access to them easier. Initially, only foreign-invested enterprises could use them. In 1988, state and collectively owned enterprises were also given access. In 1991, to preempt the black market, both local and foreign residents in China were permitted to buy and sell foreign currency at swap center rates, using designated banks. Despite all the restrictions, swap centers tacitly acknowledged the need for extensive trading at a market rate. They established what the market rate was, and this set a benchmark for prices that affected transactions throughout China in innumerable ways.

Initially, the market rate was significantly different in different provinces, because the centers were far apart, supply and demand conditions varied, and arbitrage was considered an illegitimate form of speculation. But as central authorities came to perceive the value of the swap centers, they spread rapidly and soon were present in every major city. In 1990, Guangdong alone (excluding Shenzhen) had ten adjustment centers, and transactions were rising rapidly. Chen Yuan stated in 1990 that the centers were handling roughly 30 percent of all of China's foreign exchange transactions and aiming at 50 percent in the next few years. Reality moved much faster than the predictions: by 1992, the swap markets were handling $25.1 billion of exchanges. In August 1992, Beijing announced the opening of the National Foreign Exchange Swap Center, a computerized sixty-seat market, in hopes of creating a unified national market rate.[11]

The practical consequence of having half or more of all transactions at a market rate will be to rapidly undermine any efforts to maintain the other half at an artificial rate. Chen Yuan and others indicated in 1992 that it was government policy to move the official rate close to the market rate and subsequently to make the currency fully convertible. This in turn would facilitate China's membership in GATT, the trade association of the market economies, and thereby free China from important threats of trade sanctions.

The progress of market-based foreign exchange systems was enhanced by the extraordinary volume of foreign currency transactions and the degree of their penetration of the Chinese economy. Trade of over $160 billion generates about that volume of foreign exchange transactions. A single American company, Continental Grain, moves billions of dollars into and out of renminbi. From Hong Kong, fifty thousand executives commute to work in Guangdong every day, spending Hong Kong dollars. Even as early as August 1990, Bank of China officials said that private foreign exchange accounts to-

[11]John Kohut, "Currencies Swap Centre for Beijing," *South China Morning Post*, Business Post section, August 10, 1992, p. 1.

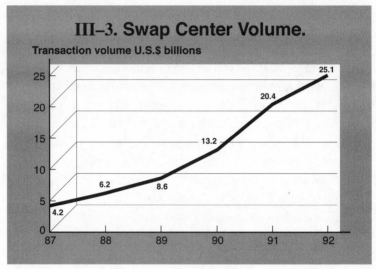

SOURCES: U.S. Treasury Department for 1987–90; Xinhua and China Daily reports for 1991–92.

taled U.S.$2.1 billion.[12] The State Administration of Foreign
Exchange Control for Guangdong Province estimated at that
time, that, excluding the capital account, foreign exchange
transactions amounted to 25 percent of the province's GNP;
including the capital account, the figure was 40 percent.[13]
Such is the volume of transactions in Guangzhou (formerly
called Canton) that an armored car full of Hong Kong currency is transferred every day from Guangzhou to Hong
Kong.

The reality of China's use of foreign exchange goes far
beyond what these numbers suggest. During a 1992 trip
across the country, I noticed volumes of foreign exchange in

[12]Meeting with Lei Zuhua and other Bank of China officials, August 13,
1990.

[13]Discussion with Ou Yang Shi Pu, State Administration of Foreign Exchange Control, August 9, 1990.

use everywhere. These monies are probably a large multiple of what the official statistics record. For instance, in Kashgar, one of the most distant outposts of the Muslim area of northwest China, when I wanted to change U.S. dollars into renminbi, the cashier at a tiny hotel pulled out an eight-inch stack of hundred-dollar bills and used a rubber band to add mine to the pile. Every hotel cashier along the Silk Road seemed to have such a stack, and most merchants of any scale seemed to have their own private ones.

China's banks began accepting deposits in foreign currency; in August 1990, banks in Guangzhou were quoting interest rates not just in the major currencies (U.S. dollars, yen, sterling, Deutschmarks, Swiss francs, Hong Kong dollars), but also in such minor currencies as Swedish kronor and Belgian francs. The rates quoted were very close to international market rates. The differences between buying and selling rates were much narrower than in Hong Kong, so the customer was getting a better deal in Guangzhou than in cartelized Hong Kong banks.

The Hong Kong dollar rather than the renminbi is the currency of choice throughout much of this province of 61 million people, and Guangzhou's taxi drivers accept fares in Hong Kong dollars at a uniform market rate which precludes any necessity for bargaining. In early 1993, a study by Hong Kong and Shanghai Bank estimated that 30 percent of Hong Kong's currency now circulates in Guangdong rather than in Hong Kong itself. The Hong Kong dollar plays a much larger role in Guangdong than the U.S. dollar played in Argentina or Poland; but unlike the authorities in Argentina and Poland for most of recent history, China's managers have accommodated thus far (though with noticeable uneasiness) and tried to adjust to the market rather than fighting it. This is auspicious both for China's financial markets and for its real economy.

What it means is that China's foreign exchange system is

moving rapidly in the direction of market exchange rates and market interest rates, and that informally Guangdong Province, with a population the size of Thailand, has moved much of the way to a market foreign exchange system.

Other pressures, too, have nudged China in the direction of liberalizing foreign exchange and investment. The country's enthusiasm for foreign investment has risen recently, not fallen. But economic conditions also force the government to liberalize further if it is to maintain a high level of foreign investment. The predominance of joint ventures prior to 1989 has begun to change. Before the credit squeeze of 1989–90, Chinese firms had adequate credit to enter into joint ventures, but that squeeze severely limited the capital available to potential Chinese joint venture partners. Hence the number of wholly-foreign-owned ventures rose disproportionately, and Chinese policy accommodated this.

In addition, China came under pressure to modify a burdensome requirement that foreign-owned firms and joint ventures "balance" their foreign exchange requirements. For the most part, this requirement has been interpreted narrowly: a company's exports of its own products had to generate enough foreign exchange to pay for its imports of machinery and raw materials as well as any profits it wanted to repatriate. There have been both formal and informal barriers to satisfying this requirement indirectly. In the early and mid-eighties this requirement had become the single biggest obstacle to foreign investment in China. Now, firms are encouraged to purchase goods from other firms and export them to earn the foreign exchange. For instance, if Avon were just selling cosmetics in Guangdong and exporting nothing, it could buy Chinese herbal medicines and export those in order to generate foreign exchange. Or it could invest in import-substituting industries to save the foreign exchange. Now foreign businesses can also, in many cases, just swap renminbi for dollars in the swap markets. The advent of the swap markets minimized the great currency bottleneck for foreign investors and began to reduce exchange problems as a key impediment to foreign investment.

The official encouragement of indirect methods of balancing foreign exchange will exert further pressures on the Chinese economy. For instance, in the past, big state enterprises often generated exports by subsidizing them—at enormous cost. The government then enabled these companies to make up the cost by maintaining a monopoly on domestic sales of other goods or on exports of other highly profitable items. Henceforth, these state enterprises will have to compete directly with foreign companies eager to do the same business and able to undercut the state enterprises because they do not need the monopoly profits.

STOCK MARKETS

China has two small but fully functioning formal stock markets, in Shanghai and Shenzhen, and a third one in Beijing, along with informal markets throughout the country.

The reemergence of share trading dates to 1984, when seven state enterprises in Shanghai were designated by authorities to issue shares to the public, and to 1986, when the Industrial and Commercial Bank of China set up a share trading counter.[14] Between 1984 and 1989, several thousand Chinese

[14]The first review of Chinese stock markets was published by this author for Bankers Trust in August 1990 and subsequently republished in *Asian Survey* XXXI, 5 (May 1991). My colleagues C. K. Law and Hung Lee Lai subsequently published periodic reviews distributed by Bankers Trust Securities (Pacific). Among recent useful reviews are Lawrence Ang, "China

companies issued 3.8 billion renminbi worth of shares.[15] In 1990, share trading began in Shenzhen, the special economic zone north of Hong Kong. Beijing intended Shanghai to open first and become the dominant market, but Shenzhen opened unofficially on December 1, 1990, just before Shanghai opened officially on December 19. Shenzhen's status was formalized the following July.

Chinese officials intended these two markets to operate in identical fashion, yet they have diverged. Shanghai initially traded mainly bonds, but used its bond business as a cover to get a real stock market going. From the beginning, Shenzhen focused more on stocks. Subsequently, Shanghai became the market for China's blue chips—mainly large state enterprises which remained heavily dependent on government orders. Shenzhen became the exchange for smaller, entrepreneurial companies which were largely dependent on the free market and on export competitiveness. In addition, because of its proximity to Hong Kong, Shenzhen was quicker to understand the importance of modern settlement systems and other techniques to protect investors.

The authorities moved very slowly and carefully in allowing companies to list; only the best and most profitable were approved. When Shenzhen officially opened in mid-1991, it had five listed companies with a book value of 200 million renminbi, combined market capitalization of over 3 billion renminbi, and some two hundred companies in line hoping to list by the end of 1991. As this is written in 1992, only seven-

---

Stock Market: A Guide for Foreign Investors," SBCI Finance Asia Ltd [Hong Kong], April 24, 1992, and Sassoon Securities, "A Background to Securities Investment in Shenzhen of the People's Republic of China" (January 1992, restricted circulation).

[15]X. Simin, "China's Stock Market—Problems and Future Development," *China Newsletter* 89, p. 19.

teen companies, with a total market capitalization of 17 billion renminbi, have succeeded in listing. Shanghai had seven
listed shares in early 1991 and twenty-six by December 16,
1992 (with 103 brokers vying for the shares). Because of the
stringent requirements for listing on the stock exchange, most
companies raised money through bonds rather than stocks;
thousands of companies in Shanghai alone issued bonds,
many of which were traded on the stock exchange.

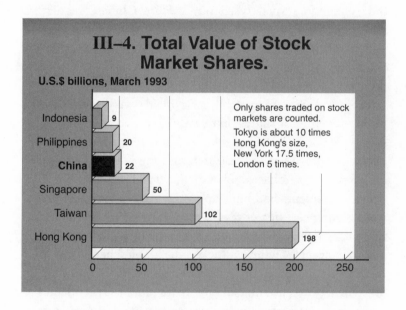

III–4. Total Value of Stock Market Shares.

U.S.$ billions, March 1993

Indonesia	9
Philippines	20
China	22
Singapore	50
Taiwan	102
Hong Kong	198

Only shares traded on stock markets are counted.

Tokyo is about 10 times Hong Kong's size, New York 17.5 times, London 5 times.

Stock market volatility presents both practical and philo-
sophical problems for Chinese authorities. Like the Japanese
and South Korean regulators in the 1980s, Chinese officials
would prefer a market that only goes up. From the beginning
they realized that, if their markets went up too fast, they
would inevitably come down with a bang. For this reason, one
senior banker in Beijing characterized regulation of the stock
markets as a failure in early 1991 because of the wild bull

markets caused by short supply and extensive demand. (Shanghai's Jing An Index appreciated 300 percent between April 1991 and November 1991.) But experience elsewhere— including major busts in Japan, Korea, and Indonesia—has demonstrated how difficult it is to manage markets. Chinese officials have meanwhile overcome some of their fear of instability. For instance, they initially issued regulations banning stock trades that moved the price up or down more than a certain percentage number in a single day. But in May 1992 they eliminated such restrictions. Here Chinese regulators moved much more quickly than, for example, Thailand, which still maintains such restrictions. By the end of 1992, Shanghai and Shenzhen had both experienced busts as well as booms.

From the beginning, Chinese officials were faced with a public demand for shares that vastly exceeded any foreseeable supply. By late 1990, Shenzhen had only five listed companies but sixteen brokers and 900 million renminbi on deposit for future share purchases. By August 1992, excitement over share investments had built up to the point where authorities were issuing certificates to the public for the right to buy future share issues; people had to buy these application forms and then accept whatever stock came along when it was their turn. Even in Shanghai, where excitement was less than in Shenzhen, it was not unusual for share purchase certificates to trade at 4,000 percent premiums to the original government charge.[16]

On August 8, 1992, about 1 million people from all over China gathered to purchase applications. Police used electric cattle prods to keep the unruly crowds under control. Key officials could not resist the opportunity to make corrupt profits

[16]"Waiting for Godot," *Far Eastern Economic Review,* July 16, 1992, p. 50.

by manipulating the application process, and major riots ensued on August 8–11. The share index plummeted 20 percent, and the government briefly closed the stock exchange. In December, several officials were convicted of corruption.

This incident may have reinforced those officials who supported a frequently reiterated decision that, instead of opening minor stock markets in many cities around China, there should be no new markets, and China would attempt to create a unified national stock market. This came as a shock to officials in Hainan, Shenyang, and other localities which had already invested in setting up local exchanges. It was a clear reversal of a policy declared by regulators to this writer and others in 1990 that many cities in the interior of China would eventually have their own stock exchanges.

By 1992, thousands of China's state enterprises had issued shares, but most were not allowed to sell their shares to individuals. Regulators faced a dilemma: They did not want ordinary people to be able to buy up the shares of state enterprises, but they needed an orderly system for trading these shares. In response, they made a distinction between "natural persons," or real people, and "legal persons," which were mostly government agencies and state enterprises. (Western law treats a limited corporation as a "legal person.") They then confined most state enterprises to selling their shares only to legal persons. The most important share trading involved these "legal person" shares, rather than "natural person" shares. In May 1992, the government issued standardized (but officially still experimental) rules for shareholding companies.[17] This development had two potentially momentous consequences. First, it could create a market mechanism for sorting out the ownership relations and financial values of

[17]Duncan Freeman, "New Options," *China Trade Report* (September 1992), p. 10.

China's state enterprises. Second, it promised a way for foreign investors to move easily in and out of stakes in Chinese companies as an alternative to joint venture contracts, which frequently locked the foreign investor into a potentially unhappy marriage for five to thirty years.

In July 1992, despite statements by high officials of People's Bank of China that no new stock markets would be permitted, Beijing began listing companies on a new Beijing stock market. But this was a different kind of stock market. Whereas Shanghai and Shenzhen trade "natural person" shares, Beijing trades "legal person" shares. That is, government entities and state enterprises trade shares in state enterprises. The purchasing enterprise gains a share of the profits and often a share of the management of the company whose shares it buys. The Beijing market emphasizes its national character, whereas Shanghai and Shenzhen have tended to confine themselves to local companies.[18] Despite the initial division of labor, there is a strong competitive push behind the new market, which unlike Shanghai and Shenzhen is not supervised by People's Bank of China. Beijing would like to do the other markets' business in natural person shares, and the others would like to do business in legal person shares.

China decided to move more quickly than predecessors like Taiwan and South Korea to open its stock markets to foreigners; after all, it is particularly useful for enterprises to be able to acquire foreign exchange for their shares. But, like other emerging markets, China wanted to ensure that foreigners were unable to come in and buy up all of the country's most successful enterprises. (Korea, Thailand, Taiwan, Indonesia, and the Philippines among others put special restrictions on foreign ownership of listed companies.) Following the exam-

---

[18]Thomas Chan, "Now It's the Peking Bourse," *China Trade Report* (December 1992), p. 10.

ple of Thailand, it created a special group of shares for foreigners, called "B shares," and limited them to a minority stake. In February 1992, both Shanghai and Shenzhen listed their first B shares. These B share issues require special approval from the central bank, and no investor is allowed to acquire more than 5 percent of a company without approval. Prices are quoted, and purchases are settled, in U.S. dollars or, more commonly in Shenzhen, in Hong Kong dollars. In mid-December 1992, Shenzhen and Shanghai each had nine companies which had issued B shares. These were hugely popular with Western fund managers, as indicated by the vast price increases after each listing; by one estimate, in mid-1992, "foreigners and overseas Chinese have already set aside U.S.$2 billion for China stocks."[19] In addition to American and European fund managers, Taiwanese investors made up a large proportion of the demand for B shares.

While foreigners surged into the Chinese market, some Chinese companies decided to list overseas. Companies such as CITIC have acquired listed subsidiaries in Hong Kong, where CITIC Pacific is considered a major China play on the Hong Kong Stock Exchange. The listing of China Travel International Investment Hong Kong in late October 1992 became a major financial event. Investors seeking shares paid out enough money to buy up the entire issue between 300 and 500 times—so much money that Hong Kong interest rates rose 2.25 percent and U.S.$25 billion had to be returned to disappointed investors.[20] A subsequent listing of Denway International in early 1993 was more than 650 times oversub-

---

[19] Lincoln Kaye and Elizabeth Cheng, "Babes in the Bourse," *Far Eastern Economic Review,* July 16, 1992, p. 48, quoting Hong Kong investment banker Robert Lloyd George.

[20] "Hong Kong Stock Scramble," *International Herald Tribune,* October 31–November 1, 1992, p. 15.

scribed; the amount of money borrowed and temporarily deposited to obtain shares was like a tidal wave disrupting the Hong Kong banking system.

Brilliance China Automotive showed that stodgy Chinese state enterprises could quickly acquire a flair for Wall Street financial gymnastics. A foundation associated with Bank of China set up a shell company in Bermuda which owned 51 percent of a Shenyang automobile manufacturer. The Shenyang company in turn was a joint venture with a Chinese assembler of Toyota minivans. The Bermuda company, Brilliance China Automotive, hired leading Western accounting firms and leading investment banks (First Boston, Merrill Lynch, and Salomon Brothers) and successfully sought listing on the New York Stock Exchange. Despite a high price for the shares, investors put up twelve times as much money as the company was seeking. On the day the stock was listed—October 9, 1992—it was the second most active stock on the exchange.

Chinese authorities announced plans that same month to list nine major state enterprises on the Hong Kong Stock Exchange. Such listings in other markets enable Chinese companies to obtain foreign exchange and to move into an environment where they can play by capitalist rules. Some even prefer to list in Hong Kong, because Hong Kong's financial disclosure requirements are less stringent than New York's. Others prefer New York, which permits supershare arrangements, prohibited in Hong Kong, enabling certain investors to retain control of the company.[21]

One Chinese company, China Venturetech, planned to list a company on the Hong Kong Stock Exchange and use it to

---

[21]Cf. "Brilliant NY Debut," *Window,* October 30, 1992, pp. 54–55, and "H. K. Bourse Unveils Plans to List China Companies," Reuters, October 6, 1992.

raise money in the West to buy up all the power plants in Guangdong Province and fund new power plants there. This would free up Chinese capital invested in those plants, while retaining ultimate Chinese control of the industry. It would eventually create the largest utility on the Hong Kong Stock Exchange. It would force the power industry in Guangdong to play by capitalist rules—a major step forward in reform of state enterprises. And, if the plan worked, it would make enormous profits for China Venturetech and other investors. It was not clear whether it would in fact work, but this kind of innovative thinking, driven by an obsession to get rich using these new capitalist ideas, had begun to drive more and more of the coastal economy.

On November 5, 1992, Shenzhen saw the first issue of warrants on a Chinese stock.[22] As in other aspects of China's financial markets, the move into derivative products was occurring faster than was typical of other emerging markets.

This process of financial innovation connects the pent-up greed of coastal China to some of the world's most powerful financial tools. In the context of China's huge problems, this was like connecting up a nuclear reactor to a grid of ancient power lines serving industries long deprived of power. It created immense potential for investment and for greater efficiency; undoubtedly it will also lead to some spectacular scandals and some gigantic financial bubbles.

China is still attempting to create a full legal framework for its stock markets. It has issued many rules, and undertaken detailed studies of regulation in Hong Kong and many other markets, but China's many special aspects preclude simple

---

[22]Warrants give the right to purchase a stock at a predetermined price on some future date. If, by that date, the price of the actual stock has risen above the level specified by the warrant, then the holder of the warrant makes a profit.

copying other countries' rules. A second major thrust of Chinese policy, announced at the end of 1992, is to impose international accounting standards—essential to a proper valuation of companies and to protect investors. But this too is a problem: At a meeting of the World Economic Forum in Beijing in October 1992, Chen Yuan spoke of the need for international accounting standards, then waved his arm at the audience and said: "There are fewer accountants of international standard in China than there are people in this room." At the time, there were fewer than fifty of us. In early 1993, the Ministry of Finance hired a major Western accounting firm, Deloitte Touche Tohmatsu, to design accounting standards and to create a training program for Western-style accountants.[23]

This willingness to charge ahead, set high standards, and then engage foreign companies in the implementation of those standards, deserves special attention. For comparison, Indonesia's stock market has a much longer history but has shown far less willingness to conform to international standards. The Indonesian authorities have talked for years about imposing such standards, but have delayed year after year because of the opposition of the local accounting profession. (China, incidentally, has a much larger local accounting profession with much more to fear from international competition, since Chinese accounting diverges far more from international practices than Indonesia's.) In the meantime, a promising stock market takeoff in the late 1980s was aborted in part by scandals over wildly exaggerated profit forecasts that were certified by local accountants.

China's stock markets are still small, but they are growing very rapidly. They are opening up faster to foreigners than

---

[23]"Deloitte to Train China Auditors," *South China Morning Post*, Business Page, February 6, 1993.

Taiwan's and South Korea's stock markets, and are moving faster toward international accounting standards than Indonesia's. They are ready to serve as a mechanism for raising money from China's huge pool of savings; to mediate the reorganization of state firms' management; to privatize state firms; to facilitate the organization of private and foreign-invested companies; and to provide local legal coloration for the vast influx of Taiwanese investments (Taiwan companies will seek to joint venture with PRC partners and then list on local stock exchanges to ensure their safety in the event of political problems between Taipei and Beijing). The rate at which these things will happen remains uncertain, but the mechanisms are largely in place.

FUTURES MARKETS

With technical support from the Chicago Board of Trade, China opened a futures market for wheat in Zhengzhou in October 1990; after its initial success, futures markets for rice in Jiangxi, Wuhan, and Anhui; for corn in Changchun; and for peanuts and peanut oil in Shandong all followed. These markets have several purposes. First, they should give farmers and firms an opportunity to hedge against the risk of future price changes. Second, they should ameliorate the traditional problem of the farmer who has to sell his crop at harvest time when prices are very low and then watch the merchant hoard the grain and sell it for very high prices later. In principle, the farmer should be able to sell his crop forward and receive a reasonable price for it. Third, this process should reduce the seasonal fluctuations of prices. Finally, in an economy where some prices are still managed by the government, the futures markets should offer the government an objective signal as to where market prices are headed, so that official policy can adapt appropriately.

The agricultural futures markets encountered several problems, aside from the instinctive ideological association of futures markets with speculation. The laws, methods of dispute resolution, and enforcement mechanisms were inadequate; systems for transferring money and communicating prices were inadequate. And infrastructure for the storage and delivery of the commodities proved weak. These problems have still not been completely resolved, but they have been firmly addressed.[24] Development has also been limited somewhat by the government's practice of guaranteeing future prices above the market price in order to encourage farmers to plant enthusiastically for the coming harvest. On balance, these markets are functioning successfully, but not at a level that will have any decisive national impact in the near future.

Over time, however, the use of a futures market to smooth grain price fluctuations could be the key to solving one of the greatest dilemmas of the rice-growing Asian economies. Throughout Pacific Asia one of the greatest sources of instability, and of reaction against the spread of the market economy, has been the uncertainty introduced into peasant lives by rapid changes in the price and availability of rice. Year-to-year price changes can deprive huge numbers of subsistence farmers of their margin of livelihood. Seasonal price changes can be politically destructive: the traditional squeeze of farmers by grain merchants created deep reservoirs of class hatred. This is the reason why even today the Indonesian government carefully controls rice prices; China has been more audacious

---

[24]This section on agricultural futures markets relies heavily on William D. Grossman, "The Development and Use of Agricultural and Financial Futures Markets in China," paper presented to an Asian Society meeting in Hong Kong, October 3, 1991.

and by the end of 1992 had freed grain prices for over 200 million people (more than the entire population of Indonesia). Draining this reservoir of class resentment somewhat through the futures market could greatly ease China's transition to a market economy.

Futures markets in metals may take off more quickly because metals are used in large quantities by huge, relatively sophisticated companies, which can operate out of the coastal centers where communications are good and money transfer is quicker. In 1992, Shenzhen set up the Shenzhen Metals Exchange and Shanghai set up the Shanghai Metals Exchange. Shenzhen began trading contracts for future delivery of aluminum, and planned contracts in copper, zinc, tin, lead, nickel, antinomy, and magnesium. The authorities permitted trading in U.S. dollars so that, when foreigners are eventually allowed to participate, they will have no currency risk. Similarly, Nanjing has opened a Petroleum Exchange.

Even before China established its own metals exchanges, Chinese firms and individuals began to use foreign futures exchanges—mostly for speculative purposes rather than legitimate business hedging. Under the direction of Mr. Gao Kongliang, CITIC's Shanghai branch alone traded more than 110,000 tons of mostly copper futures in a two-year period, although all of China imports only 130,000 to 150,000 tons.[25] Mr. Gao's salary is $1,100 per year, but he has a Reuters machine in his office and an array of telephones paid for by clients for whom he executes futures transactions on overseas markets. Speculation on this scale means there will be some large bumps on China's path to the smoothing of price fluctuations.

The most important futures market is the one that is least

[25]Julia Leung, "Shanghai Broker Pioneers Futures Trade," *Asian Wall Street Journal*, August 7, 1992.

developed: the currency. China's trade in 1992 exceeded $165 billion, and most of the traders face huge risk from currency fluctuations. For instance, if Continental Grain sells $1 billion of products in China and the value of the renminbi drops 1 percent before the money is exchanged for dollars, then the company loses $10 million. Foreign banks have been inhibited from setting up a futures market that could guarantee Continental Grain's renminbi price by a Chinese rule that prohibits foreign banks from trading renminbi. Chinese banks have made brief experiments but have not created a real market. Some trading companies have organized their own small-scale markets by matching importers with exporters. But a true currency forward or futures market still does not exist.

TAKEN AS A whole, these innovations and others have revolutionized China's financial system and accelerated the reforms of its real economy. While credit rationing by the People's Bank of China is still the major tool determining the allocation of credit, the new market-oriented banking and bond system should prove the key to making price liberalization consistent with reasonable financial stability. More broadly, the introduction of market rationality in limited areas has created enormous pressure for its extension into vast additional areas.

Less evident is a broader trend—China's discovery of the virtues of financial market efficiency has revolutionized the way officials and businessmen think about economic life. Chinese bankers and officials now speak the language of Western economists and analyze problems with the same market tools. While most are careful to justify stock and bond markets as incremental overlays on socialism, recent years have in fact seen something akin to a religious conversion among China's educated younger elite. Leading young bankers receive master's degrees in international finance from the school of their own central bank, taking classes primarily in the English language, and learning almost exclusively from British and American financial textbooks. Fourteen thousand Bank of China employees out of a total of twenty thousand are assigned to Hong Kong, where the success of free capital markets is more dramatic than anywhere else in the world. More broadly, the practical experience of managing their large debt, foreign exchange, and domestic monetary positions has taught two generations of those who run China's financial affairs that market methods work. They have studied the concepts, understood them, accepted them, and begun to employ them with considerable enthusiasm—in an environment where this employment must be creative indeed.

In the short term, a danger lurks—that China's financial reforms will so outstrip other reforms that the financial sector will inspire an ideological reaction. Financial reform needs to be done early, because reforms such as privatization simply don't work properly without it.

Over the longer term, financial reforms should provide the intellectual and market infrastructure necessary for all the other economic reforms. Like a vigorous emerging stock market, the managers of China's finances appear to have established a route that will be volatile and marked by numerous pitfalls, but that sustains a firm trend upward. This long-term rise could be challenged only by the most catastrophic political events.

|||||||||||||||||||||||||||||||||||||||||||||||||||||||||||||||||||||||||||||||

IV

THE GOLDEN AGE
OF HONG KONG
AND GUANGDONG

"Hong Kong is the shop window. We are the factory floor."
—STANDARD CHARACTERIZATION OF THE HONG KONG–GUANGDONG
RELATIONSHIP BY SENIOR GOVERNMENT OFFICIALS IN GUANGDONG.

*Lee Kwan Yew, the ex-prime minister and father of modern
Singapore, Hong Kong's great competitor, was asked what
would happen to the people of Hong Kong after 1997.
His answer: "1998."*

T he central premise of this book is that China has
grown faster economically than any other large economy in history—fully matching the smaller "Asian
Tigers" stride for stride. At the heart of that premise lies
Guangdong Province, an area with the population of France
squeezed onto about half of France's territory.

Since China's economic reform began in 1979, Guangdong, with Hong Kong management, finance, technology,
and marketing, has achieved an average annual real growth of
over 12 percent (averaging 12.3 percent from 1978 to 1990;
13.5 percent in 1991; 19.5 percent in 1992).[1] In other words,

---

[1]For an analysis of Guangdong's growth, see Toyojiro Maruya, "The Development of the Guangdong Economy and Its Ties with Beijing," *JETRO*

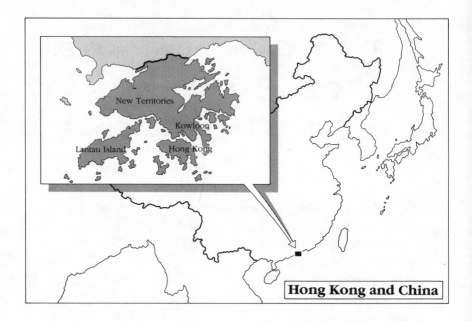

Hong Kong and China

it has grown at the rate (roughly 10 percent) achieved by
Singapore, South Korea, Taiwan, and Hong Kong in their
heyday, plus the rate of a reasonably good year for the U.S.
economy. This performance is no flash in the pan.

THE GUANGDONG–HONG KONG JOINT VENTURE

Such spectacular growth is not the fruit of Guangdong's effort
alone, but rather the result of a gigantic joint venture between

China Newsletter 96 (January–February 1992). The 1978–90 average figure
is taken from this paper. The 1991 and 1992 figures are based on Guangdong provincial statistics.

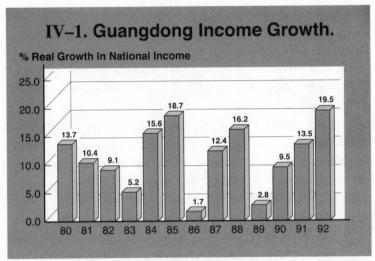

IV–1. Guangdong Income Growth.

% Real Growth in National Income

SOURCES: Guangdong Statistical Bureau; Hong Kong Trade and Development Council;
1992 estimate: Guangdong Provincial Government officials.

Hong Kong and Guangdong. Nor was it foreordained. Before economic reform, and the associated opening to Hong Kong, Guangdong was one of China's poorer provinces, starved of infrastructure investment by a Beijing leadership whose allegiances were firmly to the interior. Guangdong had even lost some infrastructure, removed and relocated to the interior by Beijing on grounds that China's security required important national assets to be placed safely inland far from a coast that was vulnerable to the imperialists.[2] Guangdong's principal asset remained a vast network of overseas Chinese businessmen, many of whom had family roots in the villages of Guangdong and still felt ties to their ancestral homeland.

Hong Kong and Guangdong were a perfect fit. Hong Kong

[2]Vogel, *One Step Ahead in China*, p. 36. Vogel's classic study is the most meticulous and wide-ranging account that has been written of life in a Chinese province, and of the details of how reform works. See also his previous book, *Canton Under Communism: Progress and Politics in a Provincial Capital* (Cambridge, MA: Harvard University Press, 1969).

had money, management talent, marketing expertise, world-wide networks, and technology. Yet its success was pushing wages and real estate prices so high that the territory was becoming uncompetitive in most of its traditional industries. Guangdong land and workers cost only about 10 percent of Hong Kong prices, but the province was desperately short of all the skills, money, and technology that were Hong Kong's forte. Bringing them together was the equivalent of pouring gasoline on a burning match. The initial relationships were small and tentative. Wary capitalists and communists fenced, each seeking an advantage. Most of the early deals involved, say, a Hong Kong company providing free machinery and materials to a Guangdong enterprise in return for the right to manage the enterprise and to receive a certain amount of final product (e.g., blue jeans, toys, plastic bags) for a certain number of years.

The communists came armed with layer upon layer of regulations, many quite secret and all designed to take in Hong Kong money and give out as little as possible in return. The capitalists brought guile and fast footwork. In the early days, more than one communist bureaucrat bought a Hong Kong company, only to discover that he was left with an old building, some obsolete technology, and some newspaper clippings about the key personnel who had skipped off to Taiwan. Hong Kong manufacturers set up factories in Guangdong, then learned that the water and electricity and roads promised by local authorities were not really available and might not be for a few years. Many of China's largest enterprises plunged into the excitement of earning fortunes in Hong Kong's volatile markets—real estate and stocks—only to discover that both the profits and the principal could evaporate overnight when something spooked the market.

Somehow both sides managed to shrug off the expensive

lessons of the early 1980s. Communist officials spoke of their experiences as "tuition money" for learning about markets. Hong Kong businessmen learned that communist regulations dissolved in a proper solution of old family connections and a dollop of hard currency. Hong Kong businessmen gradually taught their Guangdong cousins, schooled in the notion of property as theft, the value of good faith negotiations.[3] Local pragmatism began to earn fortunes even at a time when most Western investments in China flopped.

I once asked a banker for one of Hong Kong's billionaire investors in China why his ventures succeeded where Westerners so often failed. He said:

The Americans try to do everything by the book. They show up in town and immediately go to the mayor's office and ask what the rules are. He tells them the rules, and they spend months sorting out all the official details. He assigns them a factory site and they start building. As soon as they start, a pile of bricks shows up in the middle of the road. If they move the bricks, the local people sue them for breaking their bricks. When they finally get rid of the bricks, a herd of goats shows up in the road. They're always in trouble. There's always something new blocking the road or a new government regulation they never heard of before.

We do it differently. We go into town and look around for a good site. When we find what we want, we call the local people together and ask them if they'd like a new factory that pays much better wages. They always do. After this, we ask them what they want. They always want a school and a clinic and sometimes a few other things. So we build these for them; such things are very cheap in China. Then we go down to the

[3] I am indebted to Robert Theleen for pointing out the importance of this.

mayor's office with a delegation of local people and they tell
him what we're going to do. He wouldn't dare stand in their
way.

The early days of Deng Xiaoping's economic reform program coincided with his efforts to reunify China by bringing
Hong Kong and Taiwan back into the fold. Deng's plan involved a synthesis of economics and national unification. Beijing proposed to Taiwan that Taiwan accept formal reintegra-
tion. In return, it could retain its own social system, its
capitalist economy, and even its own armed forces. Its government officials would all retain their jobs and would be simultaneously appointed by the central government. While initially Taiwan rejected this, Beijing left the option open,
reasoning that Taiwan would eventually accept if the mainland become more economically successful and if Beijing
demonstrated its sincerity by implementing the same policy
successfully in Hong Kong. It is widely believed, although it
has never been conclusively proved, that Deng Xiaoping's
subsequent offer to Hong Kong of fifty years of capitalism
was based on a calculation that China could catch up with
Taiwan economically in fifty years.

Beijing negotiated for the return of Hong Kong on the basis
that the existing Hong Kong system would be continued until
the New Territories lease expired in 1997 and for an additional fifty years thereafter. (Eventually, Britain accepted
this.) Beijing gave Guangdong special privileges to move faster
in domestic reform and in foreign trade than the rest of China,
and it gave a very flexible mandate for Guangdong's reforms
so that local officials could proceed pragmatically. This created the opening for the great Guangdong–Hong Kong joint
venture.

To ease the process of reforming and opening up Guangdong, Beijing created a special economic zone called Shenzhen

on Guangdong's border with Hong Kong. Three times larger than Hong Kong, and with a mandate to liberalize far faster than the rest of Guangdong, Shenzhen was to be converted from a collection of backward villages and rice paddies into an industrial power center. Throughout this process, China's leaders and diplomats repeatedly emphasized to Westerners that the success of the "One country, two systems" policy for Hong Kong would be one key to Taiwan's eventual peaceful agreement to reunification. The other would be China's catching up with Taiwan economically.

Thus Guangdong was to be an airlock through which China dealt with the outside world. Shenzhen would be Guangdong's airlock to Hong Kong, and Hong Kong the direct window to the outside world. The example of Hong Kong's success would attract Taiwan. All this was designed in service of a nationwide economic takeoff which would restore China's internal cohesion and external prestige. The strategy seemed crippling in its complexity and bold to the point of hubris. In fact, it had only one redeeming feature: It worked. Progress so far has exceeded even the most enthusiastic expectations of the policy's creators.

By the early 1990s, the economic integration of socialist Guangdong and capitalist Hong Kong was largely complete. Shenzhen had become a mini-Hong Kong, with tall buildings, factories that saturated U.S. markets with clothes and shoes and toys, streets full of Audis and Mercedes-Benzes (some of them even paid for rather than stolen from Hong Kong), people wearing clothing with designer labels (some of which were even real), and a surfeit of London and New York investment bankers. Eighty percent of investment in Guangdong came from Hong Kong. Half of Guangdong's industrial workforce (over 3 million out of 6 million) was employed by Hong Kong companies. Three out of four Hong Kong companies had operations in China, comprising some 23,000 joint ventures. If

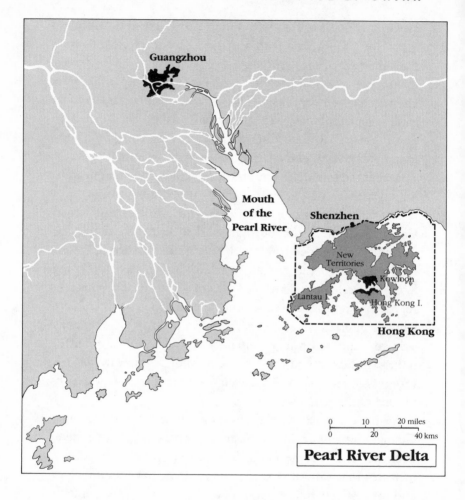

Pearl River Delta

one includes wholly-Chinese-owned companies that live primarily off contracts from Hong Kong firms, then there were
80,000 Hong Kong-related enterprises located in Guangdong.[4] Five out of six employees of Hong Kong companies

---

[4]For the number of Hong Kong firms in Guangdong, I am indebted to
Gordian Gaeta of Booze Allen Hamilton, whose firm collected data from

(over 3 million out of 3.65 million) were in the People's Republic of China (PRC). A generation earlier the two societies had lived in tense, armed isolation from one another.

For the peasantry of Guangdong, this growth brought an instant leap into modern consumerism. An underemployed population with little mobility suddenly found itself with plenty of jobs working for Hong Kong companies, and with essentially unlimited opportunities for the energetic. In half a generation good food, decent housing, nearly universal television, motorcycles, and cosmetics replaced hunger, exposure, dreary blue suits, and the trudge to work. During the Cultural Revolution, the Hong Kong border had to be carefully guarded against the hungry peasantry of Guangdong. Ezra Vogel's landmark study of Guangdong describes life before economic reform:

> The policy for the countryside by the early 1970s was cautious: to grow enough rice to avoid starvation. . . . Pork, chicken, fish, and sugar rations allowed each person only a few ounces a month. . . . The attention to rice ensured that there was basically no starvation, unlike conditions during the Great Leap Forward. . . . When the amount of consumer goods began to increase after the Cultural Revolution, the quality of even the simplest products was still marginal. Light bulbs flickered, clothes had tears, plates had chips, and hot water bottles leaked.[5]

---

officials in Guangdong Province. The other data are from published Hong Kong and Guangdong government sources. The figure usually cited in Hong Kong discussions for the number of workers in Guangdong is 4 million rather than 3 million, and the larger figure may be correct since the last published number (3 million) is several years out of date. But I have chosen to use the more conservative estimate.

[5]Vogel, *One Step Ahead in China*, pp. 29–30.

By 1990, about half of Guangdong rural households (much poorer than the urban ones) had a radio, a television, and a tape recorder.[6] Procter & Gamble was selling as much Rejoice Shampoo as it could provide; after the United States, Guangdong Province was its second largest market. Mcdonald's restaurants also profited from the new prosperity in Guangdong; the average McDonald's in America has about 1,400 customers a day, but one in Guangdong set the world record, with 14,123 customers in a single day. When 7-Eleven stores opened in 1992, the riot police had to be called out in full battle gear to control huge crowds of customers.

In early 1993, I ran into a friend who worked for a big American law firm. He was sputtering with hilarity. A former peasant from Shenzhen had come to him for advice. A decade ago, the peasant had controlled a few rice paddies in Shenzhen; he had sold his interest in the paddies to an industrialist in return for an interest in a new factory on the site. Now he had sold his interest in the factory and was asking my friend for advice. Where should he invest with 200 million U.S. dollars?

Another group that did well in Guangdong was the fishermen. The opening of Guangdong–Hong Kong trade has created a paradise for smugglers, and the most lucrative thing to smuggle has turned out to be cars, especially Mercedes-Benzes, BMWs, and Lexus. In this area the Chinese have proved that, when there is sufficient incentive, their technology can be world class. They smuggle cars in extraordinarily fast boats, built by the People's Liberation Army. They also smuggle them in very slow boats, putting the Mercedes in a rubber sheath that looks like a giant condom and towing it

[6]Economic Information Centre, Guangdong Enterprises Holdings Ltd., "Guangdong Economic Data" (July 1991), p. 33.

behind the boat, where it floats just beneath the surface. In all of this, the fishermen have the expertise and control the landing sites, so there are many millionaires among Guangdong's fishermen.

For Hong Kong, a city of roughly 5.8 million people, or about three quarters the population of metropolitan New York, China's economic growth has brought living standards higher than much of Southern Europe. Hong Kong people own more Rolls-Royces and Mercedes-Benz 500s per square kilometer than anywhere else in the world.[7] Hong Kong shops pay the highest prices for retail floor space in the entire world—by 1992 surpassing even Tokyo's Ginza. As Chart IV-2 shows, in 1992 incomes were about double those of Greece and Portugal and just barely under those of Spain. Even this understates Hong Kong's real living standards, because income taxes there take only 16 percent of income, prices are lower than in most of Europe, and the Hong Kong dollar is undervalued. Taking into account Britain's high prices and the overvaluation of the pound sterling in 1991, Hong Kong's average living standards were then probably comparable to those of Britain. By 1993, when British exchange rates fell to market levels, Hong Kong people were well ahead. Cognac manufacturers design super-expensive brands especially for the Hong Kong market. Based on the strong local demand for luxury goods, a Hong Kong company, Dickson Concepts, has been systematically buying up Asian rights to many of the world's most famous luxury brands: S. T. Dupont, Harvey Nichols (the posh London department store), Polo Ralph Lauren, Bulgari watches, and many others.

---

[7]Data on automobiles were provided by Martin Pegg of Fidelity Motors, the Hong Kong Rolls-Royce dealer.

In half a generation Hong Kong has lost its identity as primarily a manufacturer of cheap consumer goods and moved upmarket to become the services capital of Pacific Asia. By 1991 most Hong Kong manufacturing had moved north across the border, and 83 percent of the Hong Kong economy was in the service sectors.

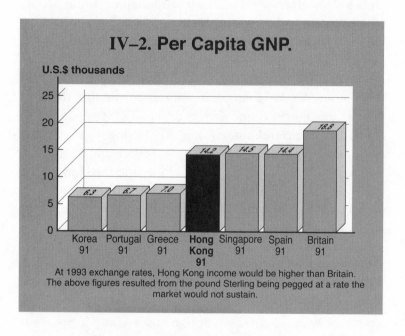

IV–2. Per Capita GNP.

U.S.$ thousands

	Korea 91	Portugal 91	Greece 91	Hong Kong 91	Singapore 91	Spain 91	Britain 91
	6.3	6.7	7.0	14.2	14.5	14.4	18.8

At 1993 exchange rates, Hong Kong income would be higher than Britain. The above figures resulted from the pound Sterling being pegged at a rate the market would not sustain.

Gross domestic product (GDP) figures showed Guangdong achieving growth in excess of 12 percent while Hong Kong, at around 5 percent in the late 1980s and early 1990s, underperformed among the Asian miracle economies. (But Hong Kong still grew two to three times as fast as Western economies of this period.) These Hong Kong statistics were surely misleading because of the integration of the two economies.[8] Hong Kong was the marketing, design, management, technology, and financial capital of the fastest-growing part of the world economy: Guangdong. It also owned most of Guangdong's modern manufacturing and trade. Even so, the concept of gross domestic product was not properly adapted to a situation where most of the manufacturing and trade by Hong Kong companies was done in Guangdong and the monies generated by these facilities were credited to the Guangdong account. (Profits reported in Hong Kong, moreover, were typically reported in a way that realized immense tax savings for the reporting company and in the process reduced Hong Kong's growth statistics.) The benefits of owning and managing the most important parts of the world's fastest-growing economy showed up in the lavish living standards of Hong Kong people, the extraordinary profitability of many companies, and the stellar level of real estate prices. (Not only retail space was expensive. In 1991, a typical middle-level American banker had to pay about U.S.$100,000 per year to rent a modest apartment, or well over $1 million to buy it.)

Although Hong Kong firms initially concentrated their efforts among their fellow Cantonese in Guangdong, the joint venture syndrome steadily broadened to involve Hong Kong with all of China. Two thirds of the huge foreign investment flowing into China from 1979 onward came from Hong Kong. Some of this was Taiwanese and Southeast Asian money using Hong Kong as a convenient political cover; but the majority originated in Hong Kong, and the fact that the remainder was channeled through Hong Kong

[8]Hong Kong publishes GDP statistics but not GNP. The Commissioner of Statistics told me in April 1993 that data now being collected show GNP growing substantially faster than GDP.

intermediaries testified to the colony's vital gateway function.

By the early 1990s, the influence of Hong Kong was pervasive throughout China. In Xian, the ancient interior capital of China, foreign tourists generally stayed at one of the top six hotels, all of them Hong Kong joint ventures, enjoyed nightlife at the premier club, the Tang Palace, another Hong Kong joint venture, and shipped home souvenirs using local bills of lading pre-printed to reassure the customer that the shipment would receive quality attention in Hong Kong rather than being shipped through such closer ports as Tianjin or Shanghai. In the distant northwest corner of China, the same situation applied: the two top hotels in the Xinjiang Uyghur Autonomous Region's capital of Urumchi are the Holiday Inn and the Universal Hotel, both Hong Kong joint ventures. Throughout China the economic takeoff has been powered most strongly by agriculture and by the dynamic Hong Kong–based industrial and service enterprises.

The success of joint ventures with Hong Kong has encouraged various Chinese authorities to engage Hong Kong ever more deeply in China's economic plans. Along the coast, Hong Kong's construction companies are building major housing developments. A Hong Kong firm, Hopewell, built a superhighway across Guangdong Province. Beijing is double-tracking a railway from the capital city to Hong Kong; this will become the backbone of north/south land transportation in China. The giant industrial city of Wuhan has engaged Wharf, one of the largest Hong Kong companies, to reconstruct its port. The Shanghai Port Authority has sold a 50 percent interest to Hutchison, the Hong Kong company which manages the world's largest container terminal; the Port Authority contributed its existing terminals to the joint venture in return for Hutchison's commitment to build three additional terminals and modernize the entire complex. In other words, management of socialist China's greatest port is now effectively in the hands of a Hong Kong company.[9] In November 1992, Hong Kong companies committed $1.4 billion to modernize some suburbs of Beijing. So the China–Hong Kong joint venture has now transcended hotels, finance, and toy companies, and is taking on some of China's biggest and most sensitive infrastructure development projects.

If Hong Kong had been close to a different province, that other province would have set the world record for economic growth. (Guangdong's competitive advantage is its network with the millions of overseas Chinese, most of whom came from this region. This advantage is tied to Hong Kong's entrepot role.) Hong Kong's institutions and underlying prosperity were in turn created by Britain, and sound British administrative institutions were an indispensable prerequisite for the initial success. But the explosion of the Hong Kong–Guangdong joint venture in the late 1980s is largely a story of Chinese vision—specifically Deng Xiaoping's vision of how to combine the capitalist skills of Hong Kong with his reform of the Chinese economy. Along with a handful of other policies—opening Chinese society to the world, giving the land back to the farmers, moving to market prices, and accepting capitalist financial markets—the pragmatic incorporation of capitalist Hong Kong into the Chinese economy was one of the vital strategies of reform success. Hong Kong became the nuclear reaction at the core of the Chinese economic explosion. Of all the instances of Deng Xiaoping's pragmatism, the incorporation of a fully capitalist Hong Kong into the Chinese system is perhaps the greatest.

This achievement was all the more remarkable because throughout the period the British firmly resisted the integration of Hong Kong with the Chinese economy. Leading Brit-

---

[9]"Hutchison Buys Into Shanghai Port," *International Herald Tribune,* September 4, 1992, p. 6.

ish firms paid huge prices to diversify themselves outward from Hong Kong. The Western press damaged Hong Kong by continually proclaiming it a failure even when the statistics showed it to be a success, and London made repeated efforts to undermine the basic compromises that supported the success.

HONG KONG'S CENTRAL DILEMMA

The extraordinary divergence between reality and Western images has derived from different assumptions about the role and purpose of Hong Kong. To Britain and much of the West, Hong Kong is now regarded primarily as a political entity. From this presupposition it follows that the basic issue in Hong Kong's future is one of political ideology: a struggle between democracy in Hong Kong and communism in China. British commentators further tend to believe—falsely—that China agreed to accept continuation of Hong Kong's system for an additional fifty years (from the year 1997 to 2047) because of British negotiating pressure. In actuality, it arose as a crucial part of Deng's strategic vision. Given this set of British/Western assumptions, and given the relative sizes of giant China and diminutive Hong Kong, a pessimistic outcome seemed foreordained. To postpone the inevitable, this line of thought suggested, Hong Kong should be made independent of China, while retaining as many entrenched Western political institutions as possible.

From China's totally different perspective, Hong Kong is an economic utility, not primarily a political entity. Moreover, this is exactly what Hong Kong was for the British—until they had to depart, at which point they suddenly decided that the highest priority was political. In terms of the Pacific

Asian takeoff, Hong Kong is an unusually complex export processing zone. South Korea and Taiwan originated the modern version, typically a small territory where certain rules of the rest of society are suspended in order to facilitate economic activity. Export processing zones proved necessary to help start up rapid growth in these smaller Asian countries at a time when they were protectionist, relatively socialist, and lacked the infrastructure to attract foreign investment. Typically, these are free trade zones, which suspend the normal restrictions on importing and exporting goods, allow an easier inflow of capital, and provide concentrated infrastructure. Frequently they suspend restrictive labor practices. Export zones, which are now popular even as Sri Lanka and India, compensate for these societies' general imposition of socialist, protectionist rules that, although politically advantageous, have proved unduly restrictive for economic growth.

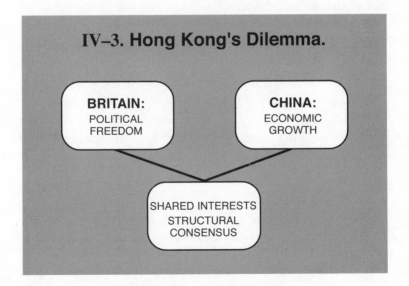

IV–3. Hong Kong's Dilemma.

BRITAIN:
POLITICAL
FREEDOM

CHINA:
ECONOMIC
GROWTH

SHARED INTERESTS
STRUCTURAL
CONSENSUS

In historical perspective, China was an early beneficiary of the idea of export processing zones. China has long felt endangered by the activities of Westerners and yet has needed to deal with them on a fairly large scale. The Imperial Maritime Customs Service, through which China delegated management of customs functions to the British, was an early example of adaptation to these contradictory requirements. Later the treaty ports, which were large areas of coastal cities where Western law and customs prevailed, evolved as conduits through which China could deal effectively with the Western world but still contain deleterious foreign influences within a narrow geographic space. For the most part the treaty ports were imposed on China, but much of their functioning was accepted because they also served an important Chinese purpose.

Hong Kong is the last survivor of the old enclaves, but it is far more than an obsolete remnant of the colonial era. It is also the most complex and successful of the modern export processing zones. Critically, it is deals primarily in services rather than goods.[10] And rather than just modifying the rules for import and export of goods in order to facilitate manufacturing, Hong Kong modifies a broad range of rules in order to facilitate a broad range of modern service functions: global financial center, regional headquarters for manufacturing firms, regional center for other services such as accounting and taxation, trade window for China, technology purchase window for China, international financial capital for China, and management consulting and design center for southern China.

---

[10]In 1990 the services sectors produced 83 percent of Hong Kong's GDP. Cf. "Service Sector Statistics on Hong Kong," *Hong Kong Coalition of Service Industries* (1992) with data compiled from official Hong Kong government statistics.

In order to fulfill all these functions, Hong Kong has to have different rules from those of the People's Republic: it must ensure free inflow and outflow of capital, free inflow and outflow of people, a convertible currency, free flow of a wide range of information (including political information that affects financial markets), and an independent Western legal system. It was these aspects of Hong Kong that China promised to maintain; China made this promise because it was advantageous for the mainland's economic development—and also as an example to Taiwan.

The overlap of economic requirements with the prerequisites of freedom that the British want to preserve made the Joint Declaration possible. (The Joint Declaration of 1984 was the British-Chinese agreement to transfer sovereignty over Hong Kong back to China but retain Hong Kong's free and capitalist system until the year 2047.) Where this overlap does not occur, British and Chinese interests diverge. For instance, the British have periodically debated a shift to full Westminster democracy for Hong Kong. That would serve no Chinese economic requirement and might create a political threat, so the Chinese have always been unwilling to concur with anything more than very gradual, cautious movement in that direction. The Joint Declaration says nothing about democracy. When the two sides agreed to maintain the existing system until the year 2047, China had in mind the economic system, together with the social and political prerequisites of that system which just happen to coincide with Western freedoms. Those prerequisites ensure a high degree of freedom for the people of Hong Kong, together with a greater degree of democracy than ever existed under the British. They do not necessarily include full electoral democracy. This was understood and accepted by the British negotiators at the time. But most British commentators have focused on the political system per se and insisted that full-blown and early Western democracy is the sole criterion of success or failure.

Remarkably, the two approaches coincide to a very high degree. Without the promises China has made for economic reasons—free movement of goods, people, and capital, a convertible currency, continuation of the British legal system, and a variety of other freedoms that cover much the same ground as the U.S. Bill of Rights—Hong Kong's highly skilled entrepreneurs, bankers, lawyers, and accountants would move elsewhere. These promises ensure the maintenance of existing freedoms. Inevitably there remains a fuzzy political boundary region. Hong Kong can maintain its economic momentum only in an environment stable and free enough to attract and retain the most successful firms, and a large number of the most educated and ambitious people. The Joint Declaration's guarantees in this respect are quite explicit:

> The current social and economic systems in Hong Kong will remain unchanged, and so will the life-style. Rights and freedoms, including those of the person, of speech, of the press, of assembly, of associations, of travel, of movement, of correspondence, of strike, of choice of occupation, of academic research and of religious belief will be ensured by law in the Hong Kong Special Administrative Region. Private property, ownership of enterprises, legitimate right of inheritance and foreign investment will be protected by law.
> —Article 5, Sino-British Joint Declaration on the Quesion of Hong Kong, 26 September 1984.

There is also a serious divergence in the policy implications of the two views. Starting from the Chinese perspective, the way to ensure Hong Kong's success is to promote economic integration with China and thereby ensure both maximum prosperity for Hong Kong and maximum benefits for China from its export processing zone. The better this works, the more China's leaders will be committed to their view that Hong Kong is a vital force for China's economic betterment, and that the concessions of freedom and capitalism that they have made to the Hong Kong people have been a sound investment. From their perspective, their policies have been successful beyond anything they had dreamed: Hong Kong has been an economic gold mine without posing any significant political threat. Based on this, Deng Xiaoping has repeatedly said that the preservation of Hong Kong's capitalist, free system should continue for a hundred years rather than fifty, and that China needs additional Hong Kongs.

The one thing that could turn Hong Kong into a liability from Beijing's perspective would be if it became a base for political challenge to China. Here the leadership in Beijing does have serious concerns. Historically, Hong Kong and nearby areas have been loci of foreign pressure and domestic subversive movements. To take only two examples, Britain used this pressure point to begin dismantling the Qing dynasty's sovereignty in the mid-nineteenth century, and Sun Yatsen's republican movement ultimately destroyed that dynasty in 1911 from this region. Beijing's nightmare is that its export processing zone could become a base for the organized subversion of China—a base with essentially unlimited financing. This nightmare coincides almost precisely with the aspirations of outspoken British and British-style pressure groups to transform Hong Kong into a full-fledged Western democracy, led by an outspoken advocate of the overthrow of the Beijing leadership.

THE DIPLOMACY OF SHARED INTERESTS AND DIVERGENT PRIORITIES

British rule over Hong Kong originated as an overwhelming diplomatic humiliation of China. The British were determined to continue selling opium to China in huge quantities in order to finance other interests. The Chinese were determined to stop the drug trade and arrogantly rejected British requests to engage in broader trade. When the Chinese sealed off their port and seized large quantities of British opium, Britain attacked. After the ensuing Opium War, a defeated China was forced in 1842 to cede sovereignty in perpetuity over Hong Kong Island. In 1860 it was forced to cede the nearby Kowloon Peninsula in perpetuity, and in 1898 it leased the New Territories, the bulk of contemporary Hong Kong's territory, for ninety-nine years—until 1997. It was as if General Noriega of Panama, infuriated at George Bush's efforts to stop Panamanian drug sales to the United States, had seized Long Island in perpetuity and decades later had used this seizure to impose an alien political ideology on part of New York State.

In 1949, a xenophobic nationalist revolutionary movement, the Communist Party, seized power in China, determined among other things to rescue the nation from foreign humiliation and foreign-imposed divisions. The fact that the Communist Party seemed more determined than its competitors to terminate such humiliation was one of the major reasons for the Party's widespread support by the Chinese people. It decided, among other things, to liberate Taiwan, and would have done so had not the vicissitudes of the Korean War led the United States to defend Taiwan. In this context, one would naturally have expected the immediate liberation of Hong Kong from colonial rule. That was not, however, what happened. Mao Zedong, advised by Zhou Enlai, decided that Hong Kong was more useful to China as it was. Through all the political upheavals in the ensuing three decades, Beijing maintained the policy of continuity. Hong Kong's stability during that period was maintained not by British military superiority but rather by Chinese pragmatism. For most of that period China could have regained sovereignty over Hong Kong simply by walking in and taking it. The British garrison was pitifully small. It could not have been reinforced adequately to counter a Chinese invasion. In fact, to conquer Hong Kong, China had only to cut off the water supply. Hong Kong is not like the Falkland Islands either geographically, strategically, demographically, or psychologically.

Moreover, even in its moments of greatest insanity, China has chosen to protect Hong Kong. The most insane time in several centuries was 1967, the height of the Cultural Revolution, when the degree of turmoil, irrational behavior, and xenophobia exceeded anything that occurred in the Iranian Revolution. Throughout the entire twentieth century, only the Cambodian revolution exceeded the Cultural Revolution in xenophobic fury. But when Red Guards approached the Hong Kong border, Beijing in the person of Zhou Enlai ordered the local army commander to clear them away. Again, most surprisingly, China—concerned among other things about the impact on Hong Kong—refused to accept sovereignty over Macau when Portugal attempted to give it back. Yet another key incident showed that China was even willing to take positive action to support Hong Kong during a period of turmoil at home: The deadline for construction of a desperately needed pipe to provide mainland water to Hong Kong fell during the worst period of the Cultural Revolution, but the Chinese side went forward anyhow, even accelerating construction in order to meet the target date.[11]

As the 1970s came to an end, Beijing had to face the question of the future of Hong Kong. The Party leadership considered three options. One was to let the situation of that time continue indefinitely. This, however, entailed ratification of the outcome of the Opium War and was politically unthinkable. The second option was to seize Hong Kong in 1997 by whatever methods were necessary. That option was the normal one that a former colonial power would have expected. In 1961, India had suddenly invade Goa, a Portuguese colony which sat on the Indian coast the way Hong Kong sat on the Chinese coast, and the world had little to say about it. In 1975, Indonesia had suddenly and bloodily seized East Timor, a former Portuguese colony which was geographically part of Indonesia but had never been under Dutch rule; because guerrilla warfare has continued in East Timor, the world has said a bit more about it. Hong Kong would in the normal course of events have been taken like Goa and East Timor. But to Chinese leaders, such a strategy seemed politically and economically counterproductive.[12]

The third option was to resume sovereignty while retaining the existing capitalist, free system in Hong Kong with all its benefits to China and others.[13] That option was judged the

[11]During the Cold War, and especially during the Cultural Revolution, Hong Kong also served other purposes, including intelligence collection and dividing Britain from the United States.

[12]Unlike Goa and East Timor, Hong Kong's status was defined by treaty. In the historical sweep of decolonization, and especially in the eyes of the countries being decolonized, this is a tiny historical footnote rather than an important distinction.

[13]On the options as China saw them, and on the earlier roles of Mao Zedong and Zhou Enlai, I am indebted to conversations with a number of

only acceptable one. Within its framework, China chose to have the system administered by Hong Kong people rather than by the British. Historians will note that, in the wake of this generous and pragmatic decision, China has received more Western criticism than the Indians, the Indonesians, and many others combined.

During tense periods of negotiation over Hong Kong's future from 1981 to 1984, China subsidized financial stability in Hong Kong. Since that time, it has made huge investments there. The Bank of China Building—Asia's tallest structure, holding many of the bank's fourteen thousand Hong Kong employees—symbolizes China's investments in Hong Kong real estate, buildings, and companies. China has large holdings in Hong Kong companies, including 20 percent of HK Telecom and 22.5 percent of Cathay Pacific Airways. Chinese companies like CITIC are rushing to list subsidiaries on the Hong Kong Stock Exchange. In fact, during the period since the British-Chinese negotiations, China has become by far the largest single investor in Hong Kong. These huge investments by a regime short of capital belie any intention to take arbitrary actions that would severely damage the Hong Kong economy and destroy the value of the investments. The only thing that could lead Beijing to abandon support of such an economically beneficial arrangement would be if Hong Kong became a security threat to the regime. In fact, as the tension has increased between China's internal fragility and its expanding contacts with the outside world, Beijing has moved to expand Hong Kong's role and to create a large variety of other special economic zones, each of which Hong Kong has come

senior Chinese officials, including Li Chuwen, a top-level adviser to successive mayors of Shanghai, and particularly to his overview at a luncheon on August 14, 1992.

to dominate. (There are signs that in the future Japan, South Korea, and Taiwan may come to dominate certain Chinese areas.)

CAN CHINA BE TRUSTED?

The pervasive concern that China cannot be trusted to honor its promises to Hong Kong has its roots in a Western misunderstanding of Chinese motives in signing the Joint Declaration. The image of a radical communist China itching to impose its own system on Hong Kong derives from the assumption that China's primary interest in Hong Kong is ideological. But the entire history of China's behavior since 1949 belies such an assumption. For two generations China has protected Hong Kong and profited from it while all other colonies around the world were simply "liberated."

The prospects for honoring the agreements over Hong Kong rest on three foundations. First, China has an excellent record in honoring past international agreements.[14] However, given the crucial importance of Hong Kong (and the high risks to China if Hong Kong somehow goes wrong), given the ambiguity of the agreement, and given that Hong Kong is predominantly a domestic issue for China, this pillar might be regarded as weak if taken alone.

Second, China's effort to promote the "One country, two systems" formula as a basis for eventual unity with Taiwan has proved both consistent and successful. Despite the psy-

[14]There is an extremely extensive literature on this point. For a review of some of it, focused on the worst of the Maoist era, see William H. Overholt, "Would Chiang Find Mao an Unacceptably Strange Bedfellow?", *Asian Survey* XIV, 8 (August 1974).

chological setback to this strategy after Tiananmen Square, China has stuck to it without deviation under both liberal and reactionary leaderships. And if unity is measured in broad functional terms, the strategy is working: Despite Tiananmen Square, Taiwan investments in China and trade with the mainland, formerly negligible, are now measured in billions of dollars, and millions of Taiwanese tourists have visited China. Even Taiwan officials visit the mainland, and Taiwan is vigorously inventing legal channels for all this trade, investment, and tourism to follow.

Third, and most important, China's vital economic self-interest is at stake. Two thirds (65.7 percent) of foreign direct investment in China comes from Hong Kong. Some 25 to 30 percent of all foreign exchange earnings come through Hong Kong, as do most of China's technology purchases and managerial advice. More broadly, the whole Chinese effort to rejuvenate the country is based on economic growth, and the payoff of Deng Xiaoping's "One country, two systems" policy has been greater than anyone could have imagined in the early 1980s. The growth in Guangdong alone more than justifies continuation of Deng's policy, and all factions in Beijing recognize this. The terms of the Joint Declaration are the minimum China needs to make Hong Kong work as an efficient enclave and relay point for capital, technology, trade, and tourism.

Finally, the post–Tiananmen Square period has severely tested China's promises to Hong Kong. The Chinese leadership was fearful of instability at home, determined to repudiate the excesses (as it saw them) of its liberal predecessor, and, not incidentally, furious at the way Hong Kong residents demonstrated against the leaders. In this difficult period, China took firm steps to control its own organizations and to prevent subversion, but its senior spokesmen repeatedly promised that there would be no retribution against people who demonstrated inside Hong Kong against Chinese policies. (China wrote into the Basic Law for Hong Kong a clause forbidding subversion of China, but that was a fundamental premise of "One country, two systems" from the beginning. In connection with this clause, it banned from executive office Martin Lee and Szeto Wah, not for activities inside Hong Kong but for specific efforts to aid dissident movements inside China.) On April 4, 1990, less than a year after Tiananmen Square, China's conservative president, Yang Shangkun, affirmed in the preamble to Hong Kong's Basic Law that "the socialist system and policies will not be practiced in Hong Kong." For this leadership, in this particular period, such commitments showed considerable restraint.

HONG KONG'S ECONOMIC VULNERABILITY

China has a powerful interest in making its Hong Kong system work, and it has established a system that could work well. But any system can be mismanaged. Although China will have great influence, it lacks Britain's post–World War II experience with light-handed colonial management. (Britain's previous management of colonies was not light-handed.) Chinese residents of Hong Kong fear that there might be circumstances under which China could invoke national security concerns to deprive them of rights to which they are accustomed. Companies fear that there might be circumstances under which, for instance, disputes with Chinese companies rose to the level of the National People's Congress and were settled under Chinese law. They fear that administration of Hong Kong will become politicized or biased. Hong Kong banks fear that the Bank of China will assert itself in damaging ways. Everyone fears China's endemic corruption and rising crime, as well as its potential instability and the possible rise of malevolent leaders.

Such fears have not, so far, damaged the economy, but they have induced widespread efforts to escape Chinese legal jurisdiction. Most major companies have relocated their legal domicile to more trustworthy jurisdictions—for instance, the Hongkong and Shanghai Bank to London. And a major proportion of the educated population has said it is interested in the possibility of emigration. To what extent has this endangered the future of Hong Kong as a prosperous, stable, free enclave?

The shift of legal domiciles by Hong Kong companies has no economic or political consequences; they do not shift their business along with their nameplates. But there are some real business shifts. Many companies have diversified their business geographically beyond what would seem justified by purely business calculations. For instance, Hong Kong and Shanghai Bank paid huge sums for Midland Bank in Britain and Marine Midland in the United States (both of which were poor uses of its funds if judged only by profit potential) in order to establish a global, primarily British identity and legal standing. Many Hong Kong companies tend to borrow heavily for Hong Kong investments and then put considerable investments overseas. Is this capital flight from a dying Hong Kong or aggressive acquisition by a dynamic Hong Kong?

Throughout the 1980s, the Western press reported vast flight of capital from Hong Kong. In fact, much of it consists of valuable acquisitions: Hong Kong's New World bought Ramada Inns and its Regal Hotels bought over two hundred U.S. hotels. The Hong Kong manufacturer Semi-Tech bought Singer, America's most famous maker of sewing machines and other household electronics. Hong Kong watch companies, far more profitable than their Swiss counterparts, bought Swiss watch companies in order to control famous brand names. When Japanese and South Korean companies did the same thing, the press called it victory, not capital flight. On balance, it was indeed victory. Even with such purchases, Hong Kong during this period achieved substantial net inflows of capital.[15]

Similarly, more individuals are keeping money offshore, and the average individual may be keeping somewhat more of his money offshore. These trends are definitely real, but easily exaggerated. Hong Kong money has always been footloose. Individuals as well as firms have always kept a high proportion of their assets overseas; the proportions have increased, but if capital flight were too vast, there would be upward pressure on real interest rates and downward pressures on the Hong Kong dollar that simply are not there. (The pressures on the Hong Kong dollar have consistently been for upward revaluation, not devaluation.) We would also expect downward pressure on real estate prices rather than the spectacular escalation that has occurred.

The most vital issue is not capital but people. People, especially the most skilled workers, are leaving Hong Kong in large numbers: about 45,000 left annually between 1987 and 1989, roughly double the rate in 1984. The rate rose to around 60,000 in 1990–92, reflecting the Tiananmen Square crisis. This high rate of emigration disrupts offices, creates skill shortages, and worsens the currently severe inflation. To pessimists, the brain drain means doom.

For perspective on an admittedly serious problem, one can compare Hong Kong with Singapore. The press is as unanimous about Singapore's economic success and excellent economic prospects as it is about Hong Kong's morbidity. Yet

---

[15]Hong Kong does not publish capital flow statistics, but the numbers can be calculated indirectly. Only two years in recent times have seen net outflows. I am indebted to Tom Sung for doing these calculations.

Prime Minister Lee Kwan Yew, in his 1989 National Day address, bemoaned the loss of 4,707 families in 1988 from Singapore's top 25 percent, up from only 1,000 earlier in the decade. Singapore has less than half the population of Hong Kong and its brain drain has risen much faster. It involves the same kinds of people emigrating to the same countries (largely Canada, Australia, and the United States) for similar reasons—in Singapore's case, disdain for the current rather than the prospective political constraints on their lives. And it is proportionately much more serious, because Singapore previously had a policy of severely restricting higher, especially postgraduate education, and consequently has a proportionately much more limited pool of high-level skills. Its loss of talent has been of proportionate magnitude.

The brain drain can hardly imply doom for Hong Kong and be consistent with rosy optimism for Singapore. It is in fact a serious but manageable problem for both countries. Hong Kong is just beginning to experience a return flow of people (10 to 15 percent of the outflow, but highly concentrated among the most talented and ambitious emigrants), who have already received their Canadian and Australian passports, and it is the recipient of a vast inflow of highly talented people from Japan, North America, Western Europe, and Southeast Asia. In addition, many of China's most talented people are also immigrating—older people who have achieved such influence that they and their families can move to Hong Kong, and younger people who have the ability to seize educational or job opportunities abroad. As against the 60,000 people moving out of Hong Kong annually, about 80,000 move in, including a large number of highly talented entrepreneurs, managers, and professionals. It is vitally important for understanding the diplomacy analyzed in the next chapter to note that virtually every Western newspaper reporting on Hong Kong during the past decade reported the outflow of 60,000 people, but I myself have never seen a report that carried any mention whatever of the inflow. Capital flight and brain drain are not in fact crippling Hong Kong, despite the vigorous efforts of local people and businesses to obtain "insurance policies" in the form of foreign legal domicile.

Moreover, since Hong Kong is much more than just a supplier for China, it can prosper even when China experiences political and economic trauma. The lesson of Tiananmen Square was not that Hong Kong businesses in China are at risk, but that, even in a time of terrible strife in Beijing, not one Hong Kong factory in southern China (where most are located) suffered any loss of production. And by 1992, remarkably few of these business were dependent on Chinese demand, because of present and past requirements that foreign investments focus primarily on production for export. Most are processing centers for goods that will eventually satisfy Japanese, European, or American demand. China can experience vast political strife, together with frightening economic downturns, as in 1958–61 and 1966–68, and Hong Kong can still grow.

Even if Hong Kong's problems are manageable, one could argue that they may sap its competitiveness—a potentially fatal problem in such a hypercompetitive region. To test this idea, we must examine each of Hong Kong's eight major roles.

HONG KONG'S MAJOR ROLES

1. Airlock. Hong Kong's first role is as an airlock for China— an entry point for technology, capital, management skills, and ideas. The airlock has expanded into a vast and busy passageway, but it still mediates between China's system and the capitalist world. No other country can compete with Hong Kong in this respect. In theory, the special economic zones could become competitors; in practice, they have become colonies of Hong Kong because its investment dominates these zones. Effectively, Hong Kong owns the zones. As China has soared, the role of airlock between China and the outside world has become far more important than in the past. While the opening up of China reduces some of the need, China's overall relations with the outside world are expanding at such a rate that any attrition is more than offset. Note that most of China's exporters seek to export from Hong Kong, even when other ports are closer, and that Hong Kong managers are assuming potentially dominant roles in China's other main ports. In the future, Shanghai or even Taiwan could become competitors, but that possibility is decades away.

2. Entrepot. Hong Kong and Singapore are the world's greatest ports primarily because of their roles as entrepots. During the 1980s it became part of the conventional wisdom that these entrepots would inevitably lose their value as other countries liberalized their trade. The entrepots were seen as important primarily because they allowed free trade at a time when other countries severely restricted or taxed trade. It followed that, with the vast liberalization under way, Hong Kong and Singapore would no longer be special. Such an analysis misses most of the rationale for an entrepot, which is a concentration of special skills for bringing together sellers and buyers.

In former decades, this was a relatively simple matter, involving a few sellers, a few buyers, and a few products. For instance, China had tungsten to sell and the United States needed to buy tungsten, and both found Hong Kong a useful intermediary.[16] Today, the situation is much more complex. A very large number of countries are sellers. Virtually all countries are buyers. The selection of products to be bought and sold ranges from raw materials to toys to petrochemicals to sophisticated software. Hong Kong's role may be to connect a Hitachi tape recorder manufactured in China to a Peruvian buyer. The permutations of seller, product, buyer, mode of transport, and financial terms have become virtually infinite, and an enormous concentration of highly specialized skills is required to make the whole process work. The role of entrepot has become more important than ever, and only Hong Kong and Singapore have the concentrations of skills to play that role.[17]

3. Financial center. Hong Kong is the world's third largest major financial center, if measured by the number of banks present, or fourth largest if measured by the number of offshore loans originated. Hong Kong is also a major center for funds management, with U.S.$114 billion under management in 1989, as compared with U.S.$15 billion in Singapore. Most potential competitors are disqualified from the start: Bangkok because its telephones and infrastructure are inadequate; Manila and Jakarta for that and many other reasons; Kuala Lumpur because it is politicized; and Taipei because its security

---

[16]Chinese tungsten has flowed to the United States throughout the post-1949 period despite trade embargoes—much of the time through the U.S. firm Union Carbide. Chinese tungsten was used to make U.S. tanks to fight China in the Korean War.

[17]I am indebted for my introduction to the theory of entrepots to Hadi Soesastro's paper, "The Changing Hong Kong Entrepot Role in the Region," Lingnan College Conference on Hong Kong's Role in the Asian Pacific Region in the 21st Century, February 28–29, 1992. I was one of the organizers of the conference, whose purpose was to explore some of the issues raised in this section on Hong Kong's roles.

environment is restrictive. Tokyo is the region's capital for the distribution of loans, but it cannot take over Hong Kong's origination role because it is too expensive a place to do business, because the language is not yet widely understood by foreigners, because Japan's culture is both esoteric and xenophobic, and because its financial markets are so large and complex that they have become all-absorbing preoccupations for Tokyo financial executives.

That leaves Singapore. A serious competitor with none of these deficiencies, Singapore has managed to surpass Hong Kong in the volume of foreign exchange transactions. But Singapore's tight controls on most markets and on the press will limit its role until those controls are loosened—and there is no prospect of early change. Most modern financial enterprises need the *Asian Wall Street Journal, Asia Week,* the *Far Eastern Economic Review,* CNN television news, and other sources of information that are banned much of the time in Singapore, and they cannot thrive in an atmosphere of heavy-handed business regulation. While a number of financial firms did move to Singapore in the period after Tiananmen Square, many subsequently moved back because of what they considered repressive regulation. Singapore is one of the world's great success stories, yet it is not particularly attractive to most of the kinds of information-intensive, freewheeling financial industries that tend to headquarter in Hong Kong.

Despite Singapore's years of campaigning to attract Hong Kong workers, only thirty-five people actually moved in the period 1985–88. I myself received almost as many résumés from Singapore wanting to move to Hong Kong as the total number of emigrants from Hong Kong to Singapore in these years. Hong Kong people seek Singapore residence permits as an insurance policy, but most do not want to live there. There are unofficial reports that after Tiananmen Square 500 to 600 people accepted Singapore's offer of permanent residence permits; but even if this is true, Singapore emigration to Hong Kong in four years (873 people) was greater than Hong Kong emigration to Singapore in five years. Proportionately, the migration to Hong Kong was more than double. Singapore officials confirm privately that such trends are continuing. Its 1980s strategy of competing confrontationally with Hong Kong and of trying to lure Hong Kong's people away simply failed. In the 1990s, Singapore has sharply changed from criticizing Hong Kong and competing directly against it to seeking chances for collaboration and to actively investing in Hong Kong.

Singapore may have a deeper problem in competing with Hong Kong. A recent analysis indicates that Singapore's over-regulated economy has been growing primarily because the government has been pouring larger and larger sums of capital into investment at ever-decreasing rates of efficiency, while the more market-driven Hong Kong has been using its resources with increasing efficiency. This is worrisome for Singapore because there are limits to the expenditure of capital in a society where the government has long forced savings rates up to around 40 percent, the highest level in the world.[18]

Despite this lack of effective competition, it is conventional wisdom among bankers that Hong Kong will lose its role as a great financial center. After all, its rise was for the purpose of recycling Middle East oil profits (petrodollars) and Japanese surpluses to Third World countries. Now that the oil boom is finished, much of that role has vanished and therefore, according to this line of argument, Hong Kong's function as a financial center should decline. Moreover, much of Hong Kong's special role has derived from its openness to interna-

---

[18]Cf. Alwyn Young, "A Tale of Two Cities: Factor Accumulation and Technical Change in Hong Kong and Singapore," mimeo, Sloan School of Management, MIT, April 25, 1992.

tional financial flows in a region of previous tight controls of capital markets.[19] As Bangkok and Taipei liberalize and seek to become financial centers, Hong Kong should lose its special advantages.

But the petrodollar argument ignores the fact that Asia has a population of nearly 2 billion people, growing at 7 percent per year, and such growth must be financed. This is the largest-scale financing job in world history. If growth must be financed in the absence of petrodollars, then it will be financed through more sophisticated methods: leases of equipment from American pension funds, global bond issues, stock market placements, private equity funds, and many others. In the absence of petrodollars, money is scarcer and (except during recessions) more expensive, so heroic efforts will be made to reduce financing costs through a variety of financial techniques. These complex techniques require a concentration of cosmopolitan bankers, accountants, lawyers, and computer services that is found only in Hong Kong. Japan has the skills but is focused on its own market; Singapore does not have the same critical mass of skills. Just as in the case of trade in goods (the entrepot role), the more complex trade in financial and other services heightens the value of Hong Kong's special concentration of skills. The reason that New York, London, and Tokyo prosper as global financial centers is not because of the protectionism of their region, but rather because of their critical mass of skills. New York does not lose its function as a global financial center just because Minneapolis has liberal financial rules and aspires to a larger role; the same applies to Hong Kong and Bangkok.

[19]The most sophisticated presentation of this argument is that of the chief economist of Bangkok Bank. See Dr. Nimit Nonthapunthawat, "Hong Kong as a Financial Center in the Region in the Twentieth Century," presented at the 1992 Lingnan University Conference cited above.

4. *Regional services headquarters.* The late 1980s and the 1990s are the era of the takeoff of the services sector in Pacific Asia. Complex cross-border trade and investment deals, governments' newfound determination to create and enforce modern tax systems, the rising role of stock markets and their associated need for analysis, and a host of other developments have created an explosion of demand for high-level, cosmopolitan, regionally oriented services from accountants, lawyers, information specialists, and computer consultants. Hong Kong and Singapore are the regional capitals of such services, with Hong Kong playing a substantially more significant role—one that is expanding exponentially.

5. *Manufacturer.* Hong Kong is in fact going out of the manufacturing business, except for certain specialized sectors. But it is becoming the manager of manufacturing in southern China, and a principal manager throughout Asia. Like New York, Hong Kong has evolved from manufacturing to management, design, and finance. The 3 million or more employees of Hong Kong firms in China represent five times the total number of industrial workers in Hong Kong itself. Before the opening to China, Hong Kong firms never employed more than about 900,000 industrial workers; now they employ 3.65 million. Thus Hong Kong's manufacturing role has expanded by nearly a factor of four, but the work done by Hong Kong people themselves has moved upmarket. As Hong Kong itself has abandoned manufacturing, its role in global manufacturing has increased tremendously; the profit derived from manufacturing has risen as it has concentrated on the higher-value-added tasks.

There are many competitors for Hong Kong's manufacturing role, but there is also plenty of work for all of them, and Hong Kong's function as a manager and designer is increasingly a regional one, with factories in Thailand, Malaysia, Indonesia, the Philippines, and even places as far away as Switzerland, the United States, and Sri Lanka. As manufacturing in China expands faster than anywhere else in the world, and as China's export manufacturing lies largely in Hong Kong hands, the market share of Hong Kong firms in world manufactures is growing rapidly.

An important change is occurring as the result of China's availability as a manufacturing base and market. For the first time, Hong Kong is capable of supporting regional- and potentially world-class firms. Until recently, the Hong Kong and Taiwan markets were simply too small to support the kinds of firms that characterize Japan (Mitsubishi, Sony) and South Korea (Hyundai, Lucky-Goldstar). Hong Kong will likely always be a more fragmented economy than that of its larger neighbors, but Cheung Kong is becoming a world-scale firm in real estate; Hutchinson in satellite television, ports, and mobile phone systems; and Hopewell as a major regional builder of infrastructure. As Chinese companies make Hong Kong their base of international operations, and as they seek to use it as a center for commercializing their broad base of scientific research, Hong Kong could well emerge for the first time as the home of recognizable firms and brand names.

6. *Regional headquarters.* Most major Pacific Asian firms require one headquarters in Tokyo and another for the rest of Asia. In addition to the other reasons for choosing Hong Kong or Singapore as a financial center, tax and other incentives make these two city-states the locations of choice. Hong Kong is regarded as a superior environment for its culture and entertainment; Singapore has a more placid physical and social ambience. Both city-states appear to have entrenched roles in this respect, depending on a particular firm's sector and geographic orientation. There is no evidence of a large net movement of headquarters from Hong Kong to Singapore, or

vice versa. Even though the number of regional headquarters in Singapore is somewhat exaggerated by many firms' tendencies to set up mini-regional headquarters there (often reporting to Hong Kong) in order to qualify for Singapore's special incentives, Hong Kong is far ahead. The most recent survey indicated that Hong Kong held 51 percent of Pacific Asia's regional headquarters, Singapore 29 percent, and Tokyo 20 percent.[20]

7. Commercializer of China's science. Despite the Cultural Revolution's devastating effect on its educational institutions, China has a huge reservoir of scientific skills, most of which have never been tapped for commercial purposes. Hong Kong has proved relatively weak in training and attracting scientists, but seems able to commercialize just about anything.Inevitably, these complementary elements will fuse into a compound that generates money.

A pioneer in such efforts is Videotech, a listed Hong Kong company that produces computers and educational toys. Videotech, which produces the majority of the world's computer educational toys, is run by Allan Wong, an American-educated Hong Kong Chinese whose huge factory in China

[20]The most recent and most thorough study of regional MNC headquarters was done by the government of New South Wales, Australia, and the city of Sydney, with the results mentioned. Cf. John C. Wilson, "Hong Kong as Regional Headquarters," presented to the 1992 Lingnan University Conference cited above. The survey also found that, on the five top criteria, most MNCs that year ranked Tokyo and Singapore ahead of Hong Kong as a favorable regional headquarters site. This apparently resulted from the fears about Hong Kong in the wake of Tiananmen Square. Two years later, Hong Kong was having a boom while Singapore was in a slump and Tokyo was suffering the aftermath of its stock market and real estate market collapses. Such events are evanescent; the only sound measure is whether MNCs actually relocate; by this criterion Hong Kong seems to be strengthening its role.

has made a point of employing highly trained but hitherto poorly paid scientists from different parts of China. Initially, such Hong Kong–mainland scientific efforts will concentrate on highly specialized areas such as the creation of Chinese-language computer software, but wide-ranging production is likely in the near future. Greater China, factoring in Taiwan, possesses an enormous range of scientific and commercial skills.

8. Press center. Hong Kong is also Asia's press center. No other country offers comparable facilities and press freedom. Singapore has superior printing capabilities but it restricts freedom severely. In the next few years, there will be no serious competitors to Hong Kong. However, Hong Kong's long-term attraction could weaken substantially at a time when one can imagine possible improvements in Singapore or Bangkok. China will certainly be tempted to curb "slander" and "rumors" about itself, although, as we have already noted, under Li Peng's conservative regime the *Asian Wall Street Journal* and the *Far Eastern Economic Review,* as well as other major news sources such as CNN television, are consistently available in China and more often than not banned or severely limited in Singapore.

IN SHORT, MOST of Hong Kong's major roles are secure—despite the brain drain—unless deterioration goes further than seems likely. China may limit press criticism of itself, Hong Kong may become more bureaucratized, the brain drain may increase, crime and corruption will certainly increase, and China may undergo severe political strife in the succession to Deng Xiaoping—but the historical record shows that Hong Kong is likely to continue to prosper. Hong Kong is now at the confluence of three of the most powerful economic forces in world history: the Chinese economic takeoff; the regional Asian economic takeoff; and the era in which the Asian services sectors take off.

HONG KONG'S COMPETITORS

A mainland version of the competition thesis holds that Shanghai is envious of Hong Kong's success and will seek to raise itself by suppressing Hong Kong. As evidence of the seriousness of this risk, some argue that China's bureaucracy dealing with Hong Kong and Macau affairs is dominated by Shanghainese.

I have sought to substantiate the thesis of Shanghai red-eye disease (the Chinese phrase for jealousy) through interviews in Guangzhou and Beijing and discussions with business leaders and officials from Shanghai. The evidence goes the other way. Shanghai perceives its problems as caused by Beijing's excessive taxation—which used to squeeze more than half of the central government's total revenues out of Shanghai—not by competition from Hong Kong. It seems keener to emulate Hong Kong than to suppress it. Guangdong officials and scholars express no such concern. They believe the Pudong economic zone outside Shanghai will follow a quite different model from their own, and they believe their proximity to Hong Kong and their superior ties to the overseas community ensure their continued success.

Objectively, there is plenty of room for both Hong Kong/ Guangdong and Shanghai to succeed. The 1992 agreement whereby the Port of Shanghai sold half of its terminal facilities to Hutchison Whampoa, with Hutchison granted a superior management role, indicates far more interest in collaboration than conflict. There will be competition, to be sure, in such areas as stock markets and banking. But shared interests and a mutually acceptable division of labor, with Shanghai as the capital of heavy industry and Hong Kong as the capital of services and light industry, seem the essence of the future relationship.

The only possible shadow is that China's tax problems, exemplified by Shanghai's excessive burden and by declining central government revenues during a period of extraordinary economic growth, presage an early reform of China's tax system. The authors of the eighth Five-Year Plan have told a group of economists (myself included) that the national tax system will be revamped and that the coastal areas are likely to lose some of their special privileges. But a fair tax system is not a Shanghai conspiracy, and Guangdong will always retain its special cultural and geographic advantages, along with its head start in developing a modern economic system.

DOES CHINA'S RISE MEAN THE LOSS OF HONG KONG'S REGIONAL ROLE?

A final piece of conventional wisdom holds that, as Hong Kong's relationship with China prospers, inevitably Hong Kong's regional role will suffer. But this need not be so. The explosion of regional Asian trade, and the explosion of the regional service industry where Hong Kong has a dominant role, create a potential as great as any provided by China. A survey of American firms in Hong Kong, which are a reasonable proxy for the multinational corporations based in Hong Kong, reveals that only about half of them (47 percent) have business related to China.[21] My informal telephone survey of

[21]"Amcham Business Study 1992: Presentation Charts," *Survey Research Hong Kong*, Table 30.

the major service firms (the fastest-growing sector in Hong Kong, albeit still a limited one) revealed an overwhelming regional role as compared with a still vestigial one with China. So, Hong Kong can walk on both the Chinese leg and the regional leg if it organizes to do so. The key question here is whether the Hong Kong government will act decisively to maintain the cosmopolitan skills and competitiveness needed for its regional role.

THE CENTRAL ISSUES IN HONG KONG'S FUTURE

There remain some critical balances that have to work if Hong Kong is to take full advantage of its opportunities.

Instant Democracy vs. Preservation of Freedom

Hong Kong is the freest stable society in Asia. Malaysia and Singapore have severe restrictions on the press and severe national security laws, and Malaysia has spent virtually its entire post-colonial era under a state of emergency. Japan has informal controls on the press. Hong Kong by contrast has complete freedom of speech, religion, the press, and assembly, as well as almost all of the freedoms guaranteed by British common law. If the United States ranks 100 on a freedom scale of 1 to 100, Britain ranks perhaps 97 (because of restrictions on press publication of government information), and Hong Kong ranks perhaps 94 (because Hong Kong's anti-corruption agency, the Independent Commission Against Corruption, or ICAC, can do many things that would be prohibited in the United States). No stable Third World regime ranks higher than Hong Kong.

If one ranks Hong Kong in terms of democracy, it does not fall in the same class as the major industrial democracies, but it is in the top tier of the Third World. In 1995, twenty of its legislators will be directly elected by popular vote, thirty will be elected by functional groups such as accountants and lawyers, and ten will be indirectly elected through an electoral college. The Chief Executive will be elected after 1997 through some mechanism over which Beijing will have a veto. An extensive system of consultative bodies ensures a broad representation of views, which are in fact taken seriously into account. A free and diverse press gives a very articulate voice to virtually all social groups. This falls short of full democracy, but it is much more representative than all but a handful of Third World countries. The system has also displayed some initial resilience against Chinese efforts to manipulate it; in the 1991 election, Xinhua—the New China News Agency, which manages Chinese interests in Hong Kong—made vigorous efforts to support a pro-Beijing (but non-socialist) group of politicians. Not one achieved election.

Such a system has both risks and benefits. The principal risk is that a ruthless government in Beijing could manipulate it. On the other hand, a ruthless government in Beijing might manipulate any system, and Hong Kong's principal protection is that Beijing so far has evinced no desire to do so in any way that would cause structural damage. (It *is* willing to take strong measures against unilateral British changes of the structure, but that is a different issue, as we shall see in the next chapter.) The principal benefit, shared with the other Asian miracle economies, is that Hong Kong has found a way through advisory bodies and functional constituency elections to enshrine a high level of expertise alongside a substantial degree of representation in the councils of government. Elsewhere in Asia this has been done by giving the bureaucracies tremendous power relative to politicians (Japan, South Korea,

Taiwan, Singapore, Thailand) and by enshrining for a long time the rule of a dominant party (Japan, Taiwan, Singapore, Malaysia). This reduces some of the populist politics that have led to almost universal bankruptcy in Africa and Latin America—as well as a horrendous budget deficit in the United States—and it can make government more decisive in coping with a rapidly changing economic environment.

Thus the Hong Kong system is very free by any standards, relatively democratic by Third World standards, and much more democratic than it was before China decided to take it back from the British. Moreover, China has been willing to countenance a gradual increase in democratization, indicated by a gradual increase in the number of directly rather than indirectly elected legislators. Beijing has committed itself to gradual progress toward a legislature that is wholly elected by Western-style constituencies; but it wants continuity and decisive executive leadership, and is not willing to countenance sudden radical change. This is the precise analogue of its economic strategy of gradualism, a strategy that has proved wiser than ones recommended by the West. On the other hand, powerful voices in London and Washington, together with some of the most outspoken voices in Hong Kong itself (particularly English-speaking voices), dismiss all this as meaningless and demand that Britain impose full democracy immediately. Many of these voices make the insupportable claim that Chinese resistance against such a transformation constitutes a breach of the Joint Declaration.

The question facing Hong Kong is whether a precipitous change in the system to grasp for full democracy, at the cost of possibly jeopardizing one of the world's freest and most prosperous systems, is worth it. The decision lies in the hands of a British Governor, influenced by powerful voices and constituency interests in London and by parallel voices in Washington demanding the all-or-nothing approach. To the Chinese, this sounds like the same advice the same people gave Eastern Europe.

Mutual Non-Subversion vs. Freedom

The foundation stone of "One country, two systems" will always be that China does not subvert Hong Kong and Hong Kong in turn does not attempt to subvert China. This implies mutual restraint—including restraint on organized Hong Kong groups funding Chinese dissidents, organizing them, or propagandizing in their favor. These activities may be morally just (I myself have engaged in them as a way of promoting democracy in other countries), but they jeopardize the foundation of Hong Kong's freedom if the authorities encourage or permit them.

On the other side, if Beijing takes too broad a view of what constitutes "subversion"—if for instance it includes newspaper editorials and speeches critical of Chinese leaders—then Hong Kong's freedom will be jeopardized. Fund managers and stockbroking headquarters will move away because they cannot get the information they need. Intellectuals and many others who care deeply about their freedom will leave for other areas, and Hong Kong will be impoverished.

So far, both sides have temporized. Britain has implemented some basic anti-subversion policies, but has done it in a wimpish way that depends on ancient legal technicalities (see Chapter V for details). This approach fails to confront the issue and develop a public consensus about the proper balance. China has been ambivalent. Xinhua News Agency under one leadership (Xu Jiatun) endorsed the Hong Kong people's right even to hold major demonstrations against Chinese policies as long as such activity was confined within the borders of Hong Kong. Xinhua under its 1990–93 leadership (Zhou Nan) has often bitterly criticized Hong Kong's Governor for allowing acerbic anti-Chinese editorials. At the same time, the *Asian Wall Street Journal* and the *South China Morning Post* (Hong Kong's leading English-language newspaper, which, like the *Asian Wall Street Journal,* is bitterly anti-Beijing) are available in every major Chinese city even when they carry the most fervent anti-Chinese editorials. And China has tolerated the transformation of Guangdong society under the influence of Hong Kong visitors, Hong Kong television and radio, and Hong Kong ideology. Because the process has been gradual and has been inextricably related to the economic takeoff, Beijing has seen this as a manageable and unavoidable price of economic success.

The obvious solution is a pact in which Hong Kong acknowledges the full implications of "One country, two systems," and Beijing takes a very tolerant view of any writing, speaking, or demonstrating that occurs within Hong Kong itself. It is very important that the rules be made explicit. The behavior of both parties suggests a willingness to abide by such rules. On the other hand, an explicit understanding is currently unachievable because of the level of mistrust created in Britain by Tiananmen Square and in Beijing by the British hard line on democratization and by the British breaches of the Joint Declaration (discussed in Chapter V) over the airport and political change.

Mutual Non-Subversion vs. Democracy

The rule that neither Beijing nor Hong Kong is allowed to subvert the other also means that neither government should be run by a leader who has advocated the overthrow of the other or been actively involved in such efforts. If Hong Kong is run by a governor or a group who actively seek to overthrow the leadership in China, it is fairly obvious that Beijing will react—and that Beijing will win. The Basic Law, Hong

Kong's constitutional document, includes a specific non-subversion clause. But this creates a dilemma if such groups win an election.

In 1991, the United Democrats, led by Martin Lee, who had become famous for advocating the overthrow of Beijing's leadership and for taking active measures to support dissidents in China, won twelve of the eighteen in the Legislative Council that were directly elected (out of sixty total seats). All, including Martin Lee, were allowed to take their seats in the legislature, but many of Lee's supporters also demanded that he be given a seat in the Executive Council, Hong Kong's cabinet. Beijing said that was unacceptable. Lee, a very distinguished lawyer, attempted to make a distinction between advocating overthrow of the leadership and subverting the government, but that distinction proved too subtle for Beijing. Governor Chris Patten, who took office in 1992, decided to finesse the issue by banning all members of the Legislative Council (including Martin Lee) from sitting on the Executive Council. Vocal advocates of pure democracy and of near independence for Hong Kong regard such decisions as anti-democratic, but most Hong Kong opinion rejects provoking the dragon. Mutual non-subversion remains the most fundamental assumption of "One country, two systems."

In the heat of Hong Kong politics, this observation tends to get confused with other issues, such as whether one likes Martin Lee or whether one is pro-Chinese or whether one truly values democracy. It is a reasonably objective fact that Hong Kong has two basic options. The first is "One country, two systems," which maintains Hong Kong's freedom but requires both sides to refrain from subverting one another. The second is "One country, one system"—namely, a communist system—which is the only possible outcome of either side subverting the other. Only Beijing can win a subversion game. Given this choice, someone committed to freedom would pre-

sumably choose to ban subversion. If one acknowledges this
logic, than an advocate of the overthrow of the Chinese government must not become a top leader of Hong Kong—at
least unless he publicly changes his mind. This logic is completely independent of whether one admires Lee's calls to
overthrow the Beijing leadership or not, and whether one admires Beijing's leadership or not.   ,

At the same time, Beijing would be well advised to offer
politicians like Martin Lee a path back to acceptability. Lee's
actions and statements after Tiananmen Square may have
been unwise for an ambitious politician, but at the time they
articulated very widespread sentiments. Moreover, Lee and
colleagues like Szeto Wah are universally acknowledged to be
men of great integrity and intelligence. Banning them en-
hances their substantial following. If for instance Beijing were
to allow them to compete for top leadership positions condi-
tional upon an oath of loyalty to the Basic Law, many more
people would see China's policy as balanced and flexible.

Freedom vs. Corruption

While Hong Kong is an extremely free society, it has hitherto
accepted one principal constraint on freedom—the right of
the Independent Commission Against Corruption (ICAC) to
open mail, intrude into homes and offices, and counsel business not to deal with firms believed to be corrupt. All these
and many other actions are routinely performed in Hong
Kong without the controls that are taken for granted in Britain and enforced even more strictly in the United States. Democracy advocates have insisted on a Bill of Rights that
would curtail the ICAC.

ICAC was created by the British in 1974 to cope with
debilitating corruption beyond the control of normal "democratic" mechanisms. It resolved a crisis brought on by wide-

spread corruption in government and in the police. At the time of its creation it was clearly indispensable, and it has become a model of success for other Asian societies attempting to curb corruption. Perhaps, its job now done, the ICAC can be wound up. But this is the era of integration with China, and this is the era—more precisely, one more era—of extraordinary corruption in China. The power of Chinese criminal gangs, the power of alliances between the gangs and police units in Guangdong, and the unwillingness of many Chinese companies in Hong Kong to adapt to Western anti-corruption rules, all pose a serious threat to the integrity of Hong Kong's administration and its economic system.

Until now, the ICAC has been consistent with a free society only because it has been controlled by British leaders with a commitment to freedom. In the hands of people with repressive intent, or simple lack of restraint, ICAC could become arbitrary and destructive of freedom. On the other hand, London and Washington-style mechanisms may prove inadequate. Hong Kong confronts not just ordinary criminals but also powerful triad gangs with pan-Chinese and global networks that surpass the Mafia. A highly constricted city police force can be overwhelmed. The institutional mechanisms to achieve a proper balance have not yet been formulated.

Judicial Integrity

No issue is more delicate in preserving Hong Kong's freedom and economic effectiveness than the integrity of the judicial system. In China, the state controls the courts and expects to get the results it wants. In Hong Kong, the state writes the laws, but independent courts administer and interpret them. Lawyers are accredited by the court, not the state. Hong Kong's economy could not survive a major compromise with China's legal system, because international firms expect to be able to sue the state, to sue firms belonging to the state without prejudice, and to have complex disputes adjudicated under the final authority of an independent court system. The further China goes toward ensuring the detailed continuation of such a system, excepting national security and foreign policy issues, the more prosperous Hong Kong will be. The difficulty of dovetailing the two legal systems is compounded by a second difficulty: Can the competence of a system of British common law, based on vast archives of centuries of English-language cases, be maintained in a context where the language of the law and of general social intercourse will inevitably shift toward Chinese?

So far, neither the Chinese nor the British government has articulated a strategy to deal with these difficulties. China's leaders have ensured their control of foreign affairs and national security, as well as considerable influence over the court of highest appeal. The Chinese also will have more influence over judicial appointments than is possible under the British system. This leads to understandable fears of abuse.

The Hong Kong government and legal profession have reacted defensively, sharply criticizing all changes. The Hong Kong Law Society has argued for strong safeguards on judicial independence. Unfortunately, it has also weakened its position with hypocritical arguments against reaching out to non-British and to Chinese legal institutions in ways that would safeguard Hong Kong's legal future. In particular, it has argued that it must severely restrict access by any outsiders—especially Americans—to the practice of law in Hong Kong. Hong Kong's British-trained lawyers fear that China will use any opening to swamp Hong Kong with its lawyers, and they have used this as an argument for trying to insulate themselves from any real competition. While the Hong Kong government recognizes that the Law Society is motivated primarily by a desire to preserve its members' profits, it has largely bowed to the local pressure, taking only marginal steps toward a more open system and no important initiatives toward Chinese lawyers.

Hong Kong's lawyers became particularly disgruntled over the issue of foreign appointments to the Court of Final Appeal. The Joint Declaration stated that judges from other British Commonwealth jurisdictions might be invited to sit on this Court. Britain and China agreed to interpret this as meaning that one would be invited, but only one, while the Hong Kong Bar Association argued fervently that too few indigenous judges were available and therefore it was important to invite more than one. (How the dearth of available talent squared with the restrictive policies advocated by the same groups was never addressed.) Some local lawyers even argued that limiting the number of foreign judges to one infringed the Joint Declaration. The Legislative Council voted disapproval of the deal. While the agreement probably constituted a particularly stringent interpretation of the declaration rather than an infringement of it, this was one area where British acceptance of a Chinese view was unwise. Chinese nationalism against having the highest court dominated by foreigners was comprehensible but short-sighted.

The resulting standoff is important. Indeed, the ambiguities inherent in this struggle justify the widespread tendency for individuals and firms to establish legal domiciles elsewhere. In all probability, no possible scenario between now and 1997 would untangle the legal uncertainties sufficiently for most large companies to keep their legal domicile in Hong Kong. But there is a genuine risk that real business as well as legal domiciles will migrate unless the uncertainty is limited. Such limitation can be achieved only by abandoning the fortress mentality of Hong Kong's legal system and by creating supportive links to other Western systems and to like-minded groups in China.

Three trends are inevitable. First, many of Hong Kong's lawyers will emigrate or repatriate to Britain; surveys show that the majority intend to so so. Second, the language of the law will gradually shift to Chinese. With the British gone, the local population will demand this. Third, lawyers from China will play an increasing role. Current Hong Kong policy seeks to hold back these tides; a more sensible policy would attempt to channel them in positive directions. A protectionist Hong Kong legal system—the one created by current policy—will inevitably be weakened and swamped and will detract from Hong Kong's role as a hub of regional manufacturing and of the regional services industry.

A more enlightened policy could encourage an influx of talented foreign lawyers to offset the current drain (as is happening in other areas of business). Hong Kong might, for instance, welcome Chinese lawyers, and concurrently set extremely high standards for them to be allowed to practice. Further, why not allocate modest financial assistance to enable the most promising Chinese lawyers to meet the standards? This would create the foundation for a high-quality legal system dominated by Chinese Western-style lawyers from both Hong Kong and China. Systematic training of a stratum of capable Chinese lawyers would provide the basis for negotiating a fuller understanding of the integrity of the process. Just now, local lawyers are confusing legitimate concerns over integrity with their desire to extract maximum profits and are consequently excluding mainlanders from opportunity to work within the system. Neither the government nor the Law Society has made any significant effort to prepare for an era when much of the judicial system will have to function in Chinese. Small wonder that China has legitimate doubts about the motives of Hong Kong institutions.

Laissez Faire vs. Adjustment

In adapting to economic realities, Hong Kong has an ideological problem. The colony has suffered several years of inflation rates around 10 percent during an era when its Asian neighbors limited inflation to about half that level, and Hong Kong has experienced lower growth than most of its neighbors. Although severely understated because of the statistical ramifications of the relationship with Guangdong, Hong Kong's growth could have been much faster. Lower-than-optimum growth, and—much more importantly—very high inflation can severely debilitate the economy if allowed to persist for long periods of time.

Hong Kong's inflation has many causes, including imported Chinese inflation and inflation caused by the pegging of Hong Kong's currency to the U.S. dollar. But the primary reason for both high inflation and reduced growth has been a shortage of land and labor. In turn, these shortages flow from the relatively slow speed in relocating labor- and land-intensive industries across the border into China. By Western standards, the shift of "sunset" industries out of Hong Kong has occurred rapidly. Compared with the U.S. textile industry, for instance, which has received many billions of dollars of effective subsidies to avoid the much-needed transfer overseas, Hong Kong's adjustment has taken place at lightning speed. But compared with other Asian countries, Hong Kong has been slow to adjust. Most of the Taiwan shoe industry, for example, shifted to mainland China in about two years— much to the benefit of Taiwan's economy. The Hong Kong government has been unwilling to take positive measures to speed up the adjustment. Indeed, it subsidizes low-level industry by, for instance, refusing to penalize local dying factories which pollute the environment and thereby putting the financial burden of cleanup on high-tech firms which frequently do not pollute at all.

Other Asian countries take a different approach. They charge fully for pollution, improve the appropriate infrastructure, offer retraining programs, provide adjustment assistance, and dispense information on how to organize a move. Hong Kong's regressive policies are generally justified within its government by the belief that adjustment would run counter to the territory's laissez-faire tradition, as if planning would constitute a kind of unacceptable socialism. But Hong Kong's laissez-faire tradition has never been so pervasive in reality as in current imagination. When Hong Kong had a severe housing shortage, the government became the leading builder of housing; even today, 40 percent of the housing stock is government-owned. Regulation of transport and utilities is pervasive and in many ways stricter than in the United States. The prospect of up to a decade of near-double-digit inflation is just as serious a threat to society as the earlier housing crisis, and should be addressed as such. Moreover, industrial relocation is no more a socialist idea than planning years ahead for road and airport construction. What really lies behind the government's failure to facilitate industrial adjustment is its determination to keep Hong Kong as separate from China as possible.

This "Little Hong Kong" approach leads to numerous irrationalities. The Chinese build a superhighway across Guangdong Province, but at the Hong Kong border, where the heaviest traffic is, it turns into an ordinary road on the Hong Kong side. Hong Kong's industrial area is the most densely populated territory on earth, and a similar industrial zone has arisen across the border in Shenzhen. But the British persist in zoning the Hong Kong side of the border for farmland. From a helicopter, this little strip of rice paddies looks like what it is, an absurd anachronism. Here again the British oppose the tides of history rather than channeling them. As the statistics cited at the beginning of this chapter show, China has already won the war to integrate the two economies. But the British government nonetheless mounts a series of battles to inhibit truly efficient integration. The cost to Hong Kong is immense.

Competitive Cosmopolitanism vs. Protected Interests

The end of the British era has seen a scramble to protect old monopolies, and even to create new ones. The huge new airport plans to refuse modern hubbing—at the risk of losing Hong Kong's role as an air cargo and passenger entrepot—because hubbing would threaten the local airline's protected position. The semi-monopoly exercised by Commonwealth lawyers endangers Hong Kong's prospects as the services headquarters of Pacific Area. Local doctors ban highly qualified French doctors and nurses from giving free treatment to Vietnamese refugees who lack medical care; after all, if a doctor does not hold British Commonwealth qualifications, he or she surely cannot be qualified to practice. Banking, the port, and many other areas are subject to British-era cartels. Local teachers have destroyed efforts to upgrade the territory's terrible standards of English by a number of strategems: driving out imported English teachers, rejecting high standards for local teachers of English, and even sending Department of Education investigators to harass a club formed so that people could come together and practice their English. This question of education is the single most important threat to Hong Kong's future as a regional center.

The tendencies toward entrenchment of monopolies are being fought hard by China. The Bank of China, for instance, has demanded the right to equal status with the two major British banks. And American airlines are insisting that Hong Kong be as open to hubbing as Taiwan and Singapore. On balance, though, Hong Kong is still very competitive and cosmopolitan compared to its principal neighbors. But entrenchment sets a bad precedent for the times when the major companies are from the mainland.

Little Hong Kong vs. Economic Integration

The Joint Declaration of 1984 enshrined a Hong Kong that was autonomous but also one acknowledged to be an integral part of China. What has so far emerged is a Hong Kong that retains British-style freedoms and administration but serves as a principal source of the Chinese economic takeoff. Here again there is a crucial balance between autonomy and integration. While China has never officially accepted the full implications of Hong Kong's magnetic social role in southern China, Hong Kong's economic benefits for China are so great that communist conservatives have been rapidly marginalized. Shenzhen, the Chinese territory north of Hong Kong, is much more like Hong Kong than the rest of China. People there dress like the people in Hong Kong, criticize their government freely like the people in Hong Kong, and watch Hong Kong television. They use mobile phones to place their bets at the Hong Kong Jockey Club. They have the freer sexual mores and the physical mobility of people in Hong Kong, and frequent the same kinds of karaoke bars. All of Guangdong Province is following the same path.

The embourgeoisement of southern China has gone for beyond anything Beijing anticipated. For Beijing, this has meant a painful ideological adjustment. Occasionally, it has reacted with campaigns against "bourgeois liberalization" and "spiritual pollution," but on balance China's leaders have come to accept an unexpected degree of social liberalization as the unavoidable price for an unexpected degree of economic success. Today, the campaigns more narrowly target corruption and prostitution. (Western feminists would approve the current policy of putting Hong Kong men who use Chinese prostitutes in jail for up to six months. For a while, the Chinese authorities also conducted mandatory AIDS testing of people randomly selected from those crossing the border more than a dozen times a year—apparently on the theory that such frequency indicated more interest in local girls than local business—but that policy has now ended.)

Embourgeoisement has even filtered up to the top leadership. In early 1993, Premier Li Peng addressed his colleagues wearing a Ferragamo tie. So much for Maoist austerity.

The British government in Hong Kong has found it much more difficult to aim for both autonomy and integration. Immigration rules largely deny multiple-entry visas to senior Chinese corporate executives who can travel freely elsewhere in the world. American companies based in Hong Kong must set up training facilities in Singapore for their Chinese staff because immigration rules for Chinese executives are so restrictive. Hong Kong government officials mostly view the transfer of labor-intensive firms across the border as a threat rather than an opportunity. It is not considered unusual for a top Hong Kong government official never to have taken a business trip to China. Few senior Hong Kong officials make any effort to keep in touch with their counterparts in Guangzhou (the capital of Guangdong Province). All this is because the British government in Hong Kong continues to view China as a subversive threat long after the reality of such a threat has disappeared. The government has been slow to build the infrastructure up to the border to accommodate the enormous flows. (The Chinese government has also been slow to accept round-the-clock opening of the border.) And the leaders of the local movement for full democracy have been even more resistant to intercourse with China. For instance, when Hong Kong was suffering a crime wave because of weapons and gangs moving across the border, local legislator Emily Lau denounced the government for inviting a tiny liaison team of Chinese police to Hong Kong to improve coordination.

The most telling British government policy of all has been the refusal to facilitate the learning of Mandarin Chinese by Hong Kong's Cantonese-speaking population. This was not for lack of local demand: Frank Martin, the former president of Security Pacific Asian Bank, tells how the secretaries in his bank confronted him as a group with a request for Mandarin classes. No prerequisite for smooth transition to Chinese rule was clearer than the need for Mandarin-language schools. This did not, however, move the British government to provide any such instruction.

WHEN THE DIFFICULTIES are articulated one by one, they seem to involve Hong Kong in some daunting choices. In fact, the basic choices are not particularly daunting and not at all crippling. First, will Hong Kong be willing to forbid openly organized subversion of China? If so, it will retain almost all of its customary freedom and a great deal more than its customary prosperity. The price: two to five current political figures cannot aim for top policy-making jobs unless they foreswear past positions, and residents must stop organized efforts to send money to dissidents, organize dissident movements, conduct fax campaigns across the border, and the like. Since none of this was possible in the past anyway, Hong Kong surrenders nothing of its past freedom. It remains the freest stable and prosperous society in Asia, with all the freedoms enshrined in the American Bill of Rights.[22] If it is not

[22]The qualifications "stable and prosperous" omit Manila from the comparison; Manila has a tiny additional margin of freedom, and a huge variety

willing to leave China be, it will be incorporated into the communist system.

The second basic choice: Will Hong Kong have full Western-style populist democracy, and its corollary—a standard welfare state and the slower growth, associated with a government sensitive to pressure group demands? Or will it have a system that is designed to be responsive to popular demands but is weighted in favor of economic expertise and longer-term perspectives? There are several reasons why Hong Kong might want to favor the latter choice. First, this is a transient society, with a high rate of immigration and emigration, and the resulting short-term perspective creates a danger to sound decision making. In the United States, those who advocate large government spending without the revenues to pay for them have at last acknowledged that their children will have to pay the deficit. In Hong Kong, people may well believe that their children will be elsewhere. Second, Hong Kong is vulnerable to political panics, such as the backwash to Tiananmen Square. Third, Hong Kong's internal stability derives largely from economic dynamism and in particular from a sense of universal opportunity. Unlike less well managed Western economies, Hong Kong can point to negligible unemployment and far greater opportunities for advancement. Fourth, the only reason China is willing to accept a little bastion of contradictory ideology on its southern rump is the advantage for Chinese society created by Hong Kong's extraordinary economic growth. In reality, to repeat, the real choice is between organizing systematically for economic performance or being absorbed into the communist system.

An analogy to economics might be appropriate here. In

---

of problems derived from its system of government that make it a dangerous, unpleasant, and impoverished place to live.

most Western systems it would be a serious error to peg the exchange rate firmly to another currency. The peg would either prove unstable or would exact a huge price from the real economy. But Hong Kong, unlike Britain or Germany, needs to peg. Why? Because Hong Kong faces situations of panic like the announcement that Britain and China would negotiate the territory's return to China (which eventually produced a terrible financial panic in September 1983) and fear of the consequences of the Tiananmen Square crisis in June 1989. In either of these situations, political panic could have led to loss of faith in the currency, and the currency collapse could have meant social chaos. Luckily, since September 1983 the Hong Kong dollar has been pegged at 7.80 per U.S. dollar. However, there is an economic cost to this arrangement—a cost so large as to be unacceptable elsewhere. For instance, when a strong U.S. dollar made Hong Kong exports expensive in 1985, Hong Kong fell into its only post–World War II recession. Later, a weak dollar pushed growth above 13 percent. Such volatility is undesirable and drew severe criticism from Western-oriented economists. I myself engaged in a formal critical debate on the subject with the government's leading economist, Alan McLean. Then Tiananmen Square showed the wisdom of choosing stability over Western theories and of paying a high real price for that stability. I changed my mind on the peg.

Hong Kong's economic and political institutions were built up over a century and a half. Each major institutional innovation was a response to some serious local crisis.[23] The city was

[23]For an excellent history of the development of Hong Kong's institutions, see the first four chapters of Ian Scott, *Political Change and the Crisis of Legitimacy in Hong Kong* (Honolulu: University of Hawaii Press, 1989). Much of the rest of the book is an ethnocentric and theoretically jumbled polemic on the need for Hong Kong to be run as a textbook Western system, but this does not detract from the excellence of his historical review.

always run primarily to serve British economic interests, and
the priority of the British government was always economic
efficiency. Politics was subordinated. Nonetheless, for most of
modern history Hong Kong has enjoyed the basic freedoms of
a Western society. A series of clashes over several generations
with major social groups led to the creation of a rather responsive political system: while ultimate authority remained
with the British Governor, an elaborate set of consultative
mechanisms evolved. An Executive Council serving almost as
a cabinet contained representatives of the territory's most
powerful interests and most distinguished individuals; a Legislative Council serving almost as a parliament provided
broader representation. A wide array of advisory bodies provided input from important pockets of interest and expertise.
A tradition developed that major legislation would be preceded by widespread initial community consultation, then a
government-prepared Green Paper for formal public comment, then a White Paper, then finally formal legislation. This
process succeeded in maintaining a remarkable degree of consensus on major issues. The process was not electoral democracy, but it provided broad and deep representation of interests and expertise.

Hong Kong's stability has been based on three legs. Above
all, a system designed for economic efficiency delivered superior economic growth and, with that growth, universal opportunity and near-universal employment. Second, British justice
delivered a degree of fairness that achieved popular respect.
Third, the system of consultation and representation took into
account the interests of most social groups. This system was
as different from Western democracy as Hong Kong's monetary peg was from any Western currency system. But it has
served the interests of Hong Kong people well enough to create a remarkable combination of economic growth and social
stability.

During the period from 1949 to 1979, the principal problem for Hong Kong was defending its system against successive waves of ideological fanaticism from the mainland. Particularly during the Cultural Revolution (1966–76), when the slogan in the People's Republic of China was that the "reds" should defeat the "experts," the cult of ideology over expertise threatened to slop over and destroy Hong Kong's unique successes. When the early 1980s brought the necessity of negotiating a transfer of Hong Kong back to Chinese sovereignty, and the concomitant requirement for designing a Hong Kong system that could maintain its success in the context of PRC sovereignty, both the British diplomats and the Chinese negotiators were supremely pragmatic. Had they sought to redesign the system from scratch they would have faced insuperable problems. But they didn't.

China chose to build upon this British foundation the multi-stage economic rocket of Hong Kong–Shenzhen–Guangdong–interior province takeoffs. In both its economic consequences and its influence over the Taiwan-mainland relationship, this choice proved to be one of the modern world's most successful political-economic bets. Never have so many people experienced so much prosperity so quickly as the result of a single major concept as occurred because of Deng Xiaoping's formula, "One country, two systems." But the complexity of Deng's vision and the Cold War's legacy of ideological suspicion combined to stimulate repeated bouts of fear and contention between China and Britain. China's determination to achieve the full benefits of economic synergy between Hong Kong and the rest of China has repeatedly clashed with Britain's determination to maintain a "Little Hong Kong" that would be as separate from China as possible. And British depression over the final loss of empire has given rise to a series of myths that bedevil Western understanding of Hong Kong and lose none of their vitality for being utterly inconsistent with the facts of Hong Kong's success. The story of these fears, myths, and clashes, and of the common interests that time after time overwhelmed them, is the essence of British-Chinese diplomacy since 1982. That story, summarized in the following chapter, forms an appropriate transition to the Chinese-Western geopolitics to which we turn in the final two chapters.

V

||||||||||||||||||||||||||||||||||||||||||||||||||||||||||||||||||||||||||

THE DIPLOMACY
OF HONG KONG'S
TRANSITION

*"From China's perspective, of course Hong Kong should practice
democracy. . . . The debate we are having with the British is not
whether Hong Kong will practice democracy, but rather whether
understandings and agreements between the two governments
should be observed, whether there should be convergence and
whether there should be a smooth transition."*

—ZHANG JUNSHEN, VICE DIRECTOR OF CHINA'S DIPLOMATIC ARM IN
HONG KONG, THE XINHUA NEWS AGENCY, QUOTED IN *NEWSWEEK*,
JANUARY 18, 1993, P. 52.

Contemporary Hong Kong has always maneuvered
between two countervailing forces: first, the shared
interests of China and Britain in the prosperity and
stability of Hong Kong; second, British and Chinese struggles
over different perceptions of the proper purpose and management of Hong Kong. World press reports have generally portrayed the British viewpoint almost exclusively, whereas in
fact there has been a complex interplay in which neither side
had a monopoly on justice and goodwill.

The shared interests are very powerful. For Britain, Hong
Kong remains the crown jewel of British colonial management: the last significant British colonial territory. It is also
greatly prosperous and of global financial significance. Brit-

ain's prestige and its economic stake in Hong Kong are at risk in any resolution of Hong Kong's status. The stakes in prestige were so great because the British diplomats and businessmen who built Hong Kong did such a magnificent job of turning a barren rock into a globally important center. For China, Hong Kong is the spark plug of its economic engine, a vital aspect of national sovereignty, and the fulcrum of Beijing's strategy for peaceful reunification with Taiwan.

Because of the shared interests, even very serious crises have so far always been resolved satisfactorily, even when solutions temporarily squeezed the wallets of investors in Hong Kong's stock market. Despite shared interests and China's commitment to Hong Kong, however, the divergences between British and Chinese understandings of Hong Kong have contributed to a jittery diplomacy.

MAJOR BRITISH-CHINESE DISPUTES

Hong Kong's Legal Status

Consider, first, the status of the treaties ceding and leasing Hong Kong. Britain saw the treaties as normal treaties, binding in all respects. China saw them as "unequal treaties," imposed unfairly on China by imperialists for immoral purposes—namely, forcing China to import opium from British drug traders. Under the communists, China has never recognized their validity.

In other circumstances, such a difference of views might have led to armed conflict. However, the shared interests overcame this—with some difficulty. Preliminary discussions on a very pragmatic basis between diplomats of the two countries were put on hold by a diplomatic explosion when Prime Minister Margaret Thatcher attempted to stand on principle and insist that the formal treaty was absolutely binding. But the parties achieved a compromise. Britain sought to renegotiate the lease due to expire in July 1997. China sought to regain sovereignty over Hong Kong. Britain fell back to the position that it wanted full administrative control of post-1997 Hong Kong, while China insisted on terminating colonial rule but was willing to wait for the expiration of the lease, which it did not recognize. In 1984, both concurred in a Joint Declaration that called for terminating all aspects of British rule in July 1997, but which would maintain the existing (capitalist) economic and social system for fifty years beyond that date.

Because of what was to come later, it is important to put these negotiations in historical context. The original position of Prime Minister Thatcher and leading politicians, that Hong Kong should continue as if the entire history of global decolonization and Chinese nationalism did not exist, put them in a stratosphere of political assumptions totally divorced from earthly reality. The subsequent two years of negotiation gradually brought them down close to a post-colonial earth. So far as the available historical record shows, British diplomats did not differ radically from their political masters and therefore were almost equally far from confronting post-colonial realities, but at each stage of descent toward the ground the diplomats were the first to appreciate the need to accommodate reality a bit more and they helped the politicians rationalize that accommodation. When, in 1984, this negotiation produced the Joint Declaration, it was met with universal acclaim—in Hong Kong, in Britain, and throughout the world. Substantively the Joint Declaration was a very detailed elaboration of the Twelve Points which had been China's initial negotiating position. The idea of keeping Hong Kong free and capitalist under Chinese sovereignty was what China wanted from the beginning, not something British negotiators dragged out of an unwilling Beijing.

Britain's desperate foot-dragging on the way to decolonization has several consequences. On the helpful side, the negotiating process educated Chinese leaders about how Hong Kong works, and it forged a considerable consensus in Hong Kong regarding the necessity for transition to Chinese rule and the acceptability of the system envisaged by the Joint Declaration as the best possible outcome. Moreover, the details the British added to the Chinese framework of "One country, two systems" had real value in limiting the future interpretive discretion of Chinese leaders. But the tenacity of Britain's efforts to retain colonial power also had serious negative consequences. Prime Minister Thatcher's initial unnecessary confrontation set the tone for the negotiations and maximized anxiety in Hong Kong. While serious stock market and economic problems were inevitable, given the seriousness of the Hong Kong political issues and the global economic strains of 1982, Thatcher's unrealistic negotiating posture cost stock market investors billions of dollars and worsened a great wave of corporate and personal bankruptcies that engulfed Hong Kong. In September 1983, Hong Kong society nearly shattered. A financial crisis almost destroyed the value of the currency, and social panic swept the colony. Had the currency crisis persisted, the history of Hong Kong as a free and autonomous society would have ended in September 1983. Hong Kong was saved by a gimmick, namely, a peculiar method of pegging the Hong Kong currency to the U.S. dollar, and subsequently by the new sobriety the crisis created in British policy. Thus, Hong Kong's people incurred great costs and grave risks for the politicians' efforts to prolong colonialism. Eight years later a group of politicians would seek to repudiate the accommodation to post-colonial reality and blame the accommodation on British diplomats' betrayal of their nation's values.

Democracy vs. Consultative Colonialism

The Joint Declaration led first to a period of euphoria and then to more tension. The declaration said that Britain would rule until 1997 and that the system would then be preserved until the year 2047. The British press took this to mean that Britain could have carte blanche prior to 1997, including the installation of full-blown Western democracy, and that China would be stuck with the results until 2047. In this, the press pushed well beyond what British diplomats had sought to negotiate, which was basically to preserve the existing system with a sufficient admixture of democracy to prevent the British withdrawal from creating a political vacuum. However, another section of the Joint Declaration said that prior to 1997, China would write a constitution (the Basic Law) for the territory. China took this to mean that it would write the rules to interpret the commitments to maintain the existing social system and to let Hong Kong people run Hong Kong, and that those rules would apply until 2047.

Britain proceeded to plan for the transformation of Hong Kong into a Western-style democracy. Various local groups prepared to form Western-style political parties. In October and November 1985, China announced that this was not consistent with the Joint Declaration and warned of chaos if the British made drastic changes in the way Hong Kong was governed. The British press was quick to declare—incorrectly—that China was not honoring the terms of the Joint Declaration. And so it went.

In this confrontation of 1985–86, China prevailed because it held all the power. All Beijing had to do was announce its opposition in matter-of-fact fashion, and after a few months

Hong Kong opinion forced the British to concede the weakness of their position. But the exercise of this power did not contravene the Joint Declaration. If anything contravened the spirit of the declaration's commitment to maintain Hong Kong's existing social system, it was the British effort to change Hong Kong quickly from a hierarchically governed colony (albeit with elaborate consultation) into a very different animal—a fully democratic polity. "Convergence" with the then unwritten Basic Law became the order of the day. Proposals for direct election of the legislature were confined to a minority (eighteen out of sixty) of the legislators; plans for formal political parties were abandoned; and the stock market and property prices rose once again.

The Joint Declaration as written called for the existing system to continue. There was nothing in the details, however, which would prevent some groups from advocating ever greater government control over the economy and ever greater suppression of consultation and freedom, nor other groups from advocating total abandonment of the system of consultative colonialism for full Western democracy. But in the Chinese view the underlying principle of continuity ruled out such extremes (as the chart below indicates).

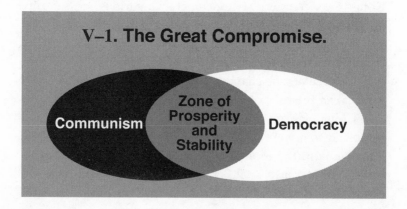

V–1. The Great Compromise.

Communism   Zone of Prosperity and Stability   Democracy

The areas labeled "Communism" and "Democracy" they regarded as unacceptable departures from the ideal of continuity, although they were willing to permit some significant democratization (more direct elections, more functional elections, election of the Governor, a smaller proportion of appointed senior roles). The intermediate area represented a very broad zone they regarded as consistent with the basic compromise.

When they wrote the Basic Law in 1990, the Chinese immediately scotched any possibility that groups might advocate moving from the intermediate zone in the direction of communism. The first sentence of the Basic Law states that the socialist system will not be practiced in Hong Kong. On the other hand, British and British-oriented pressure groups have continually advocated a breakout from compromise to full Western democracy. Such groups often justify their position not only on the basis of their own beliefs but also on the argument that a transformation is necessary to prevent the communists from breaking out in the other direction. China, with some justification, regards such efforts as an abrogation of the fundamental compromise on which the Joint Declaration was based. At a minimum, the argument that democracy is necessary to preempt a Chinese move to communism in Hong Kong is disingenuous, given the vigorous Chinese efforts to make any such move illegal.

In retrospect, it is clear that the Joint Declaration was made possible by two fortunate coincidences. The first, discussed in Chapter IV, was the extensive overlap between the prerequisites of Hong Kong's continued economic performance, as desired by Beijing, and the prerequisites of Hong Kong's continued freedom, as desired by Britain. The second was the congruence in structure between consultative colonialism as practiced by Britain and democratic centralism as practiced by China.

Under consultative colonialism, a colonial Governor is advised by an extensive network of both formal and informal structures. The Executive Council mimics the cabinet of other societies, the Legislative Council mimics the legislatures, Regional and Urban Councils represent the interests of various geographic groups, and extensive advisory bodies provide vital advice on the interests and attitudes of key segments of the community. The result is a high degree of consultative representation, despite the fact that legal authority remains firmly in the hands of the Governor. Moreover, the weight of advice and prestige is heavily biased toward community elites with an interest in rapid economic progress at the expense of the kinds of populist political pressure that influence economic policy making so heavily in the West. This system has two primary virtues: It puts a firm emphasis on economic expertise, as is common in the political systems of the Asian economic miracle countries; and it facilitates broad representation of the interests of community groups. On the other hand, it is not democracy in the sense of rule of the people.

The bare institutional structures of consultative colonialism are remarkably similar to the structures of what China calls "democratic centralism" (the Chinese people refer to it as "big centralism, little democracy"). Democratic centralism holds elections at the local level, forms broad-based consultative groups (the National People's Congress and the Chinese People's Political Consultative Committee, or CPPCC), and channels the policy-making and policy advisory process through a Central Committee, a Politburo, and a Standing Committee of the Politburo. Generally, ultimate authority is held firmly in the hands of a powerful individual at the top (not unlike Hong Kong's Governor), but even he would hesitate to take on the unified opposition of the Politburo (analogue of Hong Kong's Executive Council) or the Central Committee (analogue of the Legislative Council).

It would be wrong to ignore the structural differences. For instance, Chinese leaders rule through a political party and do not allow judicial autonomy, whereas the British put less emphasis on political parties and insist on judicial autonomy. Behind British colonial rule are the benign Westminster Parliament and British common law, whereas behind China's consultative bodies lie the rough games of the National People's Congress and the communist lack of legal protection for individual rights. "Democratic centralism" has been an instrument of oppression, whereas consultative colonialism has maintained a high degree of personal freedom.

But it would also be obtuse to miss the degree of similarity. The two sides have structures sufficiently similar to allow a workable convergence. In the case of Hong Kong, China conceded that its goals (ensuring a flow of foreign capital, technology, and market techniques into China while keeping foreigners' access to China proper limited) could be attained only by allowing the system to continue pursuing a capitalist and liberal path.

The spirit in which these two systems have been managed in Hong Kong and China has of course been radically different. Consultative colonialism really consults with a broad range of groups and takes their opinions quite seriously. Democratic centralism has hitherto been primarily a tool for manipulation; the first time significant dissent occurred in the CPPCC was in 1992, when that body, under Deng Xiaoping's influence, forced extensive amendments to Li Peng's budget and planning report.

Consultative colonialism is what the Chinese system could become at its best if it were reformed. Democratic centralism is what consultative colonialism could degenerate into if it were abused. But the fundamental point for this discussion is that the structural congruity of the two systems is what made possible the Joint Declaration. This insight is the key to understanding what can and cannot work in Hong Kong's future. If Hong Kong is reformed gradually in a way that Chinese officials view as retaining the basic virtues of its system, reform is possible.

Beijing will not tolerate several things: (1) sudden changes which create a fundamentally different system; (2) changes which seem likely to undermine the territory's economic efficiency; and (3) changes which give power to forces hostile to China's territorial integrity or political stability. To advocates of pure Westminster democracy, such restrictions are anathema. Much of the British community, certain pro-British segments of local Chinese opinion, and a good deal of sentiment in Washington takes this view. On the other side is the center of gravity of Hong Kong Chinese opinion,[1] which holds a conservative view—that improving Hong Kong's standard of living, maintaining the freedom of its people, and gradually expanding electoral democracy would constitute a remarkably positive achievement. Such an achievement, so critical to life

---

[1] A number of opinion polls have asked whether Hong Kong people desire greater democracy. The answer is invariably yes, and this answer is important. But the question is a "motherhood" question that does not deal with specific programs and real tradeoffs. Faced with concrete situations in which one choice is a drastic move in favor of British-style government at the expense of provoking China into actions that would threaten Hong Kong's existing system, and the other choice is gradual change of the kind that has been occurring, there in an almost palpable community movement in favor of the latter. This became clear in polls that were taken regarding Governor Patten's proposed reforms and showed strong net opposition to a slight speeding up of reforms at the expense of a major confrontation with China— see the *South China Morning Post* for November 22 and 29, which report trends up and through November. The reports of November 29 are especially significant because they show that the major polling organizations agree in their conclusions and that there is a very strong trend. Also, these reports predate the really serious escalation of Sino-British tension and therefore show the Hong Kong public in a reflective rather than frightened mood.

in Hong Kong, should not be jeopardized by pushing beyond the consensus that underlay the Joint Declaration.

The British press notwithstanding, China's viewpoint on the nature and role of elections does not breach the Joint Declaration, whose language is deliberately ambiguous on this point. British and Chinese negotiators faced controversies in 1983. Ultimately they agreed on ambiguous language that both could present to their respective publics as a victory. Faced with difficulties in agreeing on the precise phrasing, the negotiators had recourse to what the British called the "three little fudge words": "elections," "consultation," and "a high degree of autonomy." Hong Kong's legislature would be chosen by elections, but the kind of elections was not specified; there was a big difference between British-style elections and Chinese-style. British decisions with an important impact beyond 1997 would have to be based on consultation with China, but the nature of that consultation was ambiguous. Everyone understood that Hong Kong's autonomy would be greater than that of any Chinese province and well short of full independence, but there remained a rather wide range of alternatives. All the central conflicts after 1984 revolved around these "three little fudge words." Moreover, as British negotiators emphasized to me at the time, their chief aim was to preserve the existing system, including the consultative buffers between populist pressures and ultimate decision-making authority. There was no thought of a radically new democratic system.

The Implications of the 1991 Election

In September 1991, Hong Kong held an election for the Legislative Council. Eighteen out of the sixty seats were chosen by direct election. Twelve of these were won by liberals associated with Martin Lee, the lawyer who became famous at the time of Tiananmen Square for his vigorous support of the Chinese dissidents. Lee then presented himself to London and Washington as in effect the rightfully elected leader of Hong Kong, and came to be viewed by legislators in those capitals as speaking for Hong Kong. In effect, Martin Lee succeeded in depicting himself as the Hong Kong analogue of Burma's Aung San Suu Kyi, whose party won a national election overwhelmingly but was then deprived of any right to govern.

In this case, the difference of interpretation was not between Britain and China, but rather between the people of Hong Kong and Western politicians who interpreted the vote as if it had been held in their own countries. Hong Kong people were realistic. They were *not* voting for someone to run the government. The establishment and the British Governor would remain in firm control regardless of the outcome of the election. Most of the electorate therefore did not bother to vote, and the establishment did not organize seriously for the election. The attitude of the voting public was that they needed a gadfly to send occasional barbed messages to the establishment, and to China. Consequently, they elected a group who had distinguished themselves as gadflies *vis-à-vis* both the British and Beijing. The electorate viewed Martin Lee the way many middle-class Japanese view their representatives when they elect socialist candidates: the establishment (in this case Japan's Liberal Democratic Party) will win nationally, and they would not dream of having a socialist governing, but they sorely need a gadfly.

What the voters intended was soon put to the test. Lee demanded that his choices be appointed to the Executive Council. In response, Hong Kong's Chinese-language newspapers and radio stations filled the air with withering denunciations of his presumptuousness. Lee was forced to back down and never again asserted to the Hong Kong people that he had a mandate to govern; but in Washington and London, Lee maintained the image of having been elected to form a government. He was particularly successful with the U.S. Congress, and the initial drafts of bills such as the U.S.–Hong Kong Policy Act of 1992 were heavily influenced by his views.

Similarly, the apparent electoral endorsement of Lee's anti-China position soon turned out to have limits. The voters had indeed defeated every candidate backed by Beijing's operatives in the territory. This sent a clear message to Beijing that they resented both Tiananmen Square and the efforts of Beijing's operatives at Xinhua News Agency to elect pro-Beijing candidates. By 1992, however, the force of public opinion had pressured Martin Lee to resign from his own anti-China group, the Association in Support of the Patriotic Democratic Movement in China. Voters might unite to send a barbed message to Beijing, but they were equally united against subversive efforts that would provoke the dragon of the north.

Interpretations of Tiananmen Square: Democracy vs. "One Country, Two Systems"

The Tiananmen Square crisis profoundly affected Hong Kong in two ways. First, it cast doubt on China's ability and desire to deal sensitively with democratic movements. Second, it politicized Hong Kong, creating tension between the democratic sentiments of much of the population and the prerequisites of "One country, two systems."

The implications of Tiananmen Square could be read in opposite ways. The brutality of Chinese troops in smashing China's democratic movement undermined trust in Beijing's promises to maintain capitalist Hong Kong. If they shoot democrats in Beijing, they will surely shoot them eventually in Hong Kong, according to this logic. On the other hand, China has always brutalized its own dissidents and has always protected Hong Kong; the two aspects of Chinese policy are not logically inconsistent. Moreover, China's attitude toward Hong Kong during and after the crisis was remarkably tolerant. Ultimately, Tiananmen Square had no strong implications for future policy in Hong Kong.

The basic rule of "One country, two systems" must be that neither China nor Hong Kong is allowed to subvert the other. But during the crisis, Hong Kong people funded the Tiananmen Square dissidents, backed them with propaganda, smuggled the leaders in and out of China, channeled news of the massacre into southern China (thereby neutralizing Beijing's denial of the facts), mounted demonstrations of up to 1 million people to support the dissidents, and in the case of a group led by Martin Lee called for the overthrow of China's leadership. China responded only by complaining and by writing a non-subversion rule into the Basic Law. It made no threats, imposed no sanctions, and sent no subversive cadres to punish its opponents. In other words, while Hong Kong was ignoring the implicit rules of "One country, two systems," Beijing was honoring them impeccably. From this perspective, China's sincerity passed the test.

When China subsequently wrote a non-subversion clause into the Basic Law, many British and British-oriented sensitivities were offended. Among these groups, it was popular to argue that "we are a democracy and we have a right to do whatever we want with our money, including sending it over the Chinese border to dissidents." This view was built on a shaky foundation: Hong Kong, never a democracy, has based its stability heavily on institutions like ICAC that were inconsistent with democracy.

Westerners, already skeptical about China's ultimate intentions toward Hong Kong, grew more so after Tiananmen Square. Thus, it proved virtually impossible for Western audiences to fathom that China had honored the requirement of mutual non-subversion whereas Hong Kong had not. Western sympathy with Hong Kong was too strong, ultimately, to face the fact that, however admirable its motivations, Hong Kong had acted suicidally. The British press bitterly denounced China for insisting on the non-subversion rule; but the Hong Kong government did no such thing. Rather, it chose neither to debate the subject publicly nor to form a public consensus on the range of permissible behavior nor to write explicit laws. Instead, it quietly imposed a set of restrictions that implicitly did what the Chinese wanted. For instance, it dusted off a virtually unused law against using bullhorns without government permission and employed it against a fundraising effort by Martin Lee's group. And it cordoned off Statue Square, the most popular site for demonstrations, with signs threatening strong sanctions against anyone infringing another law by walking on the grass.

The government thereby avoided the difficult debate that would have accompanied any effort to deal with the issue straightforwardly. This policy carried a high price, for it failed to develop any public understanding or consensus. Indeed, the local British press had a field day. It routinely denounced each government effort to implement a non-subversion policy as a concession to China by a crass government whose leaders cared more about good British-Chinese commercial relations than about the democratic rights of the Hong Kong population. Such denunciations were utterly inaccurate descriptions of British motives, but the government's own unwillingness to deal with the problem publicly ensured that its decisions would be viewed as shameful.

This in turn contributed greatly to demands for a more politically decisive and astute government—demands for political leadership as well as back office maneuvering. The British business community's negative reaction to such waffling on the central issues of Hong Kong, and to unilateralism on their airport, led to a concerted demand by leading British business representatives for the replacement of Governor David Wilson, a diplomat and China scholar of great distinction, but one who lacked political skills, by a major political figure. This business community lobbying encouraged the subsequent appointment of Christopher Patten, a politician of stature, but one with no experience of Hong Kong or China. The campaign by the British business community for such a change of leadership was to have ironic consequences.

After 1997, Hong Kong may pay a price for the British government's having insisted on doing all its non-subversion work inside a closet. Meanwhile, once the excitement of Tiananmen Square had subsided, Hong Kong's Chinese community reverted to a consensus that public confrontation with Beijing could only harm Hong Kong.

In 1992, there was a successor tiff. China warned that Hong Kong's new Governor must not appoint Martin Lee to the cabinet. Governor Patten angrily retorted that he had the right to appoint anyone he wished. He gave no outward sign of deep reflection on the viability of a policy of "One country, two systems" if top Hong Kong officials were people who called for the overthrow of the Chinese leadership. If, for instance, Hong Kong officials could call for the overthrow of Chinese leaders, perhaps it was equally appropriate for Chinese leaders to call for the overthrow of Hong Kong's. No senior British official addressed the issue in any terms other than Britain's absolute autonomy and the rights derived from democracy. But in the end Martin Lee was not offered a cabinet-level position and Governor Patten announced a policy of rigidly separating the Executive Council from the Legislative Council (to which Lee had been elected) as a way of enshrining a solution to this and other problems.[2] Again the British

---

[2]Governor Patten later came to describe this decision on some occasions as a concession to China. Confidants of the Governor, including one official

government paid a heavy price for being unwilling to face publicly and forthrightly the mutual non-subversion requirement of "One country, two systems," because Patten's decision cut off the legislators from decision making and therefore would centralize the post-1997 government in a way that seemed more consistent with Chinese political management than British.

The Airport: Independence vs. Economic Integration

The controversy of 1985 over the political meaning of the Joint Declaration was largely decided through British capitulation. But it was gradually succeeded by a parallel controversy over economic management. After Tiananmen Square, Hong Kong faced a crisis of confidence, and the British government took the view that that confidence would best be restored through a dramatic demonstration that Britain could still act unilaterally and decisively. The essence of building confidence, in this view, was to prove that China would not be allowed to "meddle" or to "interfere" in Hong Kong.

From this premise, the British government set out to create a huge confidence builder—the Port and Airport Development Scheme (PADS), conceived as the largest and most expensive civil engineering project in the world during the 1990s (originally estimated to cost over $16 billion, it is now running at over U.S.$23 billion). It involved building one of the

spokesman, describe the decision to separate Legco from Exco as primarily driven by a desire to get rid of the CRC business group's representatives, while having an excuse for keeping Martin Lee off Exco was a subsidiary advantage. It is impossible to know his precise motivation. To the extent that keeping Martin Lee out of the cabinet was as strong a motive as he says it was, Governor Patten was following exactly the same path for which his predecessor was criticized, dodging this vital issue by stealth.

world's longest bridges out to an island off the coast of Hong Kong, leveling the entire island, and extending it with material obtained by huge dredging operations, then constructing an extensive infrastructure so that people could travel to this rather distant place in a reasonable time. This project lumped together all the largest projects (e.g., the port and the airport) precisely to create a dramatic example of British government decisiveness and autonomy.

The airport and port projects derived from a genuine need. The British government knew by the beginning of the 1980s that Hong Kong would require a new airport, but had procrastinated because of the economic slowdown, and then had become preoccupied with politics through the mid-eighties. Attention belatedly revived late in the decade. So there was no controversy about the need for major infrastructure projects, only about the design and packaging.

Almost from the day it was announced, the scheme was in trouble. Most of the business community doubted the wisdom of packing all the projects together, making the overall effort look so expensive. Shared wisdom of the construction fraternity agreed: one should always separate out construction projects and underprice them, so as not to frighten those who will have to pay the bill. The first crisis resulted when international banks balked at supporting the scheme as then structured. The government planned to finance PADS primarily through bank loans. However, international banks responded that since the repayments would all fall after 1997, and since China would be the beneficial owner, it was inconceivable that the banks could fund the project without both a strong Chinese endorsement and a financial contribution. Thus the British theory of totally autonomous decision making initially ran afoul not of Chinese interference but of the most basic rules of banking prudence.

There was another financial complication which was to prove fateful. The airport cost estimates published by Governor Wilson's government proved drastically low. The consequence was an endless series of embarrassing revisions that became intertwined with negotiations with Beijing.

Chinese authorities were in fact concerned. The physical structure of their window on the outside world was being made over without their participation. Chinese officials began, at first almost plaintively, to say that this project would shape southern China's transportation system for at least a generation and therefore some coordination with the Chinese infrastructure seemed appropriate. Moreover, financing the scheme would shape China's financial position for a generation in the eyes of international banks, and Chinese authorities felt they should have some say in a matter with such an impact—which incidentally was being proposed at a time of Western financial sanctions against China and hence of emergency efforts to increase reserves and decrease borrowing. Furthermore, the Joint Declaration specified that any decision with consequences beyond 1997 required consultation with China. The declaration specified particularly close consultation in the second half of the period between 1984 and 1997; that second half was now dawning. The new airport was scheduled to open only in 1997, and loan repayments would extend for many years after.

One Chinese government suggestion was to build the airport in Shenzhen, the special economic zone adjacent to Hong Kong, at a fraction of the price. Britain objected that China would control the air rights and this would infringe Hong Kong's autonomy. China then offered to cede Hong Kong the land, the access, and the air rights—a concession of sovereignty comparable to Britain giving the U.S. control of Heathrow Airport and all associated air rights for fifty years. The

British refused to discuss the offer seriously, although expert opinion on the merits of the case is at best divided.[3]

Britain's decision to insist on siting the airport on a remote island rather than in Shenzhen was not just an airport policy. It was the most important social and administrative decision Britain made for Hong Kong in the entire period after the Joint Declaration was signed. The huge incremental expenditure on the airport ruled out major initiatives elsewhere. Realization of the full magnitude of the airport's cost led to a vast effort to trim future expenditures in virtually all other areas. Among other things, the airport precluded a vitally needed modernization of Hong Kong's rickety educational and environmental protection systems. Arguably overhaul of the education and worker training systems was even more urgent than the airport, but through the end of 1992 the government

[3]This Chinese offer has been treated by the British as a closely held secret. I was told of it by a Western diplomat who was well placed to be aware of such things. During a highly publicized debate on November 25, 1992, both opponents, Marc Faber and myself, commented that acceptance of the Chinese offer would have reduced costs sufficiently to improve Hong Kong's medium-term economic outlook. (Cf. Louise Lucas, "Speculators Told to Back Off Market," *South China Morning Post*, November 26, 1992.) The following day, an official spokesman, John Elliott, called at the request of the finance secretary to inform me that the Chinese had made no such offer. When I said I was referring to an offer made earlier, he stuttered for a moment and acknowledged that there had previously been such an offer but that it had not been raised by the Chinese in the 1992 discussions. Among those who believe that the Shenzhen alternative would be substantially better for Hong Kong are top executives of both of Hong Kong's airlines, some of the highest Hong Kong government officials in charge of civil aviation, the leading American airport consultant who has looked at the issue, and the chief executive of one of America's largest airlines. The only one willing to publish his views is Stephen Miller, the founder of Hong Kong's second airline, Dragonair; see the interview with him in "One Country, Two Systems, Four Airports," *Window*, October 23, 1992, and also other issues of that weekly Hong Kong magazine.

actually planned to increase the size of already large classes in order to save money on teachers' salaries. The sums to be saved were paltry compared to even the smaller of the many port and airport projects, but the airport-induced budget pressures required officials to grasp every possible saving. Even with those savings, the first budget Patten had full control over (announced in early 1993) projected deficits every year until China resumed sovereignty. But Britain decided implicitly that avoiding a collaborative effort with China on the airport was worth starving Hong Kong's social program.[4]

The British government's handling of the airport decision was radically inconsistent with the requirement of the Joint Declaration for consultation in order to ensure a smooth transition: It made the decision unilaterally, and then, only two days before the Governor's speech announcing that decision, sent a letter in English to the Chinese government. Some British commentators argued that telling the Chinese they were going to make a decision, and then informing them of the nature of that decision, constituted consultation. But both ordinary language and diplomatic parlance have always distinguished between "informing"—which is letting the other party know what you have decided—and "consulting"—which gives the other party some opportunity to participate in the decision-making process. After the announcement, the British were adamant about refusing consultation as opposed to selective (albeit voluminous) information. One early response to the Chinese request for consultation was to ship them three huge volumes of consultant reports in English; comments filtered back that this was not exactly what the Chinese had in mind.

---

[4]In 1993, Governor Patten reversed the increase of class sizes and proclaimed strong concern for the environment, but total funding differed only incrementally from previous plans.

Moreover, Governor Wilson made it clear throughout the process that the whole reason for lumping so many projects together into one huge enterprise and then announcing it suddenly was to demonstrate to Hong Kong that the British government was still capable of acting decisively and unilaterally. Meant to raise the confidence of people in Hong Kong, the project did exactly the opposite. Anxiety rose, and the stock market began a long decline whose starting point coincided with the Governor's speech and which ended only when the British finally agreed on a detailed consultation process with China.

Britain and China agreed that China would send a consultation team to Hong Kong just as the problem with the banks was coming to a head. In October 1990, the day before the Chinese team was due to arrive, the Hong Kong government unilaterally announced that the government itself would finance much of the project. The Governor and his principal aide made strong public statements, featured on the front pages of the major newspapers, that they were under no obligation to consult with China on this huge financing decision and would not do so. Both the airport decision and this subsequent financing decision were direct and unequivocal breaches of the consultation requirement of the Joint Declaration, the first such breaches by either party. The word "consult" is very flexible, but it is not that flexible, particularly when accompanied by speeches from the Governor saying that his government recognized no obligation to consult China on the matter.

In the event, the British approach provoked the Chinese into enormous fear that the project's size risked depleting Hong Kong's finances. It also inflicted maximum damage to public confidence in the Hong Kong government's competence. Finally, it destroyed confidence that Britain could develop a working relationship with China, and gave China strong arguments that vital Chinese interests as well as national pride required its involvement in the airport project. A diplomatic impasse ensued, and a decline in public and investor confidence in Hong Kong—until in July 1991 London and Beijing signed a Memorandum of Understanding. Beijing would support the airport in return for a consultative role and for British agreement to certain limits on borrowing for the post-1997 period. The limits were low, much lower than would probably have been attainable without Governor Wilson's unilateralism; but Hong Kong business breathed a sigh of relief and the stock market began another of its great bull runs.

While Beijing had seemingly yielded, it extracted a heavy political price for the Memorandum of Understanding by requiring Prime Minister John Major to visit Beijing, making him the first of the Western political leaders to break the post–Tiananmen Square political boycott of Beijing. This embarrassed him in front of the other Western leaders. Wilson came out of the affair hopelessly crippled as British Governor. Forcing Major to Beijing had burned Wilson's bridges with his prime minister.

Fully alerted, the Chinese began to scrutinize every financial detail before approving further progress on the airport, and endless delays appeared to the British to infringe the agreement in the Memorandum of Understanding that the Chinese would respond promptly and supportively to British proposals. Britain interpreted this behavior as being driven by political motives.[5] The seeming obstructionism of the Chinese was greatly facilitated by the extraordinary confusion over

[5]Governor Patten indicated at a meeting that I attended on September 10 that Chinese obstruction infringed the Memorandum of Understanding. He also said, with an ironic tone, that the airport dispute wasn't about the airport—meaning that it was about politics.

airport financing left by Governor Wilson's administration. The Chinese insisted that their concerns were purely financial: the proposal was the world's largest construction project of the decade, the projected price of the airport nearly doubled after the Memorandum of Understanding, and the British made constant major changes such as financing much of the project with "callable equity."[6] Elderly communist bureaucrats reporting up a cumbersome chain of command on one of the biggest financial questions China faced found it difficult to keep up with the bewildering variety of British proposals. This problem seemed valid.

Moreover, quite aside from financing, British consortia were winning over 70 percent of the construction contracts for the new airport, and British design specifications were geared toward parts that would have to be procured from Britain. Chinese officials saw this as a last-minute effort to extract the maximum economic advantage from Hong Kong and to entrench the British role in Hong Kong far beyond 1997 (British arguments that the British firms just happened to be the most competitive fell rather flat with businessmen from other countries, who had never seen British firms prove so competitive anywhere else in the world). They argued that their acceptance of such British shenanigans was extraordinarily flexible and generous.

Chinese spokesmen in Hong Kong also argued that the cu-

[6]In a lunch with representatives of the American community, including this writer, former U.S. Consul General Burton Levin, and others, Li Chu Wen, by that time occupying the role of Special Adviser to Xinhua on Hong Kong affairs, emphasized the tremendous impact on Chinese thinking of the near doubling of the project's cost and the confusing concept of "callable equity." Most senior Western financial executives did not find it easy to follow the stream of revised proposals. The reader may get some sense of the situation by trying to draft a memo to the Chinese Politburo on the pluses and minuses of financing an airport with callable equity.

mulative financial commitments made by Governor Patten would make it impossible for the British to meet their promise under the Memorandum of Understanding to leave certain reserves for the post-1997 government. Here, the Chinese calculations seemed to a Westerner strained to fit their view that the British were using giant projects to drain Hong Kong's resources into British companies. (At one meeting with the leadership of the American Chamber of Commerce, Zhou Nan, China's principal representative in Hong Kong, said, "We knew the British would try to drain Hong Kong, but we had no idea they would drain it this badly.") This was unfair. Even though Hong Kong could have bought a better airport for less money, and even though many of the decisions over infrastructure showed an unwarranted bias against the Chinese, Hong Kong would have been better off if Beijing had just let Britain build the airport. Financial reserves were adequate.

When the new Governor, Christopher Patten, arrived in Hong Kong in July 1992, he was intensely conscious that the Chinese were obstructing progress. He believed this pattern to be contrary to the agreements contained in the Memorandum of Understanding. His boss and close friend, Prime Minister Major, had accepted embarrassment and obtained only further obstruction in return. Governor Patten had little experience with Hong Kong or China and little sense of Chinese grievances over his predecessor's high handedness on the airport, and no concept of how the withering complexity of financial changes twisted up the Chinese bureaucracy. Patten set forth on his own agenda, convinced that the Chinese were not people one could deal with in good faith. By the autumn of 1992, the airport had become entangled with the new Governor's efforts to impose political changes on Hong Kong.

Hong Kong's Boundaries

The scope of Hong Kong's geography and role also became a divisive issue. China, with its economic perspective, sees Hong Kong constantly enlarging and expanding its scope. Chinese reformists welcome this and Chinese ultra-conservatives fear it; but both see Hong Kong as strengthened by it. Britain, with a political and colonial perspective, sees Hong Kong as threatened by it.

As China's primary window on the world, Hong Kong's role has naturally expanded. Hong Kong investment has driven China's trade. Hong Kong firms effectively dominate China's special economic zones. Hong Kong's currency is informally the currency of choice in much of Guangdong (one can pay Hong Kong dollars on the public buses in Guangdong and receive change in Hong Kong dollars). Hainan Island is considering allowing a formal role for the Hong Kong currency. Shenzhen's stock exchange is modeled on Hong Kong's and looks to Hong Kong for support. Guangdong hopes to marry its superior basic science to Hong Kong's superior marketing and financial strength in order to create an export-oriented manufacturing powerhouse that neither could build on its own.

As Hong Kong's function expands, some Chinese officials are planning to expand its geography also. In the early 1990s, Guangdong officials would like to abolish visa requirements for Hong Kong people wanting to visit Shenzhen.[7] Within the following decade, Guangdong's leaders hope that Shenzhen's economic progress and institutional development will move so close to Hong Kong's that travel restrictions from Shenz-

---

[7]Cf. "Merger of Two Systems Proposed," *South China Morning Post,* September 6, 1991, and "Guangdong to Relax Control of Border," *South China Morning Post,* March 11, 9991.

hen can be abolished. Tight travel controls from the rest of China into Shenzhen would remain to avert the risk of the zone's being swamped by impoverished immigrants from elsewhere inside. Effectively, the border would be moved back and Hong Kong would be made several times larger.

Typically, Chinese officials perceive all this as being supportive of Hong Kong, as an expansion of Hong Kong's role. British officials see it as threatening, almost all of them denouncing the Shenzhen plans as a plot to subvert Hong Kong's autonomy. The Chinese officials, for their part, perceive the British efforts to promote an extreme version of Hong Kong autonomy as anti-Chinese. All the Chinese frustrations over Britain's "Little Hong Kong" policy coalesce around this debate.

Misperceptions of Hong Kong

The period after the Joint Declaration of 1984 was a boom time for Hong Kong. Its living standards came from far behind to surpass those in Britain. Even so, the British press— and most of the Western world's—ignored every reality and persistently reported that Hong Kong was being destroyed by China.

During the period after Chinese-British negotiations, the city's stock market rose from around 700 to over 7500 (or from 1400 to 7500 if one counts from the peak of the prerecession boom). While the Western press trumpeted that foreign companies were fleeing Hong Kong, the number of foreign companies roughly doubled. The number of Americans living in Hong Kong more than doubled. At precisely the time when the American press was reporting a vast exodus of U.S. companies from Hong Kong, the Americans in Hong Kong were desperately trying to build the American school (Hong Kong International School) fast enough to keep up with the growing number of schoolchildren created by the influx of U.S. companies. Although the new high school was huge, it nonetheless faced a shortage of space when it opened in August 1989—and 1989 was the worst year for morale in Hong Kong. We had to take emergency space on the other side of Hong Kong Island in 1992–93 to accommodate the overflow. Even with this emergency space, all twelve grades and kindergarten were overflowing by summer 1993. Other expatriate communities (except the British) faced the same problem.

When the Western press was reporting a vast exodus from Hong Kong of 45,000 people per year in the mid-1980s and 60,000 annually in the late 1980s (accurate figures as far as they went), not one major newspaper, as we have seen, reported the countervailing fact that 80,000 people per year were moving *into* Hong Kong. The total number of highly educated people in Hong Kong rose throughout the period, but all through the Western world commentators maintained that Hong Kong's talent base was being depleted.[8]

After several years of reading reports of a vast migration to Singapore, I became determined to get some figures, although they were difficult to obtain because the Singapore and Hong Kong governments treat them as confidential. Finally, some officials in both countries leaked a few emigration statistics. For the period covered by these statistics, more than eight hundred Singaporeans had moved to Hong Kong while fewer than forty Hong Kong people had moved to Singapore. I made these and other data a key point in a major speech, which created an unexpected splash. The audience was large, various organizations reprinted tens of thousands of copies of

---

[8]The point about rising numbers of highly educated people is made by a government paper, "Emigration," Hong Kong Information Note, Chief Secretary's Office, December 1992, p. 1.

the speech, and several books reprinted it as a chapter. But British-oriented newspapers almost ignored the data and went on reporting an exodus to Singapore.

V–2. Hong Kong: The "Bad Years."

	1979	1991
GDP	$21.6 billion	$81.6 billion
Total Exports	$15.3 billion	$98.6 billion
Re-Exports	$4.0 billion	$68.8 billion
Trade Rank	**20th in world**	**10th in world**
Foreign Companies	1261	2828
U.S. Expatriates	10880 (1980)	24600
Cargo	1.3 million TEU	6.1 million TEU

SOURCE: Hong Kong government statistics.

The Western press mostly reprinted such myths uncritically. Press surveys commissioned by the American Chamber of Commerce in Hong Kong showed that, throughout this long period of extraordinary success, most American newspaper stories depicted a city in a state of decline and potential collapse. After a decade of reporting by the local British press that people were fleeing to Singapore in vast numbers, there were 6,500 Singaporeans living in Hong Kong and fewer than 6,000 Hong Kong people living in Singapore. Since Hong Kong's population is twice Singapore's, this means that Singaporeans were moving to Hong Kong at twice the rate of Hong Kong emigration to Singapore. In fact, the scale of im-

migration from Singapore forced the Singaporean government to decide in 1992 to build a separate school in Hong
Kong for its citizens.[9]

Yet the writing by both British and American journalists
was often heartbreaking in its fervor:

> As I prepare my own departure, I often think of an image that
> captures the melancholy of this slowly breaking city. It is a
> scene I saw on the television news, almost surreal in its inten-
> sity, the scene of a great bulldozer crushing a mountain of fake
> gold watches, all made in Hong Kong, until there was nothing
> left but dust.[10]

Television made its own powerful contribution to the
myths by featuring interviews with Hong Kong's most colorful and least representative political figure, Emily Lau. For
many years, Lau used her position covering Hong Kong for
the *Far Eastern Economic Review* to mount a crusade for
complete Western-style democracy and what amounted to independence from China. She entered politics for the 1991
elections. Lau is Hong Kong's least representative figure in a
number of ways. She is affiliated to no substantial political
party or group. She is the only prominent political figure I am

[9]This information was provided by a Singaporean diplomat.

[10]Ian Buruma, "The Last Days of Hong Kong," *New York Review of
Books,* April 12, 1990, p. 46. Buruma, perhaps the finest cultural essayist on
Asia during this period, interviewed me for the article, but found my enthusi-
astic compilation of evidence about Hong Kong's bright prospects unworthy
of note. Buruma's article is a review of several books by distinguished jour-
nalists who are advocates of the myth of decline. One of them, by an Ameri-
can, Kevin Rafferty, *City on the Rocks: Hong Kong's Uncertain Future*
(New York: Viking Penguin, 1990), has been the most prominent book on
Hong Kong since it was published. Cf. my review of this and other books in
William H. Overholt, "Tiananmen Square and Objective Possibilities for
Hong Kong," *Journal of Politics* 53, 2 (May 1991).

aware of who has explicitly repudiated the Joint Declaration by calling it a betrayal of Hong Kong. She effectively advocates a Western welfare state, which virtually all other prominent politicians believe would be bad for Hong Kong. Nonetheless, her polished British accent, uncomplicated message, and fanatical anti-China opinions make her the perfect interviewee. She is a bit of a figure of fun in Hong Kong, due to the extremism of her views, but CNN and BBC coverage has effectively portrayed her as one of the three most important voices of Hong Kong (along with Governor Patten and Martin Lee).

No wonder that, at home, a British audience (and the Americans who read or heard the same views) began to buy the line that Britain had somehow betrayed the people of Hong Kong and should do something decisive. It was articulated with deep emotion by Paddy Ashdown, leader of the Liberal Democratic Party and a man with unusual depth of experience in earlier Hong Kong affairs, to a group of Hong Kong business leaders a few days before Chris Patten gave his famous speech on political reform in October 1992. It was frequently articulated by leaders of the Labour Party. All the while the Hong Kong stock market was regularly breaking records and Hong Kong standards of living, far below Britain's when the British press started writing about the deterioration of Hong Kong, were soaring above those of Britain. When Governor Patten arrived in Hong Kong to put things right, Hong Kong was in a mood of intense exhilaration, with the post–Tiananmen Square fears finally laid to rest and exultant celebration over the victory of the reformers at the Fourteenth Party Congress in Beijing. This was quickly to change.

Alongside the myth of decline came the myth of betrayal. Purveyors of the myth of betrayal believed that Hong Kong was declining and looked for someone to blame for it. The British diplomats became the villains. According to this myth, the British diplomats had consistently been a spineless lot who didn't care about the people of Hong Kong and who always bowed to Beijing. Instead of being one of the great triumphs of modern diplomacy, the Joint Declaration was a sell-out to the Chinese, and everything that followed constituted a betrayal. These diplomats came to be referred to as the "sinologists." In the extreme version of this myth, not only were the details of arrangement with the Chinese a sell-out, but the whole return of Hong Kong to China was an unnecessary result of the sinologists' incompetence.[11] British honor required that the spinelessness of the sinologists be compensated by confronting the Chinese and firmly upholding the value of British-style democracy.

The myth of betrayal, like the myth of decline, was so ahistorical that it could be understood only as a powerful emotion rather than as analysis. Even a cursory reading of modern Chinese history shows the power of nationalism behind the determination of Chinese leaders to reunify their country. The 1982–84 negotiations, far from being a failure, were quite rightly regarded at the time as a triumph in which the British got far more than any other decolonizing power has ever achieved. Moreover, the myth of the spineless sinologists con-

---

[11]The most explicit statement of this view is from Steven Vines, Southeast Asia correspondent of *The Observer*. Vines's book, *Awaiting the Avalanche,* which purports to document this view, has not yet become available, but it is summarized in his article, "Britain Blundered Away Hong Kong," *Asian Wall Street Journal,* March 6, 1991, p. 6. Most holders of this attitude back away when cornered into stating it so explicitly, but Vines merely makes explicit an extremely widely held attitude. Vines says that "in essence, the Chinese got what they wanted on the big issue of sovereignty, and the British got to write practically all the small print in the Joint Declaration." He sees that as proof of incompetence. I would interpret the same words to say that the British gave away the minimum that every colonial power must and managed to keep almost everything that was actually negotiable.

veniently forgets about the slaps in the face delivered to China by sinologist Governor David Wilson over the Hong Kong airport. Despite all this, the myth of betrayal became the driving force of British policy under Governor Patten.

Rapid Democratization vs. Expertise and Decisiveness

China values Hong Kong for its economy—as Britain did so long as its hold on Hong Kong was secure. Britain now judges its performance in Hong Kong by the degree of its institutionalized democracy. This has led to sharp clashes. The original British negotiators envisioned primarily an extension of Hong Kong's existing decisive-but-consultative system. But British efforts have focused on the promotion of democracy to the exclusion of considerations of efficiency and expertise.[12] After the 1991 election of only eighteen directly elected legislators (out of sixty), it took three times longer for the average bill to pass into law. More important, senior government executives no longer felt confident in making significant policy commitments. Virtually every sector of society felt the consequences of heightened uncertainty and prolonged delays.[13] When pressed about this, the government simply denied it, although the data are clear and concern in the business community was nearly universal.

[12]Responding to an earlier version of material included in Chapter IV of this book, Governor Wilson summoned me to Government House and remarked in the course of the conversation that my essay was the first time he had ever seen anyone argue the importance of Hong Kong's post-1997 government being effective.

[13]The statistics on legislative delays are from a study being conducted by Booz Allen Hamilton for the Business and Professionals Federation of Hong Kong (Gordian Gaeta, Project Leader). The slowing of government was the subject of extensive commentary in the press in the year following the election. The comments on increased uncertainty are based on interviews with key people in a variety of sectors.

Both China and the Hong Kong business community grew worried that the British administration in Hong Kong refused to address the issue of maintaining economic efficiency as democratization progressed. Many people pointed to the Philippines. There, Cory Aquino's commitment to democracy was admired, but the country's inefficient patronage politics further degraded an impoverished economy. Here was an example of what Hong Kong had to avoid. Aside from genuine concern about the integrity of the civil service, the British refused to face this problem, behind which lay China's core interest in Hong Kong as an economic utility. To Americans, this idea of another Philippines seems abstract and unlikely, but to many Asians it is immediate. When I lived in the Philippines in the early 1960s, the Filipinos were just behind Japanese in standards of living and most wealthy families had Chinese housekeepers from Hong Kong. Today the Philippines, lacking Asian-style mechanisms to ensure a priority for economic expertise, is one of the region's poorest countries; most middle-class Hong Kong families now have maids from the Philippines—in all, just under 100,000 of them. Indeed, the word "Filipina" is used routinely as a synonym for "maid." Philippine decline was not solely the result of Marcos family theft, since the decline continued under Cory Aquino's democracy and was exacerbated by her policies. The point, however, is not whether this perception was right or wrong but that it was a central concern of Hong Kong's leaders which had to be addressed.

A central feature of the Asian miracle economies has been to create institutions that give great weight to specialist expertise in the face of populist pressures. In Japan, South Korea, Taiwan, Singapore, and Thailand, the civil bureaucracies all have far more decision-making power than in the United States or the United Kingdom. Senior civil servants carry more prestige compared to senior politicians than in most Western countries. Finance ministries and the ministries of commerce hold some of the autonomous authority and prestige that in Washington is accorded to the Federal Reserve. The West frequently denigrates this bureaucratic power as a lack of democracy, but it is envious of the superior economic performance that results.

In Hong Kong, some academics have a name for systems which give priority to economic efficiency over populism—"economism," defined as "a paradigm or doctrine in which economic activities and successes are considered to be the chief objective of a society." Li Kui Wai expresses a widely held perspective when he argues that economism has been the key to the achievements of Hong Kong, Singapore, Taiwan, and South Korea, which are acknowledged as the outstanding success stories—and not just economic—of the Third World. He argues:

> The paradigm of economism has definitely served Hong Kong well. The question in front of us is whether we should stick to the same paradigm which has brought us success so far, and what mechanisms we should employ in order to prolong and strengthen our economic success. . . . The central issue is that the political system that is to replace the British colonial system after 1997 should take up the paradigm of economism and consider economic prosperity the ultimate condition of survival in Hong Kong.[14]

Hong Kong is a very transient society, and one characterized by an extremely short term view. It is a society made ner-

[14]Cf. Li Kui Wai, "The Economic Paradigm for Hong Kong," *Intellectus* [Bulletin of the Hong Kong Institute of Economic Science] 23 (July–September 1992), especially p. 10. Li is lecturer at a local university.

vous by decades of fear of the Communists and hence very volatile in its moods. Fear of a sudden panic has led the government, as we saw, to accept huge economic costs in pegging the currency to the U.S. dollar in order to eliminate the risk of a sudden currency collapse and possible subsequent social chaos. Therefore much sympathy exists in Hong Kong for special structural measures to maintain continuity and a relatively long-range perspective as well as economic expertise.

Historically, the British shared the Chinese and Hong Kong concern to emphasize economic efficiency, although their arrangements in Hong Kong for maintaining such efficiency at the expense of populism were much cruder than the ones that evolved in, say, Japan or Singapore. A colonial government did not have to come to terms so directly with local political forces. Populist politics could be suppressed by relying on consultative bodies to the almost complete exclusion of elected local officials. The principal advisory bodies were filled by appointment or by indirect elections that buffered away populist pressures before they could influence high-level decision making. Authority lay always in the hands of a Governor whose mandate was based on sound economic management, and on consultation with lawyers, accountants, and business leaders. The advisers provided the expertise and an interest in economic efficiency.

These policies lay at the core of British achievement in Hong Kong, which by all accounts was the most successful of Britain's colonies. This did not mean a lack of concern for popular welfare: a housing crisis was dealt with when the government built 40 percent of the colony's housing stock; per capita income has grown at a multiple of Britain's rates; and Hong Kong's unemployment, usually under 2 percent, has been a small fraction of Britain's own rates. The system drew legitimacy and resilience primarily from its ability to deliver universal opportunity. In American terms, Hong Kong was a Horatio Alger society.

China approved. It also agreed to gradual democratization, as we have seen, including eventual election of all members of the Legislative Council by direct democratic elections as understood by the British. But the Basic Law provided for a gradual transition, with eighteen out of sixty people directly elected in 1991, and twenty directly elected in 1995, alongside thirty representatives of functional constituencies such as the legal and accounting professions and ten individuals indirectly elected by an electoral college. Over time, these special seats would gradually be turned into normal Western-style electoral seats. It was clearly understood by China, Britain, and the people of Hong Kong that the functional constituencies were to be identifiable elite groups with some important expertise, and that the electoral college would consist of a collection of notables with special expertise and long-range commitment to Hong Kong.

This system was to perform both the representative functions of the lower houses in the United States and Britain, and the more deliberative functions of the U.S. Senate and the British House of Lords, but to do so in one house rather than two. One house makes the system more efficient because only one vote need occur, and there is no prolonged period of negotiation between different houses over nuances of a bill.

This Asian-style system was designed to satisfy both Beijing's concern to emphasize expertise and longer time horizons, and the British experts' view that a system leaning on indirect rather than pure direct democracy would be better for Hong Kong. The British view at the time was that the important goal was to preserve Hong Kong's system of consultative but expert and decisive government as far as possible, while introducing limited elements of democracy to prevent the emergence of a political vacuum when the British withdrew.[15]

The best way for a Westerner to understand this system is in the context of America's Senate or the British House of Lords. These separate houses exist because of special historical circumstances but they are acknowledged to have continuing value because they offer a needed counterweight—more reflective, more expert, and more experienced—to the more populist lower houses. Both are chosen on a less "democratic" basis than the lower houses; for instance, giant Texas gets the same number of Senate seats as tiny Rhode Island. Hong Kong also has special historical circumstances, and it lives or dies on its economic performance. But neither the British nor the Chinese sides thought efficiency would be served by having two houses, so they put both kinds of representatives in a single house. Unlike the U.S. Senate or the British House of Lords, the special seats in Hong Kong would eventually be phased out completely under the agreed Chinese-British plan, leaving a more democratic legislature in Hong Kong than in Britain.

Following Tiananmen Square, Hong Kong developed a greater political self-consciousness, and, inevitably, a greater interest in democracy. The change was very real. Prior to Tiananmen Square, Hong Kong people had been determinedly apolitical; politics just got in the way of business. Afterward, they followed it seriously and had strong feelings, but were exceedingly cautious in their approach. Life is very good and very free in Hong Kong, and there is no inclination to put freedom and prosperity at risk. In contrast with Eastern Europe or Latin America, Hong Kong has never had any significant demonstrations in favor of greater democratization.

[15]For a review of the concerns behind the Joint Declaration, based primarily on interviews with British diplomats, see my article in *Current History* (September 1985).

Polls which in various ways asked whether the populace would like more democracy showed that they would; polls which asked whether people thought it important for the Hong Kong government to restore better relations with China showed that they did. In other words, they were enthusiastic about democracy, but not at the cost of jeopardizing Hong Kong's traditional freedom and prosperity. Asked whether they wanted limited democratization, as proposed by Governor Patten, at the expense of a confrontation with China, people voted strongly in the negative.[16] Getting the balance right would have required great subtlety and extensive public discussion.

THE PATTEN PROGRAM

When the new Governor, Chris Patten, took office in July 1992, he radically changed British policy. Previous governors had been men with great knowledge of both China and Hong Kong, who believed it was essential to understand the unique history and institutional structures of Hong Kong, to understand China's goals, and to obtain the best deal possible under the circumstances. They felt that any future for Hong Kong had to acknowledge China's core interests and overwhelming power, understanding that Hong Kong could have no future in confrontation with China. Prime Minister John Major deliberated, chose for Patten a quite different perspective and gave him orders to march in a different direction. Patten approached Hong Kong from a completely different angle. He had no experience of either Hong Kong or China, and empha-

[16]Polls demonstrating this result were a front-page feature of the *South China Morning Post* on November 22, 1992.

sized in public statements that he would not attempt to become an expert. His public statements acknowledged only one criterion for judging the success or failure of Britain's relationship with Hong Kong: the extent to which he was able to make Hong Kong's legislature more like a Western legislature, in the way it was elected and in the role it played.

Patten was a politician, not an expert; a domestic politician, not a foreign affairs specialist, although he had managed much of Britain's Third World aid program; and a party politician rather than a government administrator. He had the charm and personal attractiveness of a successful politician, and these qualities, new to Hong Kong, made a hugely successful initial impression.[17] In Northern Ireland and in the aid program, he had shown an admirable instinct to side with the underdog—and, for instance, he was willing to side with the Brazilians against much of his own bureaucracy. The first time I met him in Hong Kong, less than three months into his tenure there, he showed a very impressive command of the details of economic policy and a thrusting intelligence on complex economic questions. But he also had the tough skin appropriate to the chairman of the Conservative Party.

In London Patten was known as tough and insensitive and had been a bit of a hatchet man for Prime Minister Major; libel suits dogged him after he came to Hong Kong, and he was forced to settle. (The party paid the damages; he had just been doing his job.) Having been the architect of Major's come-from-behind victory in 1992, Patten had the strong support of the prime minister and frequently told Hong Kong people and Beijing that he was the prime minister's closest political and personal friend. While he had been the architect

---

[17]Polls inquiring about Patten's personal popularity—as distinct from specific policies—remained consistently high throughout his first year. He is an enormously attractive personality.

of Major's victory, he had lost his own election, and in the British system this meant that Major could not give his friend a cabinet post. But the British business community in Hong Kong had been pushing for a major political figure to be made Governor, and Major was furious at Wilson and the Foreign Office for having persuaded him to kowtow to the Chinese over the airport. On every ground except knowledge of the subject, Patten seemed to fit the bill for Governor of Hong Kong.

Ninety days after his arrival in Hong Kong, Governor Patten presented a new plan that constituted a radical reversal of the China experts' careful rapprochement with China over Hong Kong. His approach combined several elements:

- Dispense with the traditional process of consultation, Green Papers, and White Papers in favor of a policy development approach confined to a small group of advisers and kept secret until a dramatic public announcement.
- Separate the legislature from the executive by prohibiting members of the Legislative Council from holding Executive Council positions. This removed Martin Lee and the leading representatives of the Chinese business community from direct influence over decision making.
- Appoint less well known and less powerful figures to the Executive Council, and appoint liberal young lawyers and journalists to Legislative Council seats rather than the economy-focused businesspeople who would have held them in the past.
- Redefine nine new functional constituencies in the Legislative Council so that they would be elected by the entire working population (or a little under half the total population) rather than by narrower groups with specific expertise.
- For the ten Legislative Council constituencies to be chosen

by an electoral college, substitute a popularly elected electoral college for the group of notables that was originally intended.

- Position the Legislative Council as the central organ of government, despite the previous understanding that Hong Kong would have an "executive-led" government.
- Create a Business Council with a mandate to look at issues of competition (i.e., monopolies), in compensation for having removed so much business influence from the actual decision-making process.
- Position himself as standing up for Hong Kong's interests and democracy by firmly opposing China. As part of this, Patten would reject his predecessors' imperative for ensuring a smooth transition in 1997.
- Focus media attention on the new electoral proposals, which in turn were defined as "democratic reform."

The core of the Patten "reforms" was the effective transformation of functional constituencies into popular constituencies by opening them up to the whole working population. In his reversal of past understandings about the nature and purpose of a functional constituency, Patten took a legalistic view—his extension of the functional franchise was technically consistent with the wording of the Basic Law. Many commentators said that Patten had found a loophole. Not surprisingly, the Chinese took the view that, since the whole purpose of the functional and electoral constituencies was to implement a consensus on the need to ensure special continuity and expertise, and since Governor Patten's purpose in redefining those seats was to eliminate such elitism, he had infringed the Joint Declaration and the Basic Law. To the Chinese, the reason that the functional constituencies had not been defined in great detail was that there was no controversy as to their nature and purpose. Patten had certainly used the loophole to destroy the spirit and central intent of the original deal. More-over, under British law he appears to have committed a funda-mental error. There probably was no loophole.

What Governor Patten proposed might well have been judged illegal if actually adjudicated in British courts. While Patten sold almost all British and American commentators on the view that he could effectively change functional constitu-encies into popular constituencies, since the latter were not defined precisely in the Basic Law, that is not the way consti-tutional law works under the British system. In a dispute be-tween business parties, all that counts is the text of the agree-ment; prior understandings of the original intent have no standing. In such a dispute, Patten would be correct. But in a *constitutional* dispute, such as one involving the Basic Law, the original intent of the parties is the essence of the legal issue. When I asked the leading judicial authority in Hong Kong about this, he replied:

> In a contract between subjects, only the cold print counts. Pre-contract negotiations cannot be introduced into litigation. In a constitutional controversy the rules are very different. If the Privy Council were deciding on Governor Patten's proposals it would have to take a broader, organic view of the situation, taking into account the intent of the parties, much more in line with the Chinese position on the issues and contrary to the position Governor Patten has taken. This distinction has been ruled on.[18]

He went on to say that legally the Chinese have a trump card, since the interpretation of the Basic Law is ultimately the re-sponsibility of the National People's Congress under the ad-vice of the State Council.

[18]Justice Henry Litton, remarks to Vision 2047 breakfast, December 8, 1992.

However, politically this turns into a trump card for Governor Patten, since it means that the Privy Council has no jurisdiction, and therefore will never rule on the merits. So Governor Patten was able to press forward with a legally tenuous position and denounce the Chinese position as simply representing Chinese fear of democracy. He succeeded in selling that argument to virtually all British and American observers.

The difference between obeying the fine print and obeying the spirit of the Joint Declaration was captured by Hong Kong's favorite cartoonist, who had another scenario for China's abiding by the fine print but not the spirit, namely, using the United Democrat Party as slave labor to build the airport.[19]

The central appeal of the Patten program was that it constituted "democratic reform." It is therefore vital to identify the precise consequences of the whole program for democracy in Hong Kong. His electoral proposals would somewhat democratize the election of nineteen out sixty legislators. This was quite a modest step, as the Governor himself repeatedly stated, especially since Beijing had anyway committed itself to eventual full popular election of all legislators. So it was a modest way of speeding up something that would have happened in any case. Meanwhile, on the most important issue Hong Kong had faced since the Joint Declaration itself, Patten had swept away the whole community apparatus for consultation: no more broad consultations before the Governor took his position, no Green Paper, no White Paper, only secretive meetings with close advisers from London followed by a dramatic public announcement. This new approach divided Hong Kong politically to an extent that had never occurred

[19]"The World of Lily Wrong," *South China Morning Post*, October 22, 1992.

Copyright © 1992 Larry Feign

since the first years of the Cultural Revolution in the 1960s. Meanwhile, he had weakened the Executive Council and packed the Legislative Council in order to minimize opposition to his proposals.

Moreover, Patten risked creating the perfect set-up for a future dictator. His split of the Legislative Council from the Executive Council would enable a future Chinese leader to handle all important decisions within the cabinet and cut the legislature out; this was the price he paid for finessing the Martin Lee problem rather than confronting it, and for chasing the leading representatives of Chinese business out of the Executive Council. Patten also set a potentially fatal precedent for twisting the meaning of words. If he could take functional constituencies and change them into popular constituencies, then a dictatorially minded future Chief Executive could play the same game by turning them into appointive constituencies. Following the Patten precedent, nothing stood in the way of a future Chinese Chief Executive's defining a functional constituency as consisting of the Chief Executive and his secretary. At a breakfast meeting, I asked Governor Patten whether this was not a problem; he dodged the question, giving a long, rambling answer about the maturity of the Hong Kong people and their readiness for democracy.

Patten's high-profile confrontational approach also crippled the development of local political figures. It made him an international media star, featured on the cover of *Newsweek*. Hong Kong politics became completely centered on Patten, who thereby dwarfed all other personalities and groups. This tended to defeat the British diplomats' central goal in partially democratizing Hong Kong: to avert the creation of a political vacuum that would draw China in. Since Patten filled all available space, his departure would create a vacuum. This was not inevitable; the chairman of the Conservative Party was a media genius and could have encouraged local groups to take center stage.[20]

If, as Governor Patten said, the primary purpose of his proposals was to entrench democracy in the territory, then the net effect was somewhere between vanishingly small and very negative. At best, the gain would be roughly proportional to what would happen if the Chinese sent gunboats to Washington and demanded that much of the U.S. Senate be elected on

[20]This I tried to do in the Philippine revolution of 1986.

the same purely populist basis as the House of Representatives.

If his goal was to diminish vastly the role of the business community in the Executive and Legislative councils and to emasculate the special weight of functional expertise in Hong Kong's decision making, then his approach would have to be judged a great success. At no point did Patten address the issue of the proper balance of populism and expertise. Yet there were important issues here. On the one hand, there remained the old consensus of the Chinese, the British experts on Hong Kong, and the local business community (as well as almost everyone else who had analyzed Hong Kong) that exceptional economic efficiency was the only basis for survival, because it was the only source of internal stability and the only reason for China to maintain a capitalist system there. On the other hand, Hong Kong people genuinely wanted greater control over their own destinies. Articulating the imperatives of democracy and expertise, crafting a synthesis for the unique situation, and negotiating a measured shift in the direction of democratization was a task worthy of a great statesman. This task was *the one* central issue of Hong Kong's political future. Governor Patten gave no public indication that he was aware it existed, and he antagonized everyone who differed with him by treating them as the enemies of democracy.

Patten was convinced that the issue was simply democracy versus authoritarianism, good versus evil. He was clear that the Chinese were definitely not on the side of good, and that what had been lacking in British policy under his predecessors was a willingness to stand up to a brutal China. His arrival in Hong Kong was preceded by a spate of articles about how spineless his predecessors had been and how finally a British Governor would take a firm stand against China. On arrival, he emphasized to diplomats that if it was necessary to have a confrontation with China, then it was important to do so early.[21]

Before his October 7 speech, leading Chinese businessmen emphasized to Patten (at a meeting I attended) that it was essential for him to send a signal of his interest in working with China; it would be most unusual for the new executive of a joint venture not to express an interest in fruitful cooperation. When Patten gave his speech, it was devoid of any mention of cooperation with China. Indeed, although this epic-length speech even got down to such details as where water fountains were to be placed, somehow any mention of the vital, high-priority Hong Kong–China infrastructure projects was omitted. There was, however, a boast to the legislators that he had not consulted with China prior to his speech. This dog that didn't bark was a silent declaration of war. In the ensuing controversies, Patten addressed the Chinese with scornful sarcasm—perhaps acceptable in the House of Commons but utterly unacceptable in Chinese culture. Even the Governor's supporters were embarrassed. Under public pressure he later toned down the sarcasm but took many opportunities to refer to Britain as "the present sovereign" of Hong Kong, thereby reviving the disagreement over the status of the treaties that had been resolved almost a decade earlier.

Shortly after the speech, the British armed forces planned

---

[21]Little if any of the expression of Patten's antagonistic posture toward the Chinese or his predecessors has ever been attributed to him in direct quotes. It is omnipresent in private expressions and pervades the work of journalists who have been briefed by him and his supporters. Not surprisingly, the chairman of the Conservative Party is a master of using the press without showing his own hand. American readers who want a taste of the tone should read an article by Jim Hoagland, which reads like a transcript of comments by one of Patten's confidants: cf. "Bravo, Mr. Patten, for Ending the Coddling," originally published in the *Washington Post,* then republished in the *International Herald Tribune,* December 5–6, 1992.

an exercise, "Operation Winged Dragon," to practice defense of Hong Kong against a Chinese invasion. "The scenario was to demonstrate to the invading force that the territory was still under British sovereignty."[22] This was a curious exercise, because Hong Kong is indefensible. A Chinese attacker would not use military force, but would merely turn off the water tap and have total victory in a few days. If some misguided Chinese general did invade Hong Kong, Britain would never undertake a defense that would lead to the loss of innocent life in a hopeless cause. Since the only purpose most people could imagine was to strike a hostile diplomatic posture toward China, the public disclosure caused embarrassment (the Chinese army would have known of it anyway) and the exercise was postponed for the stated purpose of avoiding diplomatic antagonism with China. High-level military sources were quoted as saying that the exercise would almost certainly be scrapped, because it would be very difficult and undiplomatic to reschedule. Subsequently, Patten's government reinstated it.

Politically, Patten's government carried the warfare across the border into China. An aide of the Governor told a reporter that large numbers of Chinese were writing to support the Governor's reforms and suggested that the paper look into it. (Anyone who believed that numerous citizens of Guangdong would risk the wrath of their government to do this had more faith in Chinese liberalization than any Hong Kong businessman.) Duly prompted, the *South China Morning Post* conducted a survey in Guangdong and reported in large headlines that the people of China strongly supported Patten-style de-

[22]Cf. Paul Tyrrell, "Diplomatic Retreat by Army over Territory Exercise," *South China Morning Post,* November 6, 1992, and Kevin Sinclair, "When Our Military Minds Go Absent Without Leave," *South China Morning Post,* January 11, 1993.

mocracy. Such episodes positioned the new Governor as the mighty British lion putting the Chinese in their proper place.

As with Governor Wilson and the airport, Governor Patten informed the Chinese of his decision. He did not consult with them. (The Chinese foreign minister was sent a letter before the speech on the broad outline of Patten's proposals.) Further, Patten sought to mobilize Hong Kong public opinion and international opinion against China, in order to present Beijing with a fait accompli. A promise to discuss his program with the Chinese after announcement meant that his speech fell just short of flagrantly violating the Joint Declaration's requirement for consultation in the manner of his predecessor's airport announcements. But Patten also made it clear that he intended to implement the proposals unilaterally unless Beijing offered counterproposals which met his criteria of free and fair elections. He defined those criteria in a way that turned elite seats into popular seats. Since it was precisely his criteria which were objectionable to the Chinese, he was in fact taking an uncompromising position, but one that he was able to present to the press as flexible.

Governor Patten followed through by announcing that he would move ahead on the airport even though the Chinese objected. In his view, the Chinese were only obstructing the airport plan in order to cause difficulty for his political reforms. In the Chinese view, Patten was linking the two instances in which Britain had broken the Joint Declaration. Swire Pacific, one of the two most prestigious British companies in Hong Kong and, as the owner of Cathay Pacific Airways, the company with the greatest interest in the new airport, waged a battle until midnight against the decision to drive ahead without China's permission. When I pointed this out to the official spokesman on the airport, he replied that CITIC, a Chinese company, had a minority stake in Cathay

Pacific. "Swires are just the thin edge of the wedge [for China]," he said.

The Chinese had obtained revenge for Governor Wilson's highhandedness by humiliating the British over the airport, Governor Patten was getting vengeance for the airport humiliation through highhandedness and sarcasm over the political proposals. The Chinese in turn were reacting with outraged nationalism. On November 20, 1992, China announced that no British government contracts would be honored after 1997. Like Governor Patten's proposals, this was consistent with the fine print of the Joint Declaration and the Basic Law, but a contradiction of their central intent. China had now itself broken with the clear and undeniable intent of the Joint Declaration. Hong Kong was entering a vicious circle with no obvious exit.

The Chinese said that Britain was breaking the deal made in the Joint Declaration and in correspondence between the two governments, as well as the intent of the Basic Law. In this, they were joined by some formidable interpreters—virtually all the British officials who had participated directly in the negotiations. One by one, the key figures who had retired came forward to express their dismay. Lord McLehose, Governor at the time; Sir Percy Cradock, the foreign policy adviser to the prime minister in 1984; Sir Jack Cater, a key diplomat and later chief secretary of the Hong Kong government; and many others denounced Patten's repudiation of earlier understandings—not only of legal documents but also of consensus on things like the nature of functional constituencies and the importance of a smooth transition in 1997. (The importance of compromising to ensure that the Legislative Council of June 1997 remained in July was called the "through train" and had been promoted by the British.) Moreover, senior officials still in office also made clear to friends how deeply they disapproved of Patten's course. Sir David Akers-Jones, one of the most highly regarded British officials in Hong Kong, announced his retirement and a few days later accepted appointment to China's Advisory Council on Hong Kong. This outpouring of dissent is almost unprecedented in the British Foreign Office, which has a much more disciplined service than America's. (In America, open dissent and leaks are far more common.) Not since the Suez Crisis of 1956 had British diplomats mounted such a massive protest against the policies of their own government.

Patten mirrored their hostility, and in fact initiated it. From the time of his arrival in Hong Kong, diplomats of other countries marveled at "the open disdain he shows for his sinologists." Patten was in the vanguard of a group of insular politicians who believed in some version of the myth of betrayal. He was sure that his differences derived from his superior devotion to British values, whereas the sinologists were convinced that they were upholding British values in the context of complex power balances and institutional differences that Patten did not understand. Patten was not alone. He was working for John Major, with the prime minister's full approval—at least until the going got too rough. And the British press was heavily committed to the myth of betrayal. *The Times* published bitter denunciations of Sir Percy Cradock. The *Daily Mail* said that "One topic makes Governor Mr Chris Patten screw up his face in disgust. . . . What is the topic? The ruthless, cold-blooded machinations of the leaders of China? No. What upsets him is any mention of the British Foreign Office . . .," and went on to suggest that the appropriate solution was to replace the Foreign and Commonwealth Office with a fax machine. American commentators largely supported their British counterparts.[23] The Hong Kong crisis of 1992–93 did not stem from a rift between Hong Kong and China but from a domestic British power struggle.

In Hong Kong, matters began to turn against Patten. Broad polling about democracy still seemed to support him, but more detailed polls quickly showed that Hong Kong people did not support his proposals in the face of Chinese opposition. The polls suddenly became less of an indicator of the will of the people for Governor Patten. He leaned heavily on initial tentative support from the Legislative Council, but this body was hardly representative. Both sides opposed a referendum. Patten said a referendum would be "divisive," but skeptics thought his opposition had more to do with the fact that polls showed he would lose. Beijing feared the precedent of making a constitutional decision by popular vote.

The Chinese business community's leadership turned against Governor Patten—a few publicly, most of the rest privately. The Business and Professionals' Federation, the Chinese Manufacturers' Association, and the Chinese Chamber of Commerce all denounced the political changes, as did various labor groups. Faced with shaky support in Hong Kong, the Governor began mobilizing fellow politicians overseas. He obtained the endorsement of Australia and Canada's foreign ministers, and generalized support from the U.S. State Department for democratization. But he had to put the best face on Japan's cannier silence. Not a single Asian diplomat offered support. The effort to internationalize what China

[23]See *The Times*, November 20, 1992. Andrew Roberts, "Time Has Come to Pull Rug from Under Mandarins," *Daily Mail*, reprinted in *South China Morning Post*, March 21, 1993. For a U.S. example, cf. Hoagland, "Bravo, Mr. Patten . . ."

saw as a question of domestic Chinese politics drew stern warnings from Beijing.[24]

To China, the economic value of Hong Kong was being put in jeopardy, and the risk that the British would institutionalize a politically hostile Hong Kong appeared severe. The effort to draw foreign countries into the quarrel was seen by Beijing as a major threat to China's sovereignty, and was put by Beijing in the context of George Bush's decision to reverse a decade of American policy and sell F-16 fighter aircraft to Taiwan—the other area of sensitivities over sovereignty. The Chinese took special note of a series of articles by Gerald Segal, Britain's best known China specialist, writing from the podium of NATO's think tank, the International Institute of Strategic Studies, who suggested that Hong Kong was the soft underbelly of China and that the West should use it to strike a blow for human rights and to weaken China. The Chinese took the Segal thesis too seriously; it was sufficiently important in their thinking that Singapore's former prime minister, Lee Kwan Yew, highlighted the idea in a series of public rebukes to Governor Patten.[25] The Chinese were becoming convinced that their sovereignty was on the negotiating table.

As the quarrel became more intense, both sides backed off. Communist Party Secretary General Jiang Zemin personally stated that he did not expect contracts to be canceled, and Lu Ping, the leading Beijing official in charge of Hong Kong af-

[24]Governor Patten denied that he was trying to internationalize the issue. But he did not turn away such endorsements, and he had a busy travel schedule for someone preoccupied with a domestic constitutional reorganization. He requested a very early meeting with President Clinton and was asked to defer his visit. In early 1993 Britain's foreign minister publicly appealed for Japanese support of Patten.

[25]Segal's article appears in the *International Herald Tribune* of December 8, 1992. The most extensive transcript of Lee Kwan Yew's remarks is in *Window,* December 18, 1992, pp. 3–5.

fairs, said the same thing.[26] Senior executives of firms involved in the most sensitive contracts, such as a new container terminal, received personal reassurances from Lu Ping.[27] Governor Patten began saying he hoped the legislature would pass a bill acceptable to Britain, the people of Hong Kong, and Beijing; the inclusion of Beijing was a remarkable novelty. The two sides began to talk about holding direct talks on the subject. Patten delayed gazetting his bill for legislative consideration. Talks came so close to success that one executive councillor publicly announced that the Governor would have favorable news the following day. (Another executive councillor told me that he found the positions of the two sides "indistinguishable," and a third said that "they were within two words of agreement.") Then suddenly Patten announced that no progress had been made and, without consulting the Executive Council, gazetted his bill, accusing the Chinese of having backtracked.

The pivotal issue had to do with the makeup of the delegation that would negotiate with the Chinese. Patten wanted the government of Hong Kong to be formally represented by Hong Kong Chinese government officials as well as British. He wanted to force the Chinese government to recognize the Hong Kong government as an official party to the talks. The Chinese government took the position that this was a constitutional issue between the British and the Chinese governments. The Hong Kong government had the right to decide on policies, but all matters having to do with the return of Hong Kong to Chinese sovereignty, and with the constitutional structure after 1997, must be negotiated directly between

---

[26]"Chinese Officials Try to Calm Hong Kong on Contracts' Status," *Asian Wall Street Journal,* January 11, 1993.

[27]Based on a conversation with the chairman of one of the companies most prominently involved.

China and Britain. Beijing was perfectly happy to have the Hong Kong government officials present as advisers to the British delegation, but Patten insisted that the Hong Kong government must be a formal party to the negotiation and broke off discussions when Beijing would not accept this.

Why was this important? All along, China had said that the central issue was sovereignty and the breaking of agreements, not democracy. Dozens of times senior Chinese officials had said that they did not object to a gradual increase of democracy, but that Britain had to keep its agreements and had to acknowledge Chinese sovereignty.[28] To China, the essence of 1997 was a return of sovereignty—a reunification of the Chinese nation. The Joint Declaration was a smooth way of assuaging the humiliation of the Opium War. Conversely, the British imposition of a constitutional structure to which China had not agreed, and pressure from Washington to accept that imposition, would constitute a ratification of the Opium War, a confirmation of foreigners' rights to tell China how to govern a piece of Chinese territory. China was willing to have Hong Kong remain capitalist and free, and it went much further than Patten's proposals in promising that the legislature would eventually be entirely elected in the way Patten liked. But it was not willing to have any new structure forced upon it. Accepting the Hong Kong government and legislature as the final authorities on constitutional structure meant in China's eyes that sovereignty was being transferred from Britain to Hong Kong, instead of from Britain to China. Hong Kong was to be autonomous within Chinese sovereignty, not an independent sovereign state.

What the breakup of this round showed was that the core

---

[28]See the *Newsweek* quotation in the epigraph to this chapter.

issue was indeed sovereignty, not democracy, and not just in China's mind but also in Patten's. Patten's defenders would say that he was just trying to establish "a high degree of autonomy." But that phrase always referred to policy and lifestyle within the established framework, for instance, to economic policy and personal freedom, never to constitutional structure.

Had Patten cared most about democracy, and had he acknowledged that the Chinese cared primarily about sovereignty, there would have been plenty of room for negotiation. Throughout the controversy, the Chinese went very far out on a limb in declaring their willingness to accept Hong Kong democracy—so long as it was done in a gradual, managed fashion. And they had in any case committed themselves to full direct elections eventually. Patten was arguing about pace, not about principle.

To the extent that Patten's goal was to establish the maximum interpretation of "a high degree of autonomy," this too was lost by his negotiating tactics. From the beginning, he had disparaged his predecessors' emphasis on the so-called through train—the importance of establishing an arrangement whereby the colonial government in July 1997 would transfer smoothly into Chinese sovereignty the following month without any major changes of structure or personnel.[29] Because its Hong Kong policy to date has been so successful in achieving China's goals, there is every reason to believe that, presented with a going concern in 1997, Beijing would simply let the through train continue on its way. But its reaction to

[29]According to Martin Lee, in remarks made at a dinner on February 1, 1993, the concept of the through train was floated by the British government via Maria Tam, then a legislator, during discussions about the Basic Law. The British diplomats believed this policy vital to Hong Kong's stability.

Patten's gazetting of the political bill was to authorize through the National People's Congress the early establishment of its own planning group on arrangements for 1997. Patten's abrogation of the through train policy means that in 1997 China will have to make a series of major decisions about Hong Kong's structure and personnel. Those decisions will naturally be affected by Beijing's ideology at the time, and will be buffeted by whatever controversies and power struggles are current then. This will draw Beijing into the intimate management of Hong Kong's affairs, just as Wilson's unilateralism on the airport drew Beijing into the intimate management of the airport. Wherever London has behaved cooperatively, Beijing has given wide latitude; but wherever it has acted with blatant unilateralism, Beijing has extracted a price.

Patten's gazetting of his proposals fundamentally changed the psychology of Hong Kong. When he did so, the stock market immediately dropped 8.1 percent and Patten's support in the public opinion polls simply collapsed. This time even the London newspapers acknowledged that the Hong Kong public was repudiating Patten's decision. Subsequently, Lu Ping called a press conference for the expected angry denunciation of Patten. The stock market prepared for another drop; angry Chinese denunciations had always—always—caused a drop. Except this time. While Lu Ping was speaking, the market rose about 200 points. His speech was very angry, but the Hong Kong Chinese sensed immediately that China had decided to denounce Britain but abjure any action that could damage Hong Kong. The market began a march to a series of new record highs—the details affected by the progress of negotiations but the central trend reflecting a change of psychology that had been gradually emerging in the business community which now broke through to the surface and spread much more widely. Now they would trust China, and henceforth they would treat 1997 primarily as an opportunity rather than a risk.[30]

Eventually both sides rediscovered the necessity to negotiate. China had to back off from its refusal to talk until Patten withdrew his electoral proposals, because protracted uncertainty about Hong Kong's future was not in China's interest. Patten had to get back to the negotiating table because his collapse in the polls would eventually make his position untenable. China swallowed its rhetoric about never negotiating until Patten repudiated his proposals. Patten fudged the status of the Hong Kong members of the delegation. While the negotiations proceeded, China pursued a two-pronged policy: supportive on economics, hard on sovereignty. Beijing agreed to an important land-use decision, made positive sounds about the Container Terminal, accepted a cable TV arrangement, and agreed to renew negotiations on the airport. On the other hand, it announced that the turnover in 1997 would include a major military parade from China into Hong Kong and that 10,000 Chinese troops, rather than the previously announced 5,000, would subsequently be stationed in Hong Kong. Previously the latter would have rattled Hong Kong; in the new mood, the stock market continued its extraordinary ascent to new records.

As this book goes to press, the negotiations continue. The point here is not the outcome but the process. Hong Kong is where the tectonic plates of Chinese and Western civilizations engage most firmly. As such, it is a microcosm of much broader relationships. British leaders dealt with a caricature of China. They underestimated China's power and overestimated their own moral position in Hong Kong. The Western

---

[30]For a written expression of this view, cf. Business and Professionals Federation of Hong Kong, *Hong Kong 21: A Ten Year Vision and Agenda for Hong Kong's Economy.* Hong Kong, May 1993, especially pp. 5–6.

press mostly magnified the caricatures, and Western leaders, especially in Washington, acted on them and were mystified when Hong Kong opinion and leaders throughout Asia moved in the opposite direction. Beijing meanwhile was so slow and indecisive on the major practical issues affecting Hong Kong that reasonable people doubted its good faith. And its diplomacy was so clumsy, threatening, and inarticulate that even when its case was undeniable, many people recoiled from association with the angry dragon.

IN ALL THESE controversies, the central problems of the British and the Chinese were complementary. Wilson and Patten alike refused to confront key issues—most notably the need to accept the rule of mutual non-subversion—that were politically difficult to explain to core British constituencies. Both the Patten and the Wilson administrations thought that minimizing Hong Kong's economic ties to China—for instance, by holding back on infrastructure to the border and refusing to enhance the teaching of Mandarin in the schools—would be beneficial to Hong Kong's future, whereas the key to success lies in fact in ensuring that Beijing gets the fullest economic benefits of a free Hong Kong. Both believed that the way to reassure Hong Kong was to take drastic unilateral actions—Wilson on the airport and Patten on both the airport and politics—that breached British promises and could not possibly have had any other outcome than major confrontations with China.

As a result, both men seriously exacerbated Hong Kong's fears and both defeated their own central goals. Wilson could have had a better airport, faster and at less cost, if he had adhered to the Joint Declaration's requirement for consultation. Patten could have negotiated a great deal more democracy for Hong Kong if he had acknowledged the elementary point that sovereignty is a sensitive issue during a decolonization. Wilson was at least aware of the tides of history, the unique value of Hong Kong's institutions, and the requirements of "One country, two systems," but seemed ashamed to proclaim them. Patten was completely insensitive to the diplomacy of decolonization and could see no value in any institutions and culture different from London's.

Ultimately, the British had good values and good intentions but had lost the cosmopolitanism of empire and were no longer capable of transcending their own insularity. A few British editors promulgated a series of myths that had only the most tenuous and distorted connections to reality, and this generation of politicians seemed to possess neither the knowledge to pierce the myths nor the determination to master a reality that did not fit the convenient categories of domestic politics. The repudiation under John Major of the expertise that had created Hong Kong and helped rescue it from the fate of Goa was not just a last-minute twist in the return of Hong Kong. It was the culminating political consequence of the loss of empire, the final loss of its political base by one of the greatest diplomatic services in all of world history. Henceforth Britain would be just a particularly insular player within the European Community.

Chinese leaders had the tides of history on their side, but lacked the finesse to ride those tides smoothly. A generation of leaders reared completely within an authoritarian bureaucracy had no skills at rallying public opinion. A generation callused by the Cultural Revolution had no knack for the quick-footed policy reformulations that would have given China what it wanted (the trappings of sovereignty) and Britain what it wanted (a bit more democracy and a little bit of favorable publicity for the constituents back home). The older generation had Zhou Enlai, one of the smoothest diplomats of the age, and the younger generation has some of the most attractive personalities in diplomacy, but those currently in power talk like Russian engineers. Each day China played the heavy, with droning bureaucrats making threats for world television to display. It was a Western flaw that the journalists and politicians of the West refused to hear a very clear message, repeated hundreds of times ("The Joint Declaration will be honored, gradual democratization is acceptable, but respect our sovereignty over Hong Kong"); but it was a Chinese flaw that the message was always delivered in such a stolid, threatening, unimaginative, humorless way that the tone overwhelmed the theme itself. Most of the great Pacific Asian takeoffs have had a similar problem. Park Chung Hee, Chiang Kai Shek, Chiang Ching Kuo of Taiwan, and Suharto have all focused so intensely on domestic economic management that they have had little time to cultivate the skills of international diplomacy. Deng Ziaoping, like Park, is a crusty genius with a firm sense of priorities that doesn't put diplomacy very high on the list.

Personalities complicated this interplay. China's representative in Hong Kong, Zhou Nan, was a leftist disciplinarian placed there to reimpose fear on China's own representatives after they took the dissidents' side at the time of Tiananmen Square. He spent his formative years as an interrogator of American prisoners during the Korean War, and his diplomacy seemed to be an extension of his interrogations. Only a God with a sardonic sense of humor would have brought together Patten, whose knowledge of China and Hong Kong was so thin that he lived on the stereotype of the brutal Chinese Communist bureaucrat, with the embodiment of that stereotype. Patten and Zhou Nan drew life from each other. When Patten arrived, Zhou Nan, old and seriously ill, was due for retirement. Word had been passed to the business community not to pay too much attention to his diatribes. His cleanup at Xinhua was done. He was going, but he had served the Party all his life, and "sometimes it's a bit difficult to know what to do with the old leftists." After Patten's October 1972 political reform speech, such talk vanished. The last self-righteous British imperialist had been dispatched to humiliate the Chinese one last time, so the last Maoist had to get out his interrogation gear one last time.

It is simply impossible to capture the resulting exchanges in the language of ordinary social science or journalism, which by convention are supposed to take these things terribly seriously. One needs Evelyn Waugh's *Black Mischief* to capture the flavor. Zhou Nan's fantasies about the British sucking Hong Kong dry, and British fantasies about the betrayal and decline of poor old Hong Kong were perfect mirror images. Neither had any connection to reality.

Meanwhile, contrary to both fantasies, the freest stable society in Asia surpassed Britain in standards of living, neighboring areas of China became the fastest-growing large populations in world history, and Chinese leaders demonstrated a broad consensus that the prosperity of Hong Kong was inextricably tied to its freedom and capitalism. Behind Zhou Nan was Lu Ping, a man of sophisticated mind who spoke many languages and looked at Hong Kong from so many perspectives that Patten could not even see the sophistication. Behind Lu Ping was the multi-tiered plan of Deng Ziaoping, which had built history's greatest decade of economic growth around Hong Kong. Deng Xiaoping's tour of the region near Hong Kong in early 1992 became the symbol around which he gathered his forces for a final, decisive lunge at reform that was blessed in the Fourteenth Party Congress in October 1992. So much success assembled here that it was difficult to imagine a scenario that would not result in a win for China, a win for Hong Kong, and even a win for the British. The ideologues on both sides would try very hard to snatch defeat from the jaws of victory; but it was a tough job.

The illusions and posturings of the British in Hong Kong,

and the fear, uncertainty, financial loss, and family anguish caused by the clash of cultures, provide a microcosm of what could happen as a West that has triumphed over the Soviet Union confronts a China that is triumphing over poverty. The emergence of China as a principal arbiter of the destiny of much of the world creates one of history's greatest opportunities—and also one of its greatest risks. The following chapter explores the international consequences of China's rise.

VI

||||||||||||||

THE
TRANSFORMATION
OF INTERNATIONAL
RELATIONS

"Taiwan has lost the ability to buy foreign embassies. It has gained the opportunity to buy China."
> —ARTHUR HUMMEL, FORMER U.S. AMBASSADOR TO CHINA,
> NOVEMBER 9, 1992

C ontemporary geopolitics is being shaped primarily by two economic trends: the collapse of communist economies in Eastern Europe, the former USSR, and Southeast Asia; and the continued dynamism of the Pacific Asian market economies. Both trends have evolved over decades; the second is not less important for lack of the drama of implosion. The current takeoff of one quarter of the human race (China plus the littoral countries) is transforming the political structure of the entire globe.

THE ASIAN MIRACLE AND POSTWAR
WESTERN CONSOLIDATION

Immediately after World War II, a chaotic Asia was brought to order by U.S. policy. During this period, some felt that Japan would never again become a major industrial power;

others knew that only raising Japan again could return stability to the whole of the Pacific basin. By the early 1960s, Japan was once more on the verge of industrial power, and during that decade Japan's economic success consolidated its domestic politics and its membership in the Western alliance. By 1970, the riots which had prevented Eisenhower from visiting Tokyo in 1960 were unimaginable and the Soviet goals of dividing or subverting Japan were unattainable.

A second wave of economic development in the 1960s and 1970s consolidated most of the periphery of Pacific Asia. The changes were dramatic. In 1959–60, South Korea had been on the verge of chaos and defeat, and even Lee Kwan Yew still regarded the Communist Party as Singapore's strongest political force.[1] Indonesia, home of the world's third largest Communist Party, was closer to the communist powers than to the West. In the 1950s, Malaysia and the Philippines were nearly overwhelmed by communist insurgencies. Through the 1970s, Thailand fought a communist insurgency so serious that much of world opinion held that it would fall like a domino after the collapse of Vietnam, Laos, and Cambodia. By the 1980s, nothing of the kind had occurred. Rather, economic development had consolidated the politics of all these non-communist states and made Thailand preeminent in its region, while lack of development had humbled the Vietnamese empire to Thailand's east and backward, isolationist Burma to Thailand's west.

Likewise, in the 1950s and 1960s virtually all Pacific Asian countries except Japan had major separatist movements and serious irredentist claims against virtually all their neighbors:

[1] This is true despite Lee's having won a democratic election in 1959. The authoritative account of the transition to the rule of Lee Kwan Yew, told from Lee's own viewpoint, is Dennis Bloodworth, *The Tiger and the Trojan Horse* (Singapore: Times Books International, 1986).

Indonesia against Malaysia and the Philippines, Malaysia against those countries as well as Thailand, and so forth. Thailand had a southern Muslim separatist movement, Malaysia serious separatism in Sabah, and Indonesia a series of separatist uprisings. By 1990, the countries which had achieved sustained growth had mostly compromised or adjudicated irredentist claims or allowed them to lapse into quiescence. Similarly, most of their separatist movements had collapsed. In contrast, the Philippines, with its Latin American-style failure of growth, and Burma, with its African socialist-style failures, continued to face multiple, serious separatist movements and to have territorial conflicts with their neighbors.[2]

This period of Asian consolidation into the Western camp largely coincided with the Vietnam War, whose negative outcome was overwhelmed geopolitically by a broader regional consolidation of pro-Western diplomatic and economic orientations. That consolidation derived from a gradual recognition that national prosperity and security could be achieved fastest by focusing on market-oriented, Western-oriented, export-driven growth.

A third wave drew China into this system. In the 1950s, China was allied with the Soviet Union and hostile to the West. In the 1960s, it was hostile to both the Soviet Union and the West. Modern China, however, is essentially rational and was eventually seduced into the Western economic and diplomatic orbit because its immediate neighbors were experienc-

[2]Burma has a wide variety of territorial problems with neighbors, some of which nearly led to warfare with Thailand during 1992. The Philippines maintains a claim to Sabah, which constitutes a major part of Malaysia's territory. Periodically the Philippine regime faces the decision to renounce this antiquated claim—it almost did so under both Marcos and Aquino—but never quite succeeds. This limits many kinds of potential cooperation with Malaysia.

ing undeniable prosperity. That nearby prosperity and China's poverty were frustrating the most urgent national policies, such as recovery of Taiwan and competition with the Soviet Union. It became clear that only superior economic growth could underwrite an effective strategic response both to Soviet superiority and to the humiliation of rising Japanese regional influence. Moreover, Chinese leaders could not escape awareness of the extraordinary success of three booming Chinese fragments—Taiwan, Hong Kong, and Singapore—or the inevitable conclusion that the policies of the fragments must be sounder than the policies of the homeland.

This phase in the rise of Pacific Asia consolidated the global role of the United States and isolated the Soviet Union. Throughout the region, America protected the growth militarily and subsidized it financially. It provided technological and administrative assistance, moderated international conflicts which threatened that growth, and provided the export market on which the growth fed. The United States celebrated Asian successes and took credit for them. In turn, because of the consolidation of Asia, the United States was able to concentrate its attention on the Soviet threat and avoid diffusing its resources over what had once been a multiplicity of dangerous Asian instabilities.

This phase greatly enhanced the weight of Pacific Asia in global politics and the global economy. In the late 1970s, North American trans-Pacific trade for the first time exceeded trans-Atlantic trade.[3] In that decade, Deng Xiaoping declared China an honorary member of NATO. Both developments foreshadowed a gradual shift in the world's political center of gravity away from the Atlantic. Henceforth, the great trade

[3]For data to support this point, see the appropriate issues of IMF, *Directions of Trade*.

battles would focus on Asia. Political influence would gradually shift toward Asia, and America's West Coast would gain at the expense of the East. Later would come the assertiveness of Nakasone and Takeshita and Japan's prominence in the club of major economic powers (the so-called G-5 and G-7). Gorbachev came forward with his Vladivostok initiative, which attempted to tilt Soviet policy toward the Pacific. To the east, South Korea conducted rapprochement with Moscow in 1990 and Beijing in 1992.

During the 1980s, after joining the market system and becoming an advocate of regional stability, China became the world's fastest-growing country. Simultaneously, Japan sped past the USSR economically, and the Soviet economy stagnated in the face of a wide-ranging American military buildup. This forced the Soviet Union seriously to reassess both its domestic economic organization and its international posture. As one of several major influences that facilitated the rise of Gorbachev, the Pacific Asian takeoff indirectly affected the entire globe.

Soviet reforms raised the priority of Soviet policy toward Asia and emulated key Asian moves. Gorbachev proclaimed greater emphasis on Asia in speeches at Vladivostok in July 1986 and Krasnoyarsk in September 1988. He repeatedly took initiatives toward Japan and sent Foreign Minister Edward Shevardnadze on trips to upgrade relations with the smaller Asian states. There was a particular effort with South Korea—first in sports, then trade in 1989, then formal relations in 1990—to learn from the South Korean experience, and to engage South Korean firms in major projects. Much of the Gorbachev reform package (but not nearly enough) was familiar to students of Asia: Cut the military budget, provide incentives for foreign investment, propose free economic zones, and praise (for a while) the Chinese model of development.[4] Obviously, the USSR's proposed five free economic zones owed much to Taiwan and South Korean export processing zones and to China's fourteen special economic zones.

Why didn't the Soviet reform work? It failed because Russia proved ambivalent, even reluctant, in most of these aspects of reform, and because it implemented reforms in the wrong sequence. Gorbachev's priorities were international politics first, domestic politics second, heavy industry third, and light industry and agriculture last. Deng Xiaoping's priorities were the exact opposite.

Nor was Russia alone in reacting to Pacific Asian growth. Professor Paul Bracken of Yale argues that "extensive interviews with leading European businessmen have convinced me that the most important single influence on the EC's decision to remove all interior barriers to trade and capital flows was the Japanese challenge."[5] He believes many West European leaders were initially attracted to a policy that would have combined a diplomatic deal with the Soviet Union, a limited European Community integration, and protectionism toward the United States. But such a scenario would not have conferred on Europeans the ability to compete with Japan. Europe's relative decline would have continued.

Simultaneously, Vietnam, Laos, and Cambodia found that the choice of a Soviet-oriented diplomatic alignment and Soviet-model economic policies condemned them to inexorable decline in the face of the challenges from the Association of Southeast Asian Nations (ASEAN). Thus they too are now belatedly trying to join the Pacific Asian system, with market-

---

[4]Cf. Scott Atkinson, "The USSR and the Pacific Century" *Asian Survey* XXX, 7 (July 1990), pp. 629–645.

[5]From comments made during the "Asia-Pacific Strategy Development Workshop," National Defense University, Washington, D.C., May 23, 1990.

oriented reforms at home and incentives for foreign investment. After a false start, Vietnam's reform efforts have
brought remarkable improvements in inflation, currency stability, and trade. They promise a rapid takeoff once international sanctions are lifted.

North Vietnam's wartime victory a decade and a half earlier, in 1975, served only as an ironic counterpoint to the
Asian economic miracle. National impoverishment followed,
along with a steady flow of refugees. The United States, while
failing in its military objectives, had protected and nurtured
the Asian takeoff when it was still a fragile blossom in Southeast Asia. Expenditures on the Vietnam War generously financed and accelerated the takeoff, just as the Korean War
had earlier financed and accelerated the takeoff of Japan.[6] The
fact that China did not attack American troops in Vietnam
(whereas it had attacked American troops in Korea) gave U.S.
leaders confidence that, if they properly considered China's
sensitivities, they could successfully manage a relationship
with China despite its hostile ideology. And the lack of any
U.S. thrust at China during the long Vietnam War persuaded
Chinese leaders that, despite Beijing's earlier fears, it was not
the United States' intention to attack China. These realiza-
tions created the confidence on both sides that made the 1972
Sino-American rapprochement possible.

ECONOMIC TAKEOFF AND REGIONAL PEACE

The process by which Pacific Asian growth facilitated stability
both within countries and between them is one of the great

[6]Cf. Richard Stubbs, "Geopolitics and the Political Economy of Southeast Asia," *International Journal* XLIV (Summer 1989).

political miracles of the modern world. Stability now charac-
terizes the internal politics of the fast-growing countries and
their international politics alike. Within countries, economic
growth has knitted countries together by demonstrating that
the way to prosperity is national collaboration rather than
tribal strife. It has replaced a mentality of "every tribe for itself" with a mentality of common nourishment from a growing pie. Growth has financed Asia's truly national infrastruc-
tures for the first time in history—roads, telephone systems,
and mass education, for instance, and the nationalism that
often accompanies mass education, and military and police
forces capable of dealing with any groups slow to comprehend the message.

Internationally, the consequences have been similar. For
centuries in Southeast Asia, regimes have enriched themselves
by plundering their neighbors. Most of regional politics previously consisted of territorial aggression and irredentism. The
possibility of sustained development at 7 percent annually has
made it much more attractive to seek prosperity via domestic
development. Moreover, with development swept in modern
military technology, which has drastically increased the risks
and cost of plundering one's neighbors. Thus the whole calcu-
lus of international politics has been transformed. War is now
far more costly and peace the only sensible path to prosperity
and power.

The change in economic environment has not worked
alone, of course. The U.S. presence has allowed countries—
including notably Japan and 1960s South Korea—to enhance
their growth further by reducing military expenditure and relying on U.S. protection. Moreover, the United States strongly
discouraged most forms of regional conflict. Such a policy
worked well in the context of Asian growth and post–World
War II West European recovery; but the absence of rapid eco-

nomic growth in Africa and Latin America deprived the policy of leverage in those areas.

China's strategic reorientation in 1968–72 preceded its change in economic strategy, but after 1978 economics because the core of national strategy. In the mid-to late seventies, China bought the whole Pacific Asian policy package, including:

- a reduced military budget;
- subordination of geopolitics to economic growth;
- strategic reliance on the United States;
- subordination of ideology to economic pragmatism;
- substantial subordination of politics to economics;
- acceptance of foreign corporations and technology;
- an increasingly market-oriented economy;
- encouragement of domestic economic competition; and
- an increasingly outward-looking economic and social posture.

Washington used the Beijing connection to press for a solution to the Vietnam War, to play the China card against the Soviet Union, and to obtain a site on Chinese territory from which to monitor Soviet missile and nuclear testing. China played the Washington card in its dealings with Moscow; when Moscow put out a feeler about bombing Chinese nuclear facilities, Washington firmly sided with Beijing. These developments created a China that was militarily and ideologically non-threatening to its neighbors and to U.S. interests, and which was locked, however uncomfortably, into doing business according to Western rules.

China benefited, and followed the Pacific Asian pattern; Beijing gradually made peace with all its neighbors. Rapprochement with the United States and Japan in the 1970s was followed by rapprochement with the Soviet Union in the 1980s. The solution of troubling border problems began much earlier. China peacefully resolved major border disputes on the basis of the status quo with all those neighbors who would negotiate with it, including Burma, Thailand, Afghanistan, and Pakistan. (A few minor ones remain.) India and the Soviet Union were the two major countries that refused to negotiate, and in both cases this led to clashes, but by the 1980s these clashes were ancient history.[7]

China abandoned international revolutionary fervor and embarked on a conservative policy of getting along with its neighbors. It withdrew support from revolutionary movements in Asia and elsewhere. In particular, the communist parties of Thailand, Malaya, the Philippines, Indonesia, and Burma, and revolutionary communists in India, lost the subsidies, arms transfers, revolutionary training, and propaganda support that China had once provided. Chinese scholars and officials made unusually frank apologies for their former support of revolutionary movements in Southeast Asia:

> China will not use its relations with other communist parties to intervene in others' internal affairs. China's relationship with communist parties in Southeast Asia is a problem formed in the Second World War, a problem left over by history. Then in the 1950s and 1960s, China had certain inappropriateness [sic] in a period in handling its relations with other communist

[7]The Indo-Soviet clash of 1962 occurred when India, having refused to negotiate, sent troops behind Chinese lines and took control of China's road between Tibet and Xinjiang. China feinted in a distant disputed area, recaptured its road, and withdrew voluntarily to roughly its initial positions. The most significant clashes with the Soviet Union occurred over disputed river boundaries, where China took the traditional legal position that a river boundary ran down the middle of the river, whereas the USSR said that it must run down the Chinese side of the river.

parties, and by drawing lessons has made corrections since then. As Deng Xiaoping said, "We did not handle this problem well in the past. We have summed up our experiences in this regard."[8]

In the course of improving its relations with ASEAN countries, and especially while normalizing diplomatic relations with Indonesia, China made a series of specific promises not to tamper in the affairs of its neighbors and to promote positive economic and political ties. By all accounts, Beijing has honored those promises. China also retracted its concrete support for revolutionary movements in Africa and Latin America. It ceased to frown on U.S. military bases in the region; particularly in private diplomatic discussions, China acknowledged that the U.S. military bases played a useful role in stabilizing the region. Previously, China had celebrated instability and even made great efforts to enhance it.

China went on the peace path in Southeast Asia, opening up diplomatic relations with both Singapore and Indonesia. Relations with Indonesia had been strained since the country's 1965–66 revolution, which Jakarta believed to have been triggered by a Beijing-supported abortive communist coup. Trade and travel increased with Singapore and Indonesia as well as with Malaysia. The latter had long been profoundly suspicious of China because of its past support for the Communist Party of Malaya, relayed through Malaysia's huge Chinese community. China also moved from antagonism toward Thailand's very capitalist, U.S.-aligned government to an effective alliance with it in opposition to Vietnam's takeover of Laos and Cambodia. In 1990–92, Beijing cooperated increasingly with Western diplomatic efforts to resolve the warfare in

[8]Ji Guoxing, "Sino-ASEAN Relationship and Its Effects on US," *Asian Profile* (February 1990), p. 4. This article also contains the detailed commitments made to Indonesia, the Philippines, and others.

Cambodia; it curtailed weapons to the Khmer Rouge from 1990 onward. In 1990, China restored diplomatic relations with Vietnam, and in 1992 Premier Li Peng personally visited that country, following an earlier visit to Laos, in an effort to improve relations.

Most noteworthy of all was China's newfound conservatism toward its erstwhile ideological enemies, South Korea and Taiwan. The Chinese abandoned support of the North Korean confrontation with South Korea; on several occasions they actively intervened to prevent North Korean actions from threatening war on the peninsula. Most important, China intervened to dissuade North Korea from invading South Korea in the wake of the 1975 U.S. defeat in Vietnam.[9] Recently, China has refused to help North Korea with its nuclear programs; Beijing actively advocated a nuclear-free zone in the Korean peninsula, and expressed willingness "to cooperate in persuading Pyongyang to give it [the nuclear weapon program] up." This came at a time when preventing North Korea from obtaining nuclear weapons was the highest U.S. security concern in East Asia,[10] and Beijing was in fact very helpful to Washington.[11]

[9]See, for instance, Harry Harding, *A Fragile Relationship: The United States and China Since 1972* (Washington, DC: Brookings Institution, 1992), "China began to offer explicit support to peace and stability on the Korean peninsula, including discouraging Kim Il Sung from launching an attack against the south in the aftermath of the fall of Saigon in 1975" (p. 45).

[10]Cf. Paul Kreisberg, "China's Relations with Asian States," mimeo, Carnegie Endowment for International Peace, January 9, 1991, p. 24; Ji Guoxing, "Regional Approaches Towards Enhancing Security Confidence, and the Disarmament Process in the Northeast Asia," Shanghai Institute for International Studies, undated (the quote is from p. 3). Kreisberg is a senior scholar and former high State Department official; Ji's senior position at the government-sponsored Shanghai Institute makes his remarks authoritative.

[11]American government officials emphasize how helpful China has been in earlier years. In March 1993, China refused to go along with efforts to use

In addition, China conducted first an economic and then a diplomatic accommodation with South Korea, establishing normal diplomatic ties on August 24, 1992. Formerly, China had held that it would not recognize South Korea until the United States recognized North Korea. Now, North Korea was isolated, and China abandoned it further by floating proposals that the two Korean regimes should extend full diplomatic recognition to each other.[12] In December 1992, China announced that it would henceforth require all North Korean purchases to be paid for in hard currency, thereby depriving the North of a desperately needed source of imports and, if fully implemented, possibly pushing the regime toward its doom.[13] This treatment of an ally once described as being "as close as lips and teeth" was the ultimate symbol of China's abandonment of ideology in its foreign policy.

China also recognized Israel, signaling its abandonment of attempts to profit from extreme positions on Middle East political disputes. When the question arose in the UN Security Council whether to permit "Operation Desert Storm" against Iraq, China merely abstained. This permitted the rescue of Kuwait to occur. The Chinese made this decision despite strong PRC traditions opposing any kind of Western intervention in a Third World country. (Beijing's leaders expected to

---

the UN Security Council to intervene after North Korea rejected the Non-Proliferation Treaty. This did not mean that China was supporting North Korea, but that by then China was convinced that supporting Security Council intervention was the wrong means. China took some action on this issue in 1993, which led to a border clash in which Chinese soldiers were reportedly killed.

[12]Ji Guoxing, "Regional Approaches . . . ," p. 8.

[13]Nicholas D. Kristof, "Beijing Asks North Korea for Cash, Ending Barter," *International Herald Tribune,* December 30, 1992, p. 1. It is not clear how far this announcement was implemented.

be rewarded by the United States for such cooperation. They were shocked when, instead, the administration expressed anger that China had merely abstained and the Congress continued to press for economic sanctions on China.)

RAPPROCHEMENT WITH TAIWAN

Perhaps most dramatically, China has conducted a rapprochement with Taiwan, which harbors Beijing's greatest opponents. From 1949 through the 1970s, leaders on opposing sides regarded each other as war criminals. In 1958, China sought nuclear backing from the Soviet Union for an attack on Kuomintang offshore forces, and some of Eisenhower's advisers proffered nuclear options for defense of the islands (fortunately, cooler heads prevailed in both Moscow and Washington). Before reform began in 1979, trade and travel between the two territories was banned and huge concentrations of armed forces faced off across the Taiwan Strait. Into the 1970s, mainland forces regularly shelled the islands. Here was a fierce situation. Consider for instance the requirements imposed on Taiwanese units stationed on Quemoy and Matsu, the Taiwan-controlled islands nearest to PRC territory—they were frequently made to go to the mainland and come back with evidence of their stay there, including movie theater tickets, but best of all the insignia and ears of mainland soldiers.

The fortifications of Quemoy needed to be seen to be believed. In 1974, I traveled with a group of American scholars from Taipei to Quemoy on Madame Chiang Kai Shek's private DC-3. We flew fifty feet above the water so that our plane would be difficult to detect, and fourteen jet fighters flew above us for protection. On landing at Quemoy, the airstrip ran directly inside a mountain. Once inside, there was no need to go back out: the entire interior of the island had been carved into a livable habitat. One could travel anywhere on roads wide enough for a tank but covered by thirty meters of granite, a roof strong enough to absorb anything less than a direct hit by a large nuclear weapon. We had a banquet in one room. Adjoining it was a huge assembly hall that in wartime could be converted into a gigantic hospital. Our military guides told us that in all the world only Sweden had comparable defenses dug into its mountains. Outside, the fortifications were equally impressive.

At the beginning of reform (as we have seen), China offered Taiwan a "One country, two systems" deal of the kind subsequently promised to Hong Kong: Taiwan could keep its freer social system, capitalist economic system, government, and army, so long as it accepted the PRC flag. Taiwan refused, and continued its policy of no contacts with the mainland. But tensions soon declined, and the concentration of military force on the PRC side thinned out. Technically illegal trade between Taiwan and the PRC through Hong Kong increased, first gradually, then spectacularly. Informal contacts at international meetings rose geometrically. In 1989 it was a great breakthrough when the Governor of Taiwan's central bank went to Beijing for an Asian Development Bank meeting. By 1992, Taiwan-PRC trade and investment were the hottest spots in the world economy. Trade exceeded $7 billion in the year 1992, and cumulative Taiwan investment in the mainland was $8.4 billion or more in over 7,500 projects.[14] Tai-

---

[14]The figure $8.4 billion (for 7,565 projects) comes from MOFERT, as cited by *China Business Gazette*, vol. 2, no. 3 (January 18, 1993), p. 1, summarizing an article in *Economic Daily* of December 30, 1992. Estimates done on the Taiwan side range from $4 billion to $10 billion—a much broader range because much of the investment was technically illegal under

wan's low-tech industries migrated en masse across the Taiwan Strait. By 1992, Taiwan's shoe and toy industries, which are among the world's largest and most successful, were primarily manufacturing and exporting from bases on the mainland. Both governments were scrambling to create legal channels for this trade and investment, despite their continued pro forma political antagonism.

Between 1987 and 1992, Taiwanese tourists made more than 3 million visits to the mainland, spreading cash and knowledge of how much better life was in Taiwan. When I traveled across China in 1992, travel guides in every city reported Taiwan as their number-one source of visitors.

The diplomatic competition has become lighthearted. At a conference in 1992, I gave a speech highlighting many of the statistics used in Chapter I of this book. John Ni, the main spokesman for Taiwan in Hong Kong, was the next speaker. As I finished, he elbowed me in the ribs and said, "Hey, Bill, do you recognize those statistics?" I replied, "No, what do you mean?" He said, "Those are our [i.e., Taiwan's] statistics from twenty years ago."

Serious competition continues over diplomatic recognition and membership in international organizations. Taiwan will refuse direct travel and mail links until Beijing recognizes Taipei as an equal government of China and renounces any future use of force against Taiwan. Competition in military technology is keen. Beijing continues to fear that elections in Taiwan will bring to power secessionist forces to replace the current leadership which considers Taiwan part of China. But the degree of political rapprochement and economic intercourse now goes for beyond anything that seemed plausible

---

Taiwan law and therefore is deliberately hidden from Taiwan authorities. Taiwan exports to China may be $4 billion higher because of illegal shipments that do not transit Hong Kong.

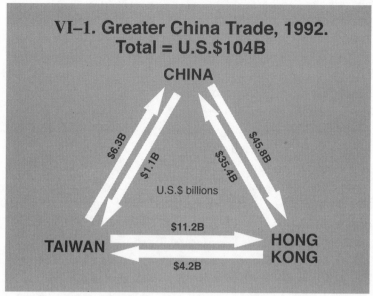

**VI–1. Greater China Trade, 1992.
Total = U.S.$104B**

CHINA

$6.3B

$1.1B

$35.4B

$45.8B

U.S.$ billions

TAIWAN

$11.2B

HONG
KONG

$4.2B

SOURCE: Hong Kong government statistics.

when reform began. Beijing's theory of the future is that China will become more prosperous and catch up economically and socially with Taiwan. Meantime Beijing will have proved in Hong Kong that the "One country, two systems" formula can be trusted.

If China's superior economic performance continues, the economic gap will indeed close, although it will take a generation or more to close completely, and reunification would become both more palatable and strategically inevitable. Meanwhile, a lot of bad things could still happen. Beijing's reform drive might weaken. A great political crisis might wrack the mainland or the Hong Kong example could go sour. Suppose a victory of independence-minded politicians on Taiwan creates a confrontation with the mainland. Then the trend of rapprochement could be at least temporarily reversed. This could happen. There are strong forces that support a Taiwanese identity separate from the mainland. The rapprochement with Beijing has mobilized those forces and elected far more of their politicians. But these separatist forces seem unlikely to push to the point of actually declaring independence. The road to accommodation is inevitably bumpy, but if properly handled not inevitably dangerous. So far, despite these important residual conflicts and uncertainties, the basic trend of the past decade has been to relax political tension, to reduce military competition, and to promote considerable economic integration. While Beijing has on principle refused to rule out the use of force for some contingency in the future, the period since reform began has seen a conflict that once threatened nuclear war and great power confrontation diminish into a politically wary economic love-fest. There is room for rapprochment to continue much further and for a very long time, and there is at least the possibility of reaching a stable relationship—not necessarily fulfilling either side's full aspirations—without military conflict or serious military tensions.

China's economic success means that the diplomatic competition between Beijing and Taipei is over—a clear victory for Beijing, despite Taipei's current efforts to regain a position in the United Nations and elsewhere. Taiwan's diplomatic position as a claimant for the whole of China has been waning since Washington went along in the 1971 shift of China's UN Security Council seat from Taipei to Beijing. Later its claim was fatally crippled in the 1979 shift of U.S. diplomatic recognition from Taipei to Beijing. Even so, the competitive behavior continues. Taipei still avidly seeks embassies and status through international organizations; it has been able to hang in on this level because of its superior trade system and the investment flows from Taiwan's economic superiority. Now

China has rejected autarky and become one of the world's great trading nations. The economic competitive advantage of Taipei has simply evaporated. It retains a key advantage, since it has moved to respect human rights and introduce democracy much faster; this too could diminish in the future.

However, the same economic opening of the mainland that has destroyed Taipei's diplomatic position has created a new and potentially far more important position for Taiwan as an influence on China's evolution. The magnetic attraction of Taiwan's higher living standards and freer society are the basis of the quotation from Ambassador Hummel in the epigraph to this chapter. The impact of Taiwan's contact with the mainland will be profound and pervasive. Already, life in Fujian Province, across the strait from Taiwan, is moving toward the Guangdong level. Taiwan has more than three times the population of Hong Kong, three times the foreign exchange reserves, and incomparably more heavy and high-technology industry. Its economic impact could be even stronger than Hong Kong's.

More important, Taiwan's potential political impact should be much greater than Hong Kong's. Taiwan evolved from a Bolshevik-type political system into, first, an extremely prosperous authoritarian system, and more recently a prosperous democracy. The enormous superiority of Taiwan's economic performance compared with the mainland's was a primary stimulus of the original mainland economic reform. The disparity in social life has been equally great. Taken together with the parallel examples of Hong Kong and neighboring countries, this will raise aspirations for comparable freedom in the mainland.

The progress of Taiwan—from near-totalitarian controls to brutal authoritarian rule to authoritarian pluralism to democracy—appeals to much of the mainland population. But not to Beijing's octogenarian leadership. They call this "peaceful evolution," and regard it as a Western plot. Chiang Kai Shek would have felt the same way about aspirations to Western-style freedom. The younger generations of China's leaders are much more flexible on taking the next steps. Already they feel the pressures that led to gradual change in Taiwan. The generation above fifty-five will usually look only one step ahead; those in their forties and younger will now debate seriously the possibility that the mainland will follow Taiwan's evolution through to a complete political liberalization when society is ready. The opening to Taiwan has assured that this debate will spread throughout all of China. Moreover, the debate will take place on very knowledgeable terms because of the omnipresence throughout China of visitors, goods, publications, and audio and video cassettes from Taiwan.

Meanwhile, the firestorm of trade and investment among Taiwan, Hong Kong, and the PRC consistently outpaces the growth of trade and investment anywhere else in the world. China's cheap land and labor (including highly educated labor) were the tinder for this firestorm. The money, technology, and marketing skills of Taiwan and Hong Kong were the oxygen. And the entrepreneurial organizations of Taiwan, Hong Kong, and increasingly Guangdong constituted the match that set off the firestorm.

THE COLLAPSE OF NIEO AND THE DIFFUSION OF TRADE TENSIONS

The late 1970s and early 1980s saw another great strategic development—the destruction of the Third World movement. In the mid-seventies, leading Democratic thinkers who subsequently occupied high foreign policy positions in Jimmy

Carter's administration held as an article of faith that the North-South split (between the rich and poor countries) was going to displace the East-West conflict (between the communist countries and the free world) as the central divide of global politics. The West appeared to be coming under successful challenge—morally, politically, and economically—by a Third World committed to radical reorganization of the world economy.

The sponsors of the New International Economic Order (NIEO) represented a majority of the world's countries and an overwhelming majority of the world's population. They believed that the world economy was unfairly organized by the rich countries in a way that condemned the poor countries to permanent dependence on the rich countries and therefore to insurmountable poverty. In this view, the rich countries were not partners in development but rather class enemies. The only way to break out of this poverty was a program that rejected multinational corporations, repudiated international banks, insisted upon national self-reliance rather than increasing interdependence, replaced the market for raw materials with a system of cartels, and reshaped world politics by building on the movement for such a new economic order. The real core of this program was the system of cartels. Each major commodity was to be controlled by a Third World cartel which would raise prices above market levels. Over all the individual cartels would be a supercartel. Similarly, the resources of the seabed would fall under the control of a gigantic organization run by the United Nations.

This political coalition, the institutions of the New International Economic Order, and the associated ideology of dependency theory were shattered by the rise of the smaller Asian economies and the subsequent success of China in following their lead.

By 1980, the combined trade of the smaller Asian economies exceeded Japan's, and their trade has subsequently expanded far more rapidly than that of Japan. Taiwan, South Korea, Thailand and Singapore broke all the shibboleths of the New International Economic Order. They exploited international markets rather than defying them; they tamed multinational corporations rather than banning them; they focused on education and competitive organization—that is, on human resources—rather than on natural resource cartels as the keys to development. They emphasized serving Western markets rather than self-sufficiency as the key to national revival. In all of this, they successfully challenged the West rather than being condemned to impoverished dependency.

This economic success split the Third World politically, defeated Latin America and Africa economically, and left the Third World movement intellectually bankrupt. Thus, the Third World movement lost its hold on the West, which was willing to feel responsible for underdevelopment if Third World countries were structurally trapped, but not if their poverty flowed from stubbornly wrong policies. In addition, the Third World movement became badly divided in interests—for instance, between those countries like Argentina which were pursuing a strategy of financial default and those (mostly Asian) countries like Indonesia which were benefiting immensely from traditional Western financial mechanisms.

China's example played a decisive role in the decline of the NIEO, even though China never disavowed the movement. Its switch into the Western camp moved a fifth of humanity out of the NIEO camp, and destroyed the alliance between communist radicalism and NIEO pauperism. While the success of the smaller countries had damaged the theory that Third World countries could not escape impoverished dependency, China's success undercut the popular argument that Taiwan and the others were just small special cases, and that the world economy could not accommodate any more entrants with this strategy.[15] At the end of the 1970s, when China's strategy was a gleam in Deng Xiaoping's eye, dependency theory was popular among leading professors in leading Western universities. At the end of the 1980s, it was a fading force in Western universities, far less important than Marxism had been in the 1960s. In contrast to the earlier view of the Non-Aligned

[15]There is a powerful desire in many circles to believe that the Asian pattern of success has come to an end and cannot be replicated elsewhere. For one version of this argument, see Robin Broad and John Cavanagh, "No More NICs," *Foreign Policy* 72 (Fall 1988). Their study is not just a straw man, because it was supported by the two most prestigious foreign policy institutes in the United States. They rely heavily on a case study of the Philippines, which they portray as a failed effort to create an NIC. But the Philippines never really followed the competitive model of the NICs, instead forming vast highly protected monopolies to siphon monopoly rents into the pockets of the leaders. The Broad/Cavanagh argument that the world is running out of markets for developing nations' products was first used by Nehru's economic planners shortly after India's independence. India had a dominant position in world textile trade, and India's planners were sure that the market was saturated, so they deliberately stifled the industry. Such foolishness greatly facilitated the poorer East Asian countries' subsequent takeoff; starting far behind India in every index of modernity, they soared past. When Herman Kahn and I gave the first briefings on the coming Pacific Asian takeoff in 1971–72, identical arguments were used to demonstrate that Taiwan and South Korea could not continue their growth for more than a few years. Roughly every three years, someone re-invents the argument. It is fallacious because there are so many diverse markets to be served. The shoe market started with just cheap sandals and now includes Nike Air Jordans and expensive Italian-designed women's shoes. Thailand makes the leather seat covers for BMWs and has a major industry pasting cashew-nut-halves back together. (One whole cashew nut is worth a lot more than two half cashew nuts.) The Asian takeoffs expand each of these markets. Broad and Cavanagh also misunderstand the nature of the model, saying that the PRC is not an example because its primary growth is domestic. Even when countries grow primarily from domestic sources, as virtually all the NICs do these days, the export orientation plays a crucial role in driving competitive efficiency.

Movement that the rich countries were the class enemy, the Jakarta Message summarizing the conclusions of the Non-Aligned Movement in 1992 stressed "a constructive dialogue between developed and developing countries . . . based on genuine interdependence."[16]

The superior performance of China and its smaller export-oriented neighbors has had other important consequences. The knowledge that even small countries without great resources can succeed economically has influenced national development policies as far away as Zimbabwe. Most important for geopolitics, it has diffused American and European responses to Japan. The smaller powers' successes belie any U.S. or EC argument that their trade problems are caused exclusively by malicious Japanese policies or exotic facets of Japanese culture. It therefore does limited good to rail at Japan. This diffusion of the trade problem has so far averted the risk of an early fracture of the Western alliance system by a trade crisis caused, say, by an American spasm of anti-Japanese protectionism, or an EC effort to cultivate its Russian option while dealing with Japan by economic isolation. Once again, China's success is decisive in this respect. In earlier times, it was not unusual for Americans to argue that the smaller countries were the arms of a Japanese octopus that had spread its tentacles to a group of smaller neighboring economies. But China is far too big and independent to be one arm of a Japanese octopus.

Thus China's seduction by the Pacific Asian miracle has created a turning point in world politics and economics. It has transformed the regional successes of a limited number of small countries into a decisive defeat for Communist insur-

[16]Quoted in Charles Smith and Suhaini Axnam, "Reason and Rhetoric," *Far Eastern Economic Review*, September 17, 1992, p. 10.

gencies, for disruptive regional irredentism, and for the global economic radicalism of the NIEO.

SEA BOUNDARIES

All of China's land borders are peaceful, but trouble remains over its territorial waters claims. China claims major island chains far from its mainland borders, together with territorial waters stretching virtually to the beaches of Malaysia and the Philippines. These claims are not just dormant history. Beijing has long made claims to the areas and has printed maps showing them as Chinese territory. On February 25, 1992, it passed a law specifically reinforcing its claim to vast territorial waters and demanding that ships passing through them obey PRC regulations: According to these, all submarines must now surface and aircraft must avoid the area overhead except as provided by agreements with the PRC.[17] These claims conflict with those of Japan, Vietnam, and most ASEAN countries, and they are more extensive than would be allowed under the archipelagic principle now generally accepted in international law.[18] They conflict with U.S. interests too, affect-

[17]Law of the People's Republic of China on the Territorial Sea and the Contiguous Zone, Order of the President of the People's Republic of China, No. 55, February 25, 1992. For a broad Chinese view of the historical background of the most intense dispute, that with Vietnam, see "China's Indisputable Sovereignty Over the Xisha and Nansha Islands," Document of the Ministry of Foreign Affairs of the People's Republic of China, January 30, 1980.

[18]The archipelagic principle specifies how far out from a archipelago the country concerned may claim, and specifies some of the details for drawing the resulting map.

ing, for instance, clandestine submarine transit of these waters.

Now China is hardly alone in these disputes. Territorial water claims, and associated claims to islands, remain a troubling issue throughout much of Asia. The most serious disputes pit Japan against Russia. The United States administers vast island archipelagos thousands of miles from its shores; while various fig leaves have been applied, these are basically strategic outposts that fell to the United States in World War II. Even under Cory Aquino, the Philippines had difficulty resisting the temptation to claim Guam, thousands of miles from the Philippines and the strategic headquarters of America's island empire. The Philippines also claims Sabah, which constitutes a large proportion of Malaysia's total land area.

The South China Sea island groupings called the Spratlys and the Paracels, along with the territorial waters rights associated with those islands, are subject to the conflicting claims of China, Taiwan, Vietnam, Malaysia, Brunei, and the Philippines. Originally, only Vietnam maintained significant garrisons in the South China Sea islands. The Vietnamese sent a force of troops to occupy islands among the Spratlys in 1975 and has since occupied numerous other islands. The Philippines has occupied a number of islands at least since the 1970s and garrisoned them with marines. Taiwan uses six hundred troops to garrison the Spratlys' biggest island, the only one with fresh water and a landing strip for aircraft. Among the several contending parties, Taiwanese officials have taken the most aggressive approach to controlling the islands, advocating surprise attacks by submarine and the like. In December 1992, a Taiwan interministerial committee published a draft "South China Sea Policy Outline" that characterized the regime's right to the Spratlys as "indisputable." Malaysia only began claiming islands in the 1980s. It occupied some in 1983 and 1986, and has been the most aggressive country in attempting economic development of disputed islands by building an airport and constructing tourist projects.[19]

As island competition heated up, China and Vietnam clashed in March 1988 in the Spratlys. In 1992, China leased oil rights to an American company, Crestone, and promised military protection to that company in case Vietnam reacted. (The Crestone lease infringed on sea areas claimed offshore from Vietnam's mainland, so this dispute went beyond island-based claims.) China's superior economic growth is gradually giving it a strategic advantage over Vietnam and the Philippines, whose inferior economies cannot sustain a naval competition.[20] China was among the earliest to stake its oil claims, and took no military action until long after Vietnam began seizing islands. Its strategy parallels that of the other claimants: to stake out as strong a negotiating position as possible before entering into talks. China has repeatedly said that developmental (but not sovereignty) issues are negotiable, and in 1992 publicly assured Vietnam, the most intense opponent, of its willingness to join negotiations. Former Indonesian Foreign Minister Mochtar Kusumaatmadja—Indonesia has the world's largest territorial waters claims—has expressed confidence that "China is not going to risk its relations with its South East Asian neighbors over the issue."[21] In sum, most of

[19]The most helpful brief summary of these issues is Robert G. Sutter, "East Asia: Disputed Islands and Offshore Claims—Issues for U.S. Policy," Congressional Research Service, Library of Congress of the United States, July 28, 1992. I am indebted to Professor Frances Lai and to U.S. military intelligence officers for accounts of how Taiwan officials have advocated very strong military action, such as quick submarine attacks, to dislodge their opponents from the disputed islands.

[20]Interview with Colonel Joanne DeLora, August 27, 1992.

[21]Dr. Mochtar Kusumaatmadja, "South East Asia: An Evolving New Regional Order," paper for International Workshop on "Challenges to Fishery Policy and Diplomacy in Southeast Asia," December 6–10, 1992.

the nearby countries are pursuing excessive claims but low-key tactics, looking toward eventual negotiation. China is running no major risks, making limited expenditures, and has been slower to move military forces than several of its neighbors.

DECLINING MILITARY EXPENDITURES

Many Asian states rode to prosperity in the 1980s in part by limiting their military expenditures and focusing budget priorities on economic development. Japan's military budget remained below 1 percent of GNP throughout the late eighties. In South Korea, Park Chung Hee, despite his background as an army general, cut military spending to 4 percent of GNP although his country was at that time the most severely threatened in the world. He raised it to 6 percent later, after the United States withdrew a division from his country. (The United States was spending 9 percent of GNP on defense.)[22] China followed: military expenditures as a share of GNP declined from 16 percent of GNP in the 1960s to 10.4 percent at the beginning of Deng's reform in 1979 to 3.7 percent in 1989. (The United States spent about 6 percent of GNP on the military in the 1980s.) Similarly, China cut the number of soldiers in its armed forces from 4.6 million in 1979 to 3.8 million in 1989.[23]

[22] *World Military Expenditures and Arms Trade 1963–1973* (Washington D.C.: U.S. Arms Control and Disarmament Agency, Publication 74, 1975), pp. 41, 61.

[23] *World Military Expenditures and Arms Transfers 1990* (Washington, D.C.: U.S. Arms Control and Disarmament Agency, 1990), p. 58, for both the budget figures and the manpower figures. There are methodologically confounding problems in comparing China with other countries and the sta-

A particularly startling indicator of China's reduction of military priorities is the country's tiny share of total regional arms imports.[24] As Chart VI-3 (page 344) shows, China's arms imports during its first decade of reform were one sixth of Vietnam's, half of near-pacifist Japan's, and only half of Taiwan's. While a big country can obviously make more of its arms domestically than a small country, China's arms imports are extraordinarily small compared to its size.

From 1988 onward, China began rebuilding its military selectively. After Tiananmen Square, internal security require-

---

tistics for one year in China with the statistics for another year. The source cited is the most authoritative U.S. government publication on the subject and the U.S. government has the best data. Pentagon and CIA publications are bedeviled by frequent changes in the way the statistics are calculated, making it difficult to get any consistent time series. Cf. the CIA's annual *Handbook of Economic Statistics* series, which presents a bewildering array of changes in the estimates for past years. There are also problems comparing Chinese statistics with other countries. Compared to U.S. figures, Chinese military budgets do not include many personnel and pension costs., nor do they include research and development, equipment modernization, local subsidies to soldiers, and the costs of conscription and demobilization. To get a military figure comparable to the U.S. figure, one would have to roughly double the Chinese military budget; on the other hand, to get a GNP figure comparable to the U.S. figure, one would have to quadruple the Chinese GNP number, for reasons reviewed in Chapter I. The ratio of military expenditures to GNP is therefore probably a conservative estimate compared with the U.S. figure. Moreover, the important point for this book is the downward trend in the first decade of reform, and this trend is so overwhelmingly strong that the data problems are dwarfed by its force.

[24]The chart and some of the comments about the changed regional environment are adapted from Andrew Mack, "Arms Proliferation in the Asian Pacific: Causes and Prospects for Control," Research School of Pacific Studies, Australian National University, mimeo, 1992. Mack is Australia's leading scholar of arms control issues. The paper, which summarizes a major research effort involving numerous scholars, is scheduled for future publication by the Carnegie Endowment.

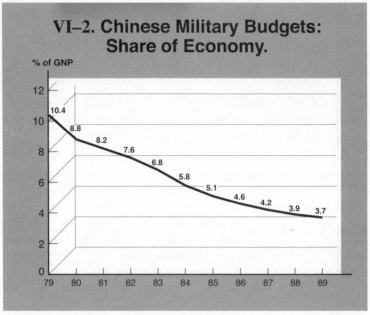

VI–2. Chinese Military Budgets: Share of Economy.

% of GNP

SOURCE: U.S. Arms Control and Disarmament Agency, 1990.
See text for the very substantial post-1989 rise for which no consistent data are available.

ments appeared more pressing. After the end of the Iran-Iraq War, military exports—one of the chief means by which the Chinese Army was supporting itself—simply collapsed. The smaller countries engaged in an arms race, and particularly strengthened their air and naval forces, a concern to China after the 1988 clash with Vietnam over the Paracels. And the major arms suppliers, particularly the Soviet Union and Western Europe, engaged in an arms fire sale that made arms purchases very attractive.

In this changed environment, China's number of soldiers hit bottom and then increased somewhat. In constant dollars, the army regained its earlier level of expenditure. As a CIA report to the U.S. Congress argued, "When adjusted for inflation, budgeted defense spending—which may account for only half of the country's military spending—fell 21 percent from 1984 to 1988, when the leadership faced no pressing security needs, but has risen 22 percent since 1988."[25] Because of the intervening growth of the economy, this means that military spending as a share of the economy remains very low—estimated by an expert at the U.S. Consulate General in Hong Kong at about 3.5 percent of GNP.[26] Adjusted for inflation, Chinese military expenditure has been growing at about 5 percent per year since 1988. Since GNP has been growing faster than that, the share of the military in the economy has continued to decline. The number of military personnel is expected by the CIA to resume its downward trend quite decisively, according to the same document, but the future spending trend is unclear. Most of the recent increase is for domestic security reasons.

[25]Directorate of Intelligence, Central Intelligence Agency, "The Chinese Economy in 1991 and 1992: Pressure to Revisit Reform Mounts," July 1992, p. 12. The report also notes that the budget had to increase somewhat to make up for lost profits from arms sales, which had declined 80 percent since the end of the Iran-Iraq War (p. 12). On the upturn in military expenditures, see Sheryl WuDunn, "China to Raise Arms Spending Again," *New York Times,* March 27, 1991, p. A3; and Nicholas D. Kristof, "China to Reward Army with 13% Increase in Military Budget," *New York Times,* March 22, 1992, p. 10; Daniel Southerland, "China Increases Spending on Military by 15 Percent," *Washington Post,* March 22, 1990, p. A33.

[26]Military analysts point out that journalists looking at the Chinese military budget drastically exaggerate the increases in military expenditure (typically stating that it has increased over 50 percent since 1989) by failing to discount for inflation. If the same journalistic criteria were applied to the Soviet military budget, they would say it has increased by hundreds of times, whereas it has actually fallen.

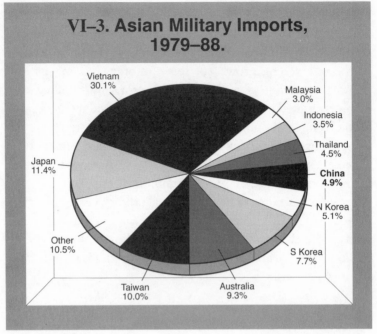

VI–3. Asian Military Imports, 1979–88.

Vietnam 30.1%

Malaysia 3.0%

Indonesia 3.5%

Thailand 4.5%

China 4.9%

N Korea 5.1%

S Korea 7.7%

Australia 9.3%

Taiwan 10.0%

Other 10.5%

Japan 11.4%

SOURCE: Andrew Mack, Arms Proliferation in the Asian Pacific, Canberra: Australian National University, 1992.

THE STRENGTHENING OF CHINA

A paradox of Pacific Asia turns history on its head: He who foregoes military ambitions gains in prosperity and power. This has been true of Japan, Thailand, and South Korea. The logic of the situation is clearer in a historical example. In 1963, North Korea's GNP was $2.3 billion and South Korea's was $3.8 billion. North Korea spent 12.2 percent of GNP ($280 million) on its military, while South Korea spent only 4.2 percent ($158 million). For a time, such figures implied total North Korean military superiority over South Korea. Although American troops corrected the imbalance, for many years there were widespread fears that the effort to defend the vulnerable South would eventually prove hopeless.

However, by 1991 North Korea's GNP was a mere $20.5 billion, while the South's had grown to $283 billion. South Korea was therefore very comfortably able to spend $10.8 billion on its military while the North's expenditure of half that much—$5.5 billion—was a crippling burden.[27] Meanwhile, all of North Korea's former allies were becoming friendly with South Korea. They wanted its trade and recognized its growing regional influence. Now South Korea is gaining an overwhelmingly superior position both militarily and diplomatically, while still spending only a moderate fraction of its economy on defense.

The same thing has happened to China. Over the past generation China has cut tremendously the burden of the military on the economy, and has reduced systematically other forms of geopolitical entanglement so that the country can focus its resources and its leaders' attention on economic development. The result has been an economic growth so fast that, even if military expenditure just grows proportionately with the economy, it can create a formidable power within a generation. In the meantime, national cohesion and international respect also improve. This raises China's international influence.

In the early 1990s, for the first time since before the Opium War, China faces no threat to its territorial integrity or national survival. British forces can no longer invade and partially dismember China for trying to curtail drug traffic. Japan no longer threatens to invade as it did throughout the first half of the twentieth century. The Soviet threat, which like North Korea put all its bets on military power, has collapsed. China is at peace with all its neighbors and has the respect of all of them. True, it has important differences with the United

---

[27]The 1991 figures are from International Institute of Strategic Studies, *The Military Balance 1992–1993* (London: Brassey's 1992), pp. 152–153.

States, but America does not threaten military invasion, and China's economic strengths limit its vulnerability to economic sanctions.

By contrast, the Soviet role in Asia has always been more limited than public image suggested. Soviet priorities focused on Europe and China. The USSR failed to come to terms with Japan. Had Moscow returned Japan's northern islands when Washington returned Okinawa, and then made economic ties to Japan a top priority, history could have been different. But Moscow did not choose to do this. Nor did it cultivate the dynamic smaller states of non-communist Asia. Because it remained autarkic and discounted the strategic importance of trade, it lacked the base to sustain a major presence in Asia. It could only fish in troubled waters, using its ideology and its limited military presence. As the ideology became less attractive, the waters became less troubled, and funds for military expansion dried up, Moscow almost vanished from Asian diplomacy. Despite the Vladivostok Initiative and a diplomatic effort far more vigorous than Washington's, Gorbachev once again failed to agree with Japan. He conferred on Boris Yeltsin a political base so weak that Yeltsin could not return Japan's Northern Islands and thereby gain its assistance in rebuilding Russia's economy. This series of failures adds up to as great a strategic debacle as any in Soviet postwar history.

Moreover, China's strengths are no longer just the mirror image of its neighbors' weaknesses. The best measure of potential military power is GNP measured on a purchasing power parity basis. By this measure, China's economy is already becoming a competitor of Japan and within a generation may well be comparable to the United States'. China is a major nuclear power, with moderately sophisticated nuclear warheads and fairly long range delivery systems. Its military, shrinking in size, will soon have the ability to project limited force overseas. It has longer range aircraft, with a new refueling capability, and its navy is being modernized. So short-term restraint is leading to long-term power. If economic growth continues, China will become a major power by any standards.

A crucial consequence of China's success has been to integrate its economy with the economies of Hong Kong and Taiwan and to begin a process of political healing. China by itself is the world's third biggest economy. If one treats Taiwan and Hong Kong as component parts of China, then greater China already has the production and trade of a big power. These are the statistics of a potential superpower. Because the three economies are effectively integrated already, this is not just a fanciful theoretical calculation. Any country competing with China competes with the integrated economy of greater China.

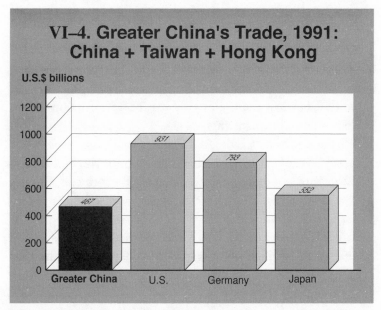

VI–4. Greater China's Trade, 1991: China + Taiwan + Hong Kong

U.S.$ billions

SOURCE: IMF, Taiwan, and Hong Kong government statistics.

CHINA'S PACIFIC ASIAN INFLUENCE

China's economic success has had a more subtle effect on the morale, sense of identity, and direction of the overseas Chinese communities in Singapore, Malaysia, Indonesia, Thailand, and elsewhere. There is a widespread sense of exhilaration here, a feeling that after centuries of weakness China is once again on the path to greatness. This unwritten pleasure is seldom expressed to non-Chinese, but it exists, and it is having a palpable impact as the business leaders of the overseas Chinese communities visit their ancient home villages, invest there, build schools and temples and hospitals, provide advice to local authorities and, in the case of the more influential, to planners in Beijing. To take just the most prominent example, former Singapore Prime Minister Lee Kwan Yew has become a regular commuter to Beijing, where he is a respected adviser.

In Southeast Asia, China's success is mainly positive, creating a new economic stimulus. But Indonesia and the Philippines, which have moved up the development ladder more slowly than the others, now have reason to regret their dawdling with economic reform. China has moved so far ahead of them that in most industries they can no longer compete for export-oriented investment.

Throughout the Chinese communities of Asia, there is a specific sense of China's finally gearing up for successful competition with Japan. Ever since the Meiji Restoration, China's adjustment to the West's intrusion has been consistently inferior to that of Japan. China was militarily humiliated by the British and others in the nineteenth century; Japan was not. China was humiliated diplomatically by Japan's Twenty One Demands in 1915 and militarily by the establishment of Manchukuo in 1931 and the full-scale Japanese invasion in 1937. Economically, following World War II Japan outstripped everybody, including especially China—a case of the loser climbing over the winner. Now there is a sense that China can hold more than its own in competition with Japan, if Chinese leaders maintain the momentum of reform. Japan's government is responding warily but with general approval to this development, preferring the regional stability that would accompany Chinese success. The Japanese certainly hope that China's success will be moderate rather than spectacular, because they do not want to have to compete with a neighboring superpower. But one thing is certain—Japan does not want to see China break down like the Soviet Union and create floods of refugees, an ecological disaster, and outbreaks of civil warfare.

Japanese businesses are keen to exploit the China market and the export platform but are particularly hesitant about transferring technology to China, and more hesitant too, about becoming dependent on a Chinese manufacturing base than they were with the smaller countries.[28] Clearly, already in the Japanese mind lies a fear of Chinese competition that is quantitatively different from, say, any fear of Malaysian competition.

The hesitation over the China market, combined with the bursting of Japan's financial bubble in the early 1990s, created an opportunity for non-Japanese firms to move into China's big new market without facing the full brunt of Japanese competition. Hong Kong and Taiwan got far ahead of Japan. American firms (Motorola, Avon, Procter & Gamble, Kodak, and many others) seized a strategic position that they might otherwise have had difficulty obtaining. China aided in

[28]On the point about technology transfer, I am indebted to Robert Scalapino, "China and Its Neighbors—Old and New Trends," paper for Asia Society Conference on China and East Asia: Implications for American Policy, 1991, p. 10.

achieving this balance. It certainly strongly preferred not to have its leading firms dominated by Japanese investment in the way South Korean firms have been.

Against this, West Europeans were delayed when they became preoccupied by unrealistic expectations of success in Eastern Europe, but they were beginning to stampede into China by 1992.[29] As an investment adviser, I ridiculed the idea, prominent from the time of the Berlin Wall's collapse, that Eastern Europe would replace Pacific Asia as the center of world growth. Few European firms listened at that time. But by 1992 they were disillusioned with Eastern Europe and had developed a mania for China. So great was the pressure in my office that it became difficult to justify working on other countries. In the meantime some shrewd American firms had acquired a crucial head start.

Can this trend continue? The American predilection for using economic sanctions or the threat of sanctions to influence China's domestic policies may well shift the balance of advantage away from the United States and toward enthusiastic European firms and even toward the Japanese. Threats by the U.S. Congress to China's most-favored-nation status slowed down American investment into China, and in important cases, including that of a major telephone company, actually convinced firms that they had to scale back existing commitments. Because the Chinese economy is so large, and constitutes such a large share of the available new opportuni-

[29]These comments are based on the writer's personal experience as an investment adviser to West European firms, whose interest in China swamped all other demands on his professional life in the second half of 1992, and as a governor of the American Chamber of Commerce in Hong Kong, which is an ideal perch from which to observe what American firms are doing. Japanese companies swarmed into Dalian and other Northeast Chinese areas in 1992 to a degree that could eventually see a Japanese-dominated enclave of considerable size.

ties in the 1990s, this competitive scramble for position will strongly influence the shape of global economic competition, and ultimately of geopolitical competition, in the early twenty-first century.

CHINA AND CENTRAL ASIA

In Central and South Asia, China is becoming a major power by default. The fragmentation of the Soviet Union has reopened the ancient contest for influence in Central Asia, a region three times the size of Western Europe. Prior to Soviet dominance, this area was one of the great trade, cultural, and political crossroads of the world. Along with Afghanistan and Pakistan, Central Asia includes the ex-Soviet states of Kazakhstan, Kyrgyzstan, Tajikistan, Turkmenistan, and Uzbekistan (familiarly known as the "stans"), impoverished, ethnically fragmented, politically unstable societies with all the problems of post-Soviet Russia and little of its education and industrialization. Some of them still possess major weapons stores, armaments factories, nuclear facilities, and even nuclear weapons. They are, in short, important, desperate, and greatly in need of stability. Will China provide it?

The primary potential influences on Central Asia are India, Russia, Turkey, Iran, and China.[30] India—non-Islamic,

[30]A useful survey of Central Asian strategic developments can be found in Rajan Menon and Henri J. Barkey, "The Transformation of Central Asia: Implications for Regional and International Security," *Survival,* vol. 34, no. 4 (Winter 1992–93), pp. 68ff. However, this survey neglects the China factor. See "The Silk Road Catches Fire," *The Economist,* December 26, 1992–January 8, 1993, pp. 30–32, for some current economic perspectives, and Martha Brill Olcott, "Central Asia On Its Own," *Journal of Democracy,* vol. 4, no. 1 (January 1993), for a foretaste of the potentially catastrophic political disintegration that is occurring.

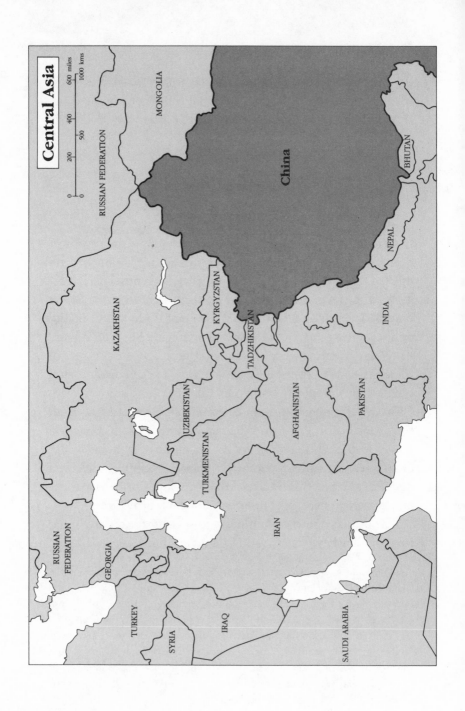

economically weak, and preoccupied with internal troubles—
is not a major contestant in this era of history. Russia is not
only the hated former imperialist country but also a model of
failure. Moreover, a large part of the Russian population is
heading back to Russia. The Soviet legacy (and Russia's
source of influence at present) is a collection of floundering
former communist bureaucracies which may well look to each
other for ideas and support.

There are some counterbalancing forces. Russia still feels
responsible for the 9 million Russians living in Central Asia.
There remain powerful Russian traditions, supported by powerful government and military interest groups, that tie Russia
to the power struggle in Central Asia. Moreover, although the
Russian economy has collapsed, the country retains enormous
military power. If the civilian democratic authorities continue
to fail to revive the economy, the prestige and power of the
Russian military could return.

The other three countries—politically secular and cultur-
ally Islamic Turkey, fundamentalist Islamic Iran, and secular
China—all exercise rising influence. An increasingly prosperous Turkey serves as a beacon of relative affluence and therefore a model for Muslims who have strong hopes for modernization. Crucially, the languages of Central Asia, except for
Tajikistan, are Turkic. Fundamentalist Iran offers ideological
solace and a strong sense of identity for Central Asians who
feel cast adrift and hopeless in the quest for modernization.
Iran is the strongest influence in Tajikistan, whose people
speak Persian. However, Turkey and Iran are both hampered
in their search for hegemony by major separatist movements,
most notably the Kurds in Turkey and the Azeris in Iran.

China is hampered by being largely non-Muslim and having restive Muslim minority groups, particularly in the Turkic
area of the Xinjiang Uyghur Autonomous Region. But
whereas the Azeris form 25 percent of the Iranian population,

the Uyghurs (the principal Turkic minority of northwest China, along with smaller ones such as the Kazakhs) are only 7 million out of 1.2 billion, and other Muslim minorities are also dismissively small. China has by far the biggest economic magnet. For formerly communist countries, it is simply the sole successful model of how to get from today's socialist poverty to the economic modernization they all seek. According to journalists traveling in the region, China is also attractive because it has merely sought to trade and, in contrast with Iran and Turkey, has not made assertive efforts to obtain political influence.[31] Beijing's political interests have been defensive—the avoidance of disorder that could spread into Xinjiang—rather than national assertion in the mode of Iran and Turkey.

The strategy has worked. Indeed, China's trade with the area is spectacularly successful. Xinjiang, the vast autonomous region of the Uyghur minority, is growing as fast as Guangdong; Chinese officials eagerly seek assignment to a region that was once a social analogue of Soviet Siberia, because the explosion of trade now offers so many opportunities for wealth. The Silk Road has effectively reopened, and, not to put too fine a point on it, the impoverished inhabitants of the former Soviet Union are willing to sell virtually anything they have and eager to buy the attractive modern goods, as well as the delicious melons and other foods, that are now abundant in China. So great has been the rush of impoverished Russians to China that the Chinese authorities find themselves in a dilemma over how to cope with the social and health problems caused by the large number of Russian women who have mi-

---

[31]This comment has been made by a number of analysts and travelers, but my understanding of the point is particularly indebted to James Clad, a former correspondent who is presently a senior associate at the Carnegie Endowment in Washington, D.C.

grated into Chinese cities to become prostitutes. On a more salutary basis, the vitality of Kashgar, a closed city until a few years ago which is now once again one of the world's most colorful and exciting markets, symbolizes Chinese commercial centrality in the reopened bazaar of Central Asia.

The speed with which the old Silk Road has reopened is so rapid as to be hard to describe. A few years ago, even my daughter's high school class was barred from visiting Kashgar. In July 1992, my family visited Urumchi, the provincial capital of the Xinjiang Uyghur Autonomous Region. We stayed at the Holiday Inn, a Hong Kong joint venture with Swiss management. I received a fax saying my older daughter was undergoing emergency surgery in Tokyo, and was able to communicate with Tokyo and Hong Kong effortlessly by international direct-dialing telephone. The following day, we watched a CNN broadcast of Governor Patten's arrival in Hong Kong. The content of the broadcast was extremely anti-Chinese, emphasizing an interview with Hong Kong's most anti-Chinese personality (Emily Lau), and containing factually inaccurate statements that China had broken its agreements over Hong Kong; but it was broadcast without interruption. All of this would have been unimaginable just five years earlier.

No nation will dominate Central Asia, but in the near future China's influence seems likely to increase more rapidly than that of any other power. The battle for influence will be a classic game of "Scissors, Paper, Stone." China will have the money. Russia will have the weapons. Iran will have the disruptive populist ideology. Turkey will have the model of successful Islamic modernization. To the east in Mongolia, which is the size of Western Europe, China will be a hegemon because there is simply no economic alternative and because Mongolia is full of resentment at Moscow's colonial-style treatment during the period of Soviet domination. Throughout the region, the world may come to welcome whatever degree of stabilizing influence China can provide. The other countries are either too politically fragmented (Russia), too economically weak (Turkey and India), or too interested in creating instability (Iran) to serve as foundations of stability. Already between twenty and forty thousand people have died in the civil war in Tajikistan, and it seems likely that many more will die there and elsewhere. Foreign aid will not stabilize such chaotic situations; it will merely go in the front door as aid and out the back door as capital flight. There is only one geopolitical foundation for stability in the region: China. There is only one model for successful reform of these kinds of economies: China.

CHINA AND SOUTH ASIA

The Chinese connection to Central Asia adds up to another defeat for India, which has long seen itself as a major competitor of China for the future of Asia. India has long pursued a much more expansive policy than China, with thrusts toward Pakistan, Sri Lanka, and Bangladesh that have no counterpart in contemporary Chinese policy. India has had a navy more configured for overseas power projection—two carriers versus none for China—whereas China's has been more configured for coastal defense.[32] (China does have one strategic submarine for which India has no counterpart, since China had a potential nuclear problem with both superpowers

[32]China has recently considered buying one carrier from Ukraine, but does not presently have one. China's fleet is more numerous than India's but for most of modern history has had no significant blue water capability. India has tried harder but its capability remains very limited.

whereas India did not). Most important of all, India is a Soviet-style economy based far more on support for national military ambitions than China's has been. India was not only trade-dependent on the Soviet Union but organized with the same priority for military-related heavy industry and electronics that was the key to Soviet industrial management.

The Chinese situation is different. China made horrific errors in its efforts to build its civilian economy during the Great Leap Forward and the Cultural Revolution. It also made some very costly strategic decisions, such as resorting to autarky and relocating much of its industry to the interior to render it more defensible. But the chief task for most of the past generation has been to build a civil society and a civilian economy, and to render them defensible. Misleading ideological labels have long obscured the fact that in its international ambitions and industrial organization India was closer to the Soviet Union than China was. As a result, India faces many of the former Soviet Union's problems.

India has only been saved from bankruptcy and even worse impoverishment by its market-oriented agriculture, and by a more rapid breakdown of state controls over light and medium industry than occurred in the Soviet Union. The breakdown of controls has been more rapid and important than deliberate liberalization, although significant policy liberalization has occurred. However, because India's central government is too weak to force through the painful reforms that China has imposed, the prospects for decisive improvement are poor, even though the efforts of the Rao government in 1992 and 1993 show that the senior leaders know what is required.

There was a time when India's economy was a serious competitor to China. No longer. In March 1993, I attended a conference of the Young Presidents Organization in Guangzhou, along with chief executives from companies all over the world. When I arrived at dinner the second night, the Indian delegates all clustered around me in a state of excitement. They had played hookey from the conference and gone out to visit the local markets. When they saw up close the way people dressed, the shops full of high-quality goods, and the availability of luxury goods from all over the world, they were astounded. Weren't all these things smuggled, they asked. Why didn't the police put a stop to it, as they would have done in India? How could people be living so well? (They also argued forcefully that an irreversible tide of reform is gathering in India, so the future of India may prove better than the present.)

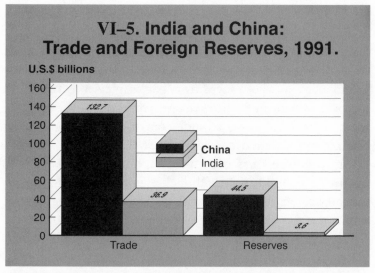

SOURCES: IMF; International Financial Statistics, December 1992; Directions of Trade, June 1992.

While China's understated official GNP statistics mask its superiority even today, in reality it is outstripping India in the same way that South Korea outstripped North Korea, and for much the same reasons. For the future, one might posit a scenario for China becoming immobilized and for India successfully implementing a reform policy along the lines of the present program of Prime Minister Rao; but for the time being, China's success has created a commanding lead and considerable momentum, while India's relative failure brought it to the brink of bankruptcy in the second quarter of 1991. The level of political violence and bloodshed is so much higher in India than in China that they cannot be compared on the same scale. This violence constitutes a great impediment to economic development and unified national policy. In sum, a combination of economic magnetism and non-threatening politics will make China a principal arbiter of Central Asia's future and will—more unwittingly than from ambition—quash for at least a generation the geopolitical ambitions that India has pursued from independence through the 1980s.

WHAT CAN GO WRONG?

The current situation appears almost idyllic. Chinese people's lives are improving immensely, and Chinese economic growth is stimulating growth elsewhere. While Chinese influence is spreading, so far the spread is peaceful, Japanese-style. China's focus on economic development reduces potential geopolitical enthusiasms—as in other countries. But this peaceful Chinese economic expansion and graceful regional reequilibration could break down. The risks are very different from the 1990s onward than they were in the previous generation because Soviet influence has vanished, Central Asia has become a vacuum, China has rejuvenated, U.S. military power and regional political support have declined, and Japan has been somewhat cast adrift.

One risk derives primarily from other countries' reactions to the Chinese takeoff. Like the Japanese, the rest of Asia is happy to see China's economy growing and happy to see China stable for once, but potentially very unhappy at China's becoming a dominant regional power. The Mongolians, cut loose from the embrace of the former Soviet Union, are happy to be free but terrified to be alone with no big neighbor but China. While China has so far done nothing untoward, the long history of mutual conquest (the Mongols ruled China from the year 1279 to 1368 and China has dominated the Mongols for long periods) creates anxiety. Likewise, Vietnam's current disputes with China over offshore islands appear more manageable than the legacy of a millennium of conflict. Non-communist Southeast Asians alternate between happiness over their current relationships with China and concern that this growing whale will fill the whole pond. Japan, which felt comfortable relying on the United States for protection during the Cold War, may feel compelled to build its own forces in an era when Washington takes an increasingly tough line with Tokyo and does not feel as compelled to shelter Japan from China as it once did from Russia. In short, Asia fears that China's economic dynamism and military power could some day become harnessed to an assertive nationalism. The policy consequences of these fears could themselves trigger a vicious circle of conflict.

A regional arms buildup provides one early warning of potential future problems. Russia's fire sale on armaments, anxiety over the weakening U.S. role, and concern about China's future intentions could stimulate a major regional arms race and a vicious circle of mutual anxieties.

Another regional problem could arise from inside China as a consequence of an enormous error the reformist regime has made. Under Deng, the government has gone much too far in abandoning central responsibility for a variety of functions, from education to the military, telling teachers and soldiers to become entrepreneurs and support themselves. English departments and platoons should not become too entrepreneurial, and the entrepreneurship of the Chinese military could turn it—or parts of it—into a dangerous force independent of the government. The Thai and Indonesian examples demonstrate that the outcome of an entrepreneurial military need not be bad for either the country or the region, but the risks are real. In 1992, the senior leadership of the Thai army got temporarily out of control and threatened to wreck the Thai system. In 1980, elements of the Korean military seized political power and used it for nearly a decade in ways that threatened the national development consensus. Fortunately, both those episodes ended in humiliation of what could have become rogue leaderships. China runs greater risks, because the national political leadership has in the past made such disastrous errors, because the military has such huge enterprises so divorced from central political control, and because the hostility of the United States toward China can potentially be employed as an excuse for a strong military role to protect national sovereignty.

The risk here is that some combination of internal breakdown and foreign hostility could lead to a rogue military leadership on the model of Japan in the 1930s. In other Asian countries this risk has declined over time because economic success has stimulated broad public support for the civilians who implemented the strategy of economic rejuvenation, because the successful economies have become self-evidently too complex to be run by soldiers, and because foreign threats have diminished as the successful economies funded more capable armies. These trends will also emerge in China, but they work slowly and more things can go wrong in China's case.

A third form of regional breakdown could occur because the United States loses its capacity to mediate Pacific Asia's conflicts and buffer the huge bursts of energy created by its development. The U.S. presence is a principal reason why there has been no second Korean War, no serious warfare between Beijing and Taipei, no major war between neighboring Southeast Asian states, no dangerous worsening of Japanese-Chinese tensions. The sublimation of national ambitions into domestic economic development has created a powerful trend toward more peaceful relations, but that trend would have been interrupted time after time without the moderating diplomacy of Washington backed by the indispensable presence of American military forces.

At the end of the Cold War, Washington is much more ideologically assertive, especially about communism in China, and much more economically assertive, especially about capitalism in Japan, than it was in the mid-1980s. This new assertiveness, and the fact that most Asian countries do not back it, weakens Washington's acceptance as regional arbiter even if the United States continued to hold its earlier economic and military stature. In fact, America's economic and military stature have declined enormously. For instance, the loss of the Philippine bases (Clark Air Base to a volcano, Subic Naval Base to then-Vice President Quayle's diplomacy)[33] has put in doubt U.S. ability to support a conventional defense of South

---

[33]For some reason the politics of the loss of Subic have never been explained to the American public. During a coup attempt in the Philippines, which occurred while George Bush was abroad negotiating with Gorbachev, Vice President Quayle pressed a decision to stage an American show of air support for Cory Aquino. Up to that point, the left in the Philippine Congress had opposed the bases while the right had supported them. (The majority of Filipinos strongly supported them.) After the coup, the right, whose leading figures had backed the coup attempt, joined the left in voting out the bases. Whether Quayle's move was a good one depends on one's perspective; what does not depend on perspective is the resultant huge reduction of American power in the Western Pacific.

Korea even if the U.S. defense budget were not declining. This leaves American defense of South Korea completely dependent on Chinese good will in not supporting North Korea.

These three scenarios are not mutually exclusive. They could occur in combination or in sequence. It is in the context of such scenarios that some of the local conflicts could assume much larger significance. By themselves, a regional arms race, or a clash in the South China Sea, or a local confrontation over Taiwan or North Korea, or even a long-term rivalry between Japan and China, should be quite manageable. But if U.S.-Chinese relations have broken down, or if Japan feels undefended against a resurgent China, or the Chinese military is looking for an excuse to assert itself and developments have made the Chinese public sympathetic to its assertions, or if some other combination of the breakdown scenarios should occur, then local conflicts could easily escalate into a regionally dangerous confrontation. In all of these scenarios, the power of China and the importance of the Chinese-American relationship are increasingly important.

IN THE MEANTIME, China's conversion to the Pacific Asian formula has not just created an economic success. It has both seduced China into abandoning its principal geopolitical ambitions and paradoxically granted it a geopolitical position superior to anything China has experienced in several centuries. It has fundamentally altered regional and global politics. In the process, it has delivered the *coup de grâce* to regional communist insurgencies, to leftist radicalism in many regions of the world, and to the Third World movement. This transformation of China's position began a decade before the Soviet collapse, and its most important attendant consequences were locked in before the Soviet debacle. The new situation created by the transformation of Chinese policies helped the United States fulfill almost every major goal of Washington in the past generation. Regional stability and the consolidation of the free world regimes have been the holy grails of American policy, and China has moved from being the greatest antagonist of those goals to becoming, along with Japan, the strongest regional supporter of them. Meanwhile, however, success has led Washington to move the goal posts, and the new situation has created new dilemmas for the United States.

VII

||||||||||||||||||||||||||||||||||||||||||||||||||||||

THE UNITED
STATES AND CHINA

*There are essential differences between China and the United
States in their social systems and foreign policies. However, the
two sides agreed that countries, regardless of their social systems,
should conduct their relations on the principles of . . . non-
interference in the internal affairs of other states. . . .*

—THE SHANGHAI COMMUNIQÚE, FEBRUARY 27, 1972, ESTABLISHING THE
TERMS OF RENEWED RELATIONSHIPS BETWEEN CHINA AND THE UNITED STATES.

*"Our policy will seek to facilitate a peaceful evolution of China
from communism to democracy. . . ."*

—WARREN CHRISTOPHER, SECRETARY OF STATE-DESIGNATE, TESTIFYING AT HIS
CONFIRMATION HEARINGS ON THE CLINTON ADMINISTRATION'S FOREIGN POLICY
PRIORITIES, JANUARY 13, 1993

Much of the future of the world will depend on the
U.S.-Chinese relationship. Economically, China
presents the United States with the greatest opportunities of the coming generation, for instance, the largest
market in the 1990s for aircraft, power plants, and telecom-
munications, and also the greatest difficulties in ensuring fair
dealing. Strategically, China's emphasis on stability and
peaceful relations with its neighbors resolves all the largest
strategic problems the United States traditionally faced in

Asia, but China's arms sales create the risk of chains of nuclear proliferation and instability. In human rights, China's new prosperity and diminution of totalitarian controls constitute one of the most positive contributions to human dignity that has occurred in the twentieth century, but China remains a harshly authoritarian country with the whole gamut of political prisoners, arbitrary rule, restrictions on freedom, and undemocratic politics. Depending on how the two nations manage these balances, China and the United States will settle into either Cold War II or a conflictual collaboration for stability and prosperity.

The central strategic reality of the relationship is a huge shared interest in continued regional peace and the continuation of the great Asian economic takeoff that has improved the lives and consolidated the politics of almost 2 billion people. The United States has stated regional stability as its core interest for at least two generations, and for China it is the primary assumption behind the national strategy of rejuvenation through economic growth. The other core strategic realities are straightforward. China is an extremely important influence on global politics and the global economy. China is not an aggressive power, but rather is committed for the indefinite future to a focus on domestic economic development. It is extremely unlikely to disintegrate as the Soviet Union did, and it would be bad for the Chinese people and disruptive for the entire world if it did. China's economy is sufficiently sound, and its financial position so strong, that it can only be hurt, not defeated, by U.S. trade sanctions. The United States seems to have committed itself to working through the UN Security Council on major international issues such as the civil war in the former Yugoslavia, and such action requires Chinese acquiescence. The United States also needs Chinese cooperation in Korea and elsewhere.

To put the relationship in perspective, it is useful to suppose that in February 1972, either Richard Nixon or Henry Kissinger had predicted that by 1991, Chinese foreign policy would be at peace with all its neighbors. It would have succeeded in rapprochement with the Soviet Union, both before and after the Soviet collapse of 1989, and developed a highly cooperative relationship with Japan. It would intervene diplomatically against aggressive North Korean moves toward South Korea, would oppose North Korean acquisition of nuclear weapons, would perceive South Korea as a mentor, would open diplomatic relations with South Korea and welcome a rapid expansion of South Korean trade and investment. It would be welcoming visits by senior officials from Taiwan, as well as several million tourist visits from that territory, would give preferential treatment in China to land ownership by Taiwanese, and would attract large investments from Taiwan. It would cut off all support of guerrilla movements in non-communist Southeast Asia, develop supportive diplomatic and economic ties with every non-communist government in the area, and even quietly support the presence of U.S. bases. China's premier would visit Vietnam to improve ties, and China would support a UN peace plan for Cambodia. It would balance its diplomacy in the Middle East by opening an embassy in Israel. And it would accede, in the face of its most dearly held anti-imperialist principles, to UN Security Council authorization of a U.S.-led war on Iraq. On the economic side, China would transform from autarky into one of the world's great trading nations. It would sign intellectual property agreements that most of the Third World had refused to sign. And it would agree to wide-ranging transformations of its economy as part of a bid to join the ultimate capitalist club, GATT.

Had Kissinger or Nixon ventured to make such predictions, they would have been ridiculed as self-serving utopian nonsense. Today, that "utopia" is reality. Since America welcomed it into the system in 1972, China has become a supporter of stability in world politics.[1]

MAJOR CHINESE-AMERICAN ISSUES

Relationships between the United States and China are bedeviled by military, sovereignty, economic, and human rights issues. The details of these are evanescent, but the problems of balance, perception, and political gamesmanship are constant, as are many structural problems.

Military Issues

China is selling Pakistan, Iran, Syria, and Algeria vital elements of the ability to build nuclear weapons and to deliver them, as well as high-technology conventional weapons that Washington fears might destabilize certain key balances in the Middle East and South Asia.[2] Since the Indian nuclear detonation of 1974, the U.S. government has worked hard and suc-

---

[1]A small number of journalists and strategic thinkers have misinterpreted China as aggressive and destabilizing by misstating key facts. The most egregious is Ross H. Munro, "Awakening Dragon: The Real Danger in Asia Is from China," *Policy Review* (Fall 1992). Such accounts rely heavily on stating China's defense budget without adjustment for inflation. (By that standard the Russian budget is now so large that Moscow is ready to conquer the universe.) They also portray China's actions in the Spratlys, as if they were unilateral actions that had no Vietnamese, Taiwan, or Filipino analogues, and portray commercial military projects, for instance in Burma, as if they represented strategic thrusts.

[2]For a survey of precisely what China is selling, see Richard A. Bitzinger, "Arms to Go: Chinese Arms Sales to the Third World," *International Security*, vol. 17, no. 2 (Fall 1992).

cessfully to limit the spread of nuclear arms, as well as biological and chemical arms. China has Washington's non-proliferation policy to thank for ending fast-moving Taiwan and South Korean nuclear weapons programs in the 1970s.[3] Nuclear non-proliferation policy is currently at a particularly delicate point where it could either collapse or be reinforced for another generation.

The Chinese military has a particular incentive to sell military technology because its budget has been cut down so drastically. As a major American study concluded: "The reforms of the Deng era left the military with less power, less unity, less money, and reduced responsibility for the modernization of China. . . . Arms sales not only produced hard currency for the military but also validated its achievement."[4] Moreover, as the same study shows, the central government often exercises very limited scrutiny over foreign sales by the major military firms. The People's Liberation Army (PLA) had a great burst of sales in the 1980s due to the Iran-Iraq hostilities, but today sales are a tiny fraction of what they once were. The 1991 Gulf War showed that most Chinese technologies were obsolete. That has left the PLA without much competitive advantage except to sell what others won't. It is reassuring that China is not making these sales out of some insidious grand strategic design. The motive is cash. But such sales can have dangerous consequences, and the diffusion of responsibility makes authoritative policy negotiations between Washington and Beijing difficult.

The United States wants full Chinese adherence to the Mis-

---

[3]On Asian nuclear non-proliferation issues in the 1970s, see William H. Overholt, *Asia's Nuclear Future* (Boulder, Co: Westview Press, 1978).

[4]John W. Lewis, Hua Di, and Xue Litai, "Beijing's Defense Establishment: Solving the Arms-Export Enigma," *International Security*, vol. 15, no. 4 (Spring 1991), p. 100.

sile Technology Control Regime (MTCR), an agreement among Western countries to limit the ranges and payloads of missiles sold to certain countries. Under U.S. pressure, China proffered in 1992 a written promise to accept the basic MTCR guidelines and parameters. While Beijing has promised to adhere to the Nuclear Non-Proliferation Treaty, it has not so far taken as stringent a view of the requirements of non-proliferation as the major industrial countries have. Moreover, it takes substantial pressure to motivate China's civil authorities to curb entrepreneurial military units from selling their hottest products. In such disputes, targeted economic sanctions,—including either trade sanctions or bans on technology transfers—can provide the United States with leverage. When the Chinese sold missiles to the Middle East after the Gulf War, the United States banned export to China of many dual-use (i.e., civilian and military) technologies. The sanction is appropriate because it targets the specific problem rather than the overall relationship, and precisely offsets any advantage the Chinese military would obtain from the military exports.

At the same time, the Chinese have some valid concerns too. The Missile Technology Control Regime, to which Washington has demanded Chinese adherence, was set up without Chinese involvement and specifically tailored to Western missiles. The United States insists that China subscribe to the MTCR rules, but does not want to admit China as a member of the club that sets those rules. The MTCR conveniently allows some standard Western missiles to be sold, but would ban Chinese missiles that go just a little further. Moreover, the Chinese ask why certain of their missiles should be proscribed when the United States sells the same countries high-performance aircraft that have a longer range, deliver a bigger payload, and deliver it with greater accuracy than the Chinese missiles. The most bitter U.S. complaints about Chinese missile sales to Iran occurred while the United States was itself secretly selling missiles to Iran. (Washington feared Chinese Silkworm missiles would be used against the U.S. Navy.) Beijing argues that in such cases, Washington is imposing a double standard. Moreover, Beijing argues—correctly—that its own arms sales are extremely limited, while Washington's are enormous and often provide similar or better capabilities to the same countries.

Beijing has drawn particular ire because it sold weapons in the immediate aftermath of the 1991 UN liberation of Kuwait. That was uniquely insensitive on Beijing's part. On the other hand, the United States has not distinguished itself for

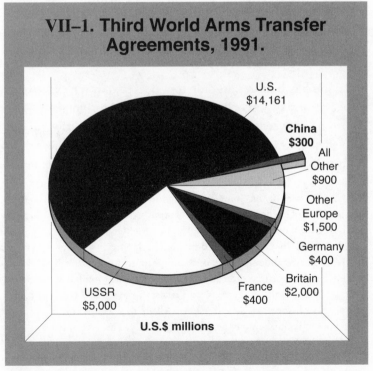

VII–1. Third World Arms Transfer Agreements, 1991.

U.S. $14,161

China $300

All Other $900

Other Europe $1,500

Germany $400

Britain $2,000

France $400

USSR $5,000

U.S.$ millions

SOURCE: Congressional Research Service Report to Congress, July 20, 1992.

sensitivity—or for keeping its word on arms sale agreements. In October 1992, facing defeat in the presidential election, President Bush approved a $6 billion sale of F-16 fighter aircraft to Taiwan. This occurred just as proponents of Taiwan independence were mounting a particularly strong campaign for greater influence—in other words, at a uniquely sensitive time. And it occurred in the context of this 1982 agreement between the United States and China:

> . . . the United States government states that it does not seek to carry out a long-term policy of arms sales to Taiwan, that its arms sales to Taiwan will not exceed, whether in qualitative or in quantitative terms, the level of those supplied in recent years since the establishment of diplomatic relations between the United States and China, and that it intends to reduce gradually its sales of arms to Taiwan, leading over a period of time to a final resolution.[5]

China has honored its side to a degree that far exceeds the expectations of anyone when the deal was signed in 1982. Tensions between Taiwan and the PRC could hardly have diminished more. The United States had banned the sale of high-performance aircraft to Taiwan for a full decade before

---

[5]United States–China Joint Communiqué on U.S. Arms Sales to Taiwan, August 17, 1982. The Reagan administration signed that document as a way of digging itself out of the hole with China created by regrettable 1980 campaign rhetoric about upgrading diplomatic relations with Taiwan. Having signed the communiqué, it indexed the promise to inflation, used a self-serving baseline for that indexing, separated the sale of military technology to Taiwan from sale of weapons, and reserved the right to replace obsolete weapons with more modern versions. All of this was within the normal stretching of language that goes on in diplomacy. The F-16 sale wasn't. For a summary of the arguments, see Robert G. Sutter, "Taiwan: Advanced Fighter Aircraft Sales—Pro and Con," Congressional Research Service, September 1, 1992.

the latest sale. While proponents of the decision justified it by pointing to PRC acquisition of 24 Su-27 aircraft from Russia, most American experts and virtually all foreign arms experts saw the sale of 150 advanced aircraft as an outright violation of U.S. commitments. The Chinese planes were not specifically directed against Taiwan (although in the future they could be), and in fact the Chinese military opposite Taiwan had thinned out a great deal. This was a desperate bid by a dying presidency to get some votes in Texas and create a symbol of presidential concern about jobs for U.S. workers. China's response has been, If you're going to break agreements and sell weapons to Taiwan, then don't talk to us about restraint on military sales to other countries. After Bush backed the sale to Taiwan, China withdrew from UN discussions armed at restricting arms sales to the Middle East.

Another pivotal issue has concerned intervention in Third World countries. As we saw in Chapter VI, Beijing has a long-standing principle of refusing to support big power intervention in Third World countries—because over recent generations China has so many times been the object of such intervention, mostly for very bad reasons such as the British wanting to sell more opium and the Japanese wanting effective control of large pieces of China. Despite this principle, the Chinese have in the past collaborated with U.S. and Japanese efforts to restrain North Korea. Moreover, as noted earlier, in the UN Security Council vote on the use of military force to liberate Kuwait, China opened the door for President Bush by abstaining; it accepted the reasonableness of the cause, but did not want to vote directly against its most cherished foreign policy principle. Beijing, as we saw, expected that Washington would be grateful and would offer important concessions in return. When Washington responded instead with angry denunciations because it wanted an affirmative vote, the Chinese were angered. In 1993, the new Secretary of State came to office proclaiming his intention to change China into a democracy and to use economic threats to force China toward Western concepts of human rights. This raised maximum concerns in Beijing about accepting any precedent for U.S. intervention.

All these issues are difficult but manageable. It is helpful for perspective to recall that in the 1970s the French attempted to sell nuclear-reprocessing facilities, and much else, to Pakistan and South Korea. The French government seemed to see the Middle East mainly as a wonderful market for French arms manufacturers rather than as a region of exceptional danger and delicacy that required extra restraint—in short, roughly the same perspective as the Chinese today. They knew exactly what the Pakistanis were doing, because they had a copy of the Pakistani contract with Libya. Still, it took some fairly boisterous conversations to dissuade them. The analogous conversation with China must be more boisterous. The ultimate goal must be not just to limit particular arms sales, but more importantly to insist that Beijing subordinate military sales to responsible foreign policy discipline. However, restraint will have to be mutual.

Sovereignty Issues

The United States has two interests at stake in the territorial disputes over the South China Sea (reviewed in Chapter VI). First, Chinese claims would turn the area into an inland lake, with restrictions on naval, maritime, and air transit. The United States is the defender of freedom of the seas globally and has a vital interest in preventing gradual restriction on international use of the sealanes. This is an issue worth a fight, and the United States needs to communicate the fact. But the fight itself should be completely unnecessary, because none of the countries has in fact tried to restrict traditional use.

Second, regional tensions are growing and there is a risk of larger military clashes. The United States has always perceived an interest in moderating such tensions and avoiding clashes. The do-nothing option now looks costly. A second option, currently in favor, is for U.S. admirals to deliver stern public warnings to China. However, it does little good to single out the Chinese when Taiwan and Vietnam have been making equally excessive claims and pursuing those claims more aggressively. The United States would serve its own interests better by serving strong and public notice on all parties that it intends to defend its interests and insists on a negotiated solution.

Meanwhile, Chinese leaders need to study the history of British and American defense of freedom of the seas, and the reasons for it, so that they understand why this is seen as a vital interest. China lacks a maritime tradition and any direct experience of the interests of the great trading nations. Now that China is becoming a great trading nation itself, it needs to join the maritime framework. The United States has been fair and responsible in defense of freedom of the seas.

Unlike some parts of the South China Sea, Hong Kong is indisputably part of China—even though the British administer it until 1997. Moreover, in the case of Hong Kong the Chinese gave Britain the most creative and far-sighted deal in the history of decolonization. China has generally honored its promises, whereas at crucial moments Britain has not. Ever since World War II, the United States has taken a strong line on decolonization and has gained the respect of the world for that stand. Washington can stand up for democracy without being totally gullible to every claim that is made in democracy's name. The long run interests of both democracy and Hong Kong's autonomy will be served best by advising Britain that it should honor its original promises. The promises China has made over the eventual democratization of the Hong

Kong legislature go far beyond anything Governor Patten is demanding; the principal issues concern timing and the trappings of sovereignty, not the ultimate degree of democratization.

The most important sovereignty issues in Asia concern a divided China and a divided Korea. The peace of the world has been imperiled by the divided regimes left over from World War II. These regimes were among the great battlegrounds of the past century: Germany, Korea, and China. Their division made already dangerous territory far more dangerous. Several times there was risk of nuclear conflict over Taiwan. Korea could be described as the Germany of Asia. It has been at the core of three big power conflicts in a single century: the Sino-Japanese War, the Russo-Japanese War, and the Korean War. Just as Germany lies at the heart of Europe, Korea lies at the juxtaposition of Japan, China, and Russia. For most of the post–World War II era, the demilitarized zone dividing North and South Korea has been the most dangerous spot on the globe. Enormous forces face off there. On innumerable occasions North Korea has probed and provoked and threatened South Korea in ways that would have led to war almost anywhere else. Since 1954, it has remained poised for surprise attack, and it has maintained a continual state of readiness for total war. Pyongyang may be capable of acquiring nuclear weapons and using them. This is no local Bosnian problem, but rather a local crevasse connected to fault lines that span the globe. Even as the North Korean regime gradually sinks, the Korean conflict remains one of the world's most dangerous.

Divided China and divided Korea are historically linked. As the Chinese civil war came to a climax, the Truman administration made the decision, after numerous dispiriting U.S. failures to shift the tides of Chinese history, that the United States could not affect the outcome and should intervene no more. But in June 1950, North Korea—armed and incited by the Soviet Union—launched an overwhelmingly successful surprise attack on South Korea. Washington interpreted this as the first phase of a global Soviet attack and assumed that the communist regime in China was simply one more tool of the Soviet Union. These two errors—that attack in Korea would be matched by attacks elsewhere and that China was just a Soviet tool like the East European regimes—dictated the decision to prevent the communists' capture of Taiwan. The U.S. sequestering of Taiwan has immensely benefited the freedom and prosperity of the people of Taiwan, and Washington can take great pride in that; but the decision was based on faulty intelligence.

Meanwhile, in Korea General Douglas MacArthur consolidated a beachhead at Pusan on the southern tip of South Korea, then catapulted to control of all South Korea through a brilliant landing at Inchon in the center of the peninsula. Allied objectives then changed from rescue of South Korea to reunification of all of Korea. In the process, MacArthur used such aggressive language against China that Truman fired the man who was probably the most able general in American history. China, listening to MacArthur and taking into account the U.S. intervention in Taiwan, feared the loss of a buffer state and probably feared that MacArthur planned to attack China. Mao Zedong argued successfully that if the United States was not stopped here, it would become a greater menace later. Thus China launched a massive attack and restored roughly the original division of the peninsula. The ensuing warfare cost America fifty thousand lives and China hundreds of thousands. Thus faulty American perceptions led Washington to ensure the continued division of China, and faulty Chinese perceptions led China to restore the division of Korea.

These wounds have become ready for healing. In China,

there is a fast-moving rapprochement between Beijing and Taipei. In Korea, the North Korean regime is financially, politically, and diplomatically bankrupt. North Korea has not been able to pay its international debts since 1974; now it receives little assistance from Russian and China, both of whom have far closer relationships with South Korea. North Koreans are cold in the winter because the regime cannot afford to import adequate fuel; in at least some areas food is being cut to two paltry meals per day. But North Korea retains one of the world's most powerful militaries. It could destroy Seoul very quickly, which would cripple South Korea for the indefinite future, even though North Korea might well be destroyed as a nation in the ensuing war.

This situation carries the seeds of peaceful reunification and the seeds of mass destruction. Washington needs Beijing's help to make sure the beneficial seeds grow. It will be very painful for China's leaders to accept the demise of a regime to which they were allied for so long. It will be impossible for them to do so if it means rapid absorption of North Korea by a South Korea that is allied to a United States which is extremely hostile to China in the manner prepared by congressional bills on China's most-favored-nation status. On the other hand, North Korea is dying and China wants stability. In many ways, that part of China is as entwined with Korea as the southwestern United States is with Mexico. If China were reassured by a gradual but perceptible easing of the U.S.-Taiwan connection, then a Chinese leader who implicitly accepted North Korean absorption into South Korea would encounter decisively less domestic political danger. And the United States could ease tensions over Taiwan without abandoning any of its demand for peaceful settlement satisfactory to the people of Taiwan because of the rapprochement that has occurred between Beijing and Taipei.

The United States can insist on the peaceful solution of the

Taiwan problem without matching every Chinese weapons purchase gun for gun with a sale to Taipei; that will soon be impossible in any case. All it has to do is to lean over backward to honor U.S. agreements regarding arms sales to Taiwan, rather than stretching them beyond the breaking point. Such a policy would not require any loudly announced agreement or any precise details. Washington could just point out to Beijing that the tilt is changing, and say that, by the way, the American president would be very grateful for any comparable cooperation in Korea. The United States could do this increments which parallel those taken in China. The result could be the defusing of the world's most dangerous situation outside Russia. If things develop badly *vis-à-vis* Taiwan in the future, then Washington can deal with those developments at the time.

A final major sovereignty issue concerns Tibet, whose peoples have suffered severely during the communist period, severely enough to justify international concern. China's sporadic rule over Tibet has a long history, dating back to the Yuan Dynasty in the thirteenth century. China subdued Tibet again in the eighteenth century—not too different in time from the period of greatest conflict between settlers and American Indians in what became the United States. For China, Tibet is a strategic buffer of great importance, and the high mountains on the far borders of Tibet provide China a natural boundary that is easily defensible. During China's period of weakness, Tibet developed substantial independence. After the revolution of 1949, it was reincorporated into China with a promise of autonomy under central leadership. Originally, when Beijing was weak, autonomy was emphasized. When Beijing became stronger, central leadership and social reforms were emphasized, and Tibetans revolted. The ensuing suppression has been harsh, and in addition Tibet has shared with the rest of China the horrors of the Great Leap Forward

and the Cultural Revolution. (Most of the worst horrors—
and they were horrors—suffered by Tibetans were shared
with the rest of China. Perhaps, though, it is worse to starve
because of the stupidity of leaders from another culture than
from the stupidity of one's own leaders.)

The Tibetans' plight is similar in some ways to that of the
American Indians. To the Chinese, Tibetan society is inferior
and feudal. Tibetans' use of human skulls for a variety of purposes, their poor hygiene, feudal rule by the monks, and much
else struck the Chinese as requiring reform. Chinese attitudes
toward the Tibetans have been similar to those of European
settlers toward the American Indians—except that for the
most part the Chinese have not forced Tibetans from their
lands, the Tibetan population has not declined as severely as
the American Indians, and Tibetans' income is a much higher
proportion of national per capita income (77 percent) than
the American Indians'. Since the current economic reform
began in 1978, China's treatment of minorities has improved
substantially, but Tibetans continue to protest and Beijing
continues to suppress Tibetan resistance ruthlessly. Recently,
China has moved substantial numbers of Han Chinese into
the vast, underpopulated area of Tibet to ensure future control.

There are about 4 million Tibetans, of whom about 2 million live in Tibet. Thus Tibetans in Tibet constitute about 0.17
percent of China's population. They are not, therefore, comparable to the Ukraine. Nor, since China is not falling apart, is
their cultural or strategic situation even comparable to Latvia.
For good or ill, their chances of achieving independence are
poorer than the chances of any major American Indian tribe.
Advocacy of the hopeless cause of independence can only
bring greater suppression and suffering—as would happen if
someone egged the Apaches into a bid for independence from
the United States. International human rights concerns there-

fore need to be expressed through efforts to improve human rights conditions in Tibet and to achieve respect for Tibetan cultural traditions, without supporting independence movements. This is easier in principle than in practice because so many of the abuses arise in connection with the independence movement. But if the principle is conspicuously respected, then campaigns to denounce abuses and to enhance respect for Tibetan culture could greatly improve conditions there.

ECONOMIC ISSUES

In recent years, China has run a huge trade surplus with the United States—in fact, the second largest surplus of any country—and it arose at a very bad time: right after Tiananmen Square and during the 1991–92 recession. The surplus stems from several factors. One is unfair trade practices. As former Ambassador Hummel says, "China is trying to export like a capitalist and import like a communist." China has sought liberal access to others' markets while restricting access to its own. It has done this by restricting the availability of foreign exchange for imports, subsidizing exports, using secret rules to manage imports, and so on. It has also made free use of foreign intellectual property without paying for it.

A second factor is U.S. policies. The United States has kept economic sanctions on China far longer than any other country; these naturally depress U.S. exports. Moreover, for several years the U.S. Congress, and recently the executive branch, have constantly threatened the most dire trade sanction of all short of quarantine: removal of China's most-favored-nation (MFN) trade status. Because American companies must hedge against the risk of such sanctions, many have limited their business with China. In addition, most of the biggest deals go to non-American companies because U.S.

export credits are not as generous as those of other nations. This is a global problem, not one caused by U.S. sanctions. Almost all deals for power plants, aircraft, telephone systems, and similar large infrastructure projects are decided on the basis of export credits. One American company recently had to hire a chief financial officer whose specialty was moving companies' production sites around so that the company could access the superior export funding of other countries.

Third, many Chinese exports are from U.S. companies making things cheaply in China and exporting them to other places, including the United States. This helps American companies compete successfully on a global basis, but it leads to an initial surge of exports from China back into the United States. High-technology and infrastructure purchases by China take longer.

Fourth, and this is the main factor, Hong Kong and Taiwan have exported their labor-intensive industries to China proper to take advantage of the lower land and labor costs there. In doing so, they have exported their surpluses to the mainland. Now it is China's problem. The chart of the total trade deficit with China (VII-2) shows what is happening. Note that all of Asia's exports, and particularly Hong Kong's, were severely depressed in 1985, the year this chart begins. Also, China's exports to the United States were exaggerated in 1992 by traders rushing to do their deals before the threatened imposition of Section 301 trade sanctions. The total deficit was roughly flat in the "normal" years from 1986 to 1991, when the expansion of China's surplus provoked such a controversy. This left the U.S. Congress howling in anger at China's unfairness while Taiwan and Hong Kong laughed all the way to the bank.

China's trade troubles with the United States are broadly similar to those of Japan, South Korea, and Taiwan. These countries too encouraged exports and inhibited imports, un-

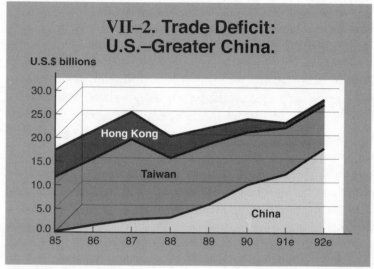

VII–2. Trade Deficit: U.S.–Greater China.

U.S.$ billions

Hong Kong

Taiwan

China

85 86 87 88 89 90 91e 92e

SOURCE: U.S. Department of Commerce.

dervalued their currencies, and pirated U.S. books, computer programs, and trademarks. But the United States is pushing China harder and faster than it pushed Taiwan, South Korea, and the ASEAN countries. It is insisting that China solve intellectual property issues in a single year that Thailand, Indonesia, Singapore, and Malaysia—proportionately much worse offenders—refused to resolve for decades.[6] China takes this to be unfair and unreasonable.

[6]U.S. diplomats estimate that pirated software comprises 90 percent of all software used in Taiwan and Singapore and 70 percent in Hong Kong, and that 90 percent of all pirated software in Southeast Asia is produced in Singapore, where tight government controls on the economy make control of such activities extremely easy for the government. This has been happening for many years without even the suggestion of drastic sanctions like those being proposed for proportionately infinitesimal infractions in China. Subsequently the United States went after Taiwan, Thailand, and others with greater fervor.

In China's eyes, Americans are disguising a political dispute as a trade dispute and are bringing unfair trade pressure to bear in order to undermine China's political system. It is true that the United States is treating China particularly harshly for political reasons. On the other hand, U.S. toleration of huge trade surpluses on the part of Asian allies cannot be regarded as a "normal" phenomenon. It was in fact an aberration that occurred, first, because for a limited period of time the U.S. economy was so strong that it seemed capable of sustaining such deficits; second, national security issues overrode short-term economic considerations; and third, the countries running the big surpluses were regarded as important allies of the United States. Moreover, the United States did have some tough trade disputes even with its allies. In the trade dispute with China, the U.S. economy is weaker; national security issues are less immediate; and since June 1989, the Chinese government has appeared to Washington as an offender against profoundly important American values. Conversely, Congress presses trade issues partly to punish China for human rights abuses, so Chinese trade concessions do not really mollify them, and China wonders whether concessions just invite more demands.

Within this broader perspective of pushing China much harder than other countries, there is a fundamental division between the "big bang" and incremental approaches. The majority of Congress has repeatedly voted to have a giant confrontation over China's most-favored-nation status that would set a deadline of six months to a year for complete Chinese capitulation on the most important human rights, trade, and strategic issues. In contrast, the Bush administration sought to channel this congressional fervor into a series of more focused negotiations. The Bush administration separated strategic, human rights, and economic issues into different negotiations, rather than accumulating them into one big fight. With the election of President Bill Clinton, the big bang approach conquered the White House, but victory has forced many proponents to look more carefully at the consequences.

Intellectual property has been one major category of contention. China has followed the Third World line in taking full advantage of Western products without paying the companies that own them. Chinese companies duplicate U.S. computer software on a very large scale without paying royalties, infringe trademarks, copy and distribute chemicals and pharmaceuticals without paying for them, exploit access to U.S. trade secrets, and copy and export legally protected hardware of many kinds, in some cases nearly driving small U.S. firms into bankruptcy. China awards trademarks to the first applicant regardless of the original owner. Because of these complaints, on May 26, 1991, the U.S. Trade Representative (USTR) designated China for investigation under the Special 301 provisions of the 1988 Trade Act and, following unsuccessful negotiations, listed items for potential retaliation on December 2, 1991. This strong stand had broad support from American businesses because such a wide range felt they were incurring serious damages.

At the same time, China has moved very fast toward accepting Western capitalist principles. The concept of intellectual property is new for China, and incorporating Western capitalist concepts of ownership into Chinese socialist law is a complex process. The vast majority of capitalist Third World countries take the position that patents on pharmaceuticals, and the resulting high prices for drugs, are not acceptable, and even a close ally like Thailand has refused for many years to protect computer software. China had previously accepted the concept of intellectual property and applied for membership in the Berne Convention. Arpad Bogsch, Director General of the UN World Intellectual Property Organization, noted that only one hundred countries even have patent laws, and that of these fifty are similar to China in not protecting chemicals and pharmaceuticals.[7]

After a series of confrontations which led to the verge of trade war, Beijing and Washington signed a Memorandum of Understanding on January 17, 1992, that terminated the USTR's investigation and threats regarding intellectual property. China agreed to very broad, modern protection of copyrights, patents, and trade secrets. On copyrights, it committed to join the Berne Convention, to join the Geneva Phonograms Convention, to protect computer software as literary works, to enforce copyright owners' right to control rental of their works, to give these international standards precedence over existing domestic law, to bring its domestic laws into line with the agreement, and to inform the United States of internal guidance related to the agreement. On patents, China promised "best efforts" to amend its patent law before January 1, 1993 (and did so), to make pharmaceuticals and agricultural chemicals (in addition to their production processes) patentable, to expand protection of production processes for these items, to protect patented items for twenty years, and to limit compulsory licensing of patents. China also agreed to make best efforts to pass implementing legislation to protect trade secrets by January 1, 1994. China already had a revised trademarks law scheduled for enactment in late 1992.

This makes China one of the leaders of the Third World in acknowledging the West's version of intellectual property. Taiwan still refuses to accept such a sweeping agreement. At the same time, further difficulties over implementation are unavoidable. The degree of sincerity with which Beijing signed the agreements remains to be tested. Many of the clauses in the agreement specify that Beijing will make "best efforts," a

---

[7]See Kennis Chu, "China Demands Fair Play Over Property Rights," *South China Morning Post*, December 1, 1991.

phrase that creates considerable room for fudging. Moreover, Beijing's writ is weak along the coast where these issues arise, and local businessmen abetted by crafty Hong Kong and Taiwan counterparts will undoubtedly elude regulation for many years.

The second area of contention is market access. China has used import licenses and high tariffs to discourage very broad categories of imports. Traditionally it has subsidized its exporting firms, although on January 1, 1991, it announced that such subsidies had been abolished. The government frequently instructs its firms as to whom they should deal with, and regulates trade and investment through secret regulations. These waste the efforts of U.S. firms and expose them to arbitrary or corrupt interpretations of the rules. In response, the U.S. Trade Representative (USTR) launched a one-year investigation on October 10, 1991. China's actual practices, which are at a level similar to those of South Korea two decades ago, are utterly unacceptable in principle to the capitalist world. Yet what it does is fairly standard Third World practice, and the pace of liberalization in China has no peers.

With one eye on congressional antipathy for China, and another on the trade deficit, U.S. negotiators again demanded much more from China than from other countries. These negotiations entailed particularly severe confrontation. Unlike the question of intellectual property, confrontations of this intensity lacked strong support in the American business community,[8] which viewed access to China's market as fairly similar to access to the markets of America's close Asian allies. In fact, China has allowed most major Western brands of goods into the Chinese market before Chinese brands have

---

[8]During this period I was a Governor of the American Chamber of Commerce in Hong Kóng and was therefore constantly involved in discussions between the business community and U.S. trade negotiators.

established dominant positions; Japan and South Korea would never have tolerated this. This was a political confrontation, to demonstrate to Congress that the Bush administration was being sufficiently tough on China. Each side threatened billions of dollars of sanctions against the other—$2.9 billion in the case of those published by USTR on August 21, 1992.

Despite the histrionics, on October 10, 1992, China and the United States announced an agreement on market access. The Chinese promised to publish most of their rules rather than keeping them secret, to remove many quotas and import controls, to reduce tariffs, to publish market information, to remove import substitution measures, and to eliminate safety and health restrictions that were not justified by scientific evidence. In return, the United States promised to "staunchly support China's achievement of contracting party status to the GATT and . . . work constructively with the Chinese Government and other GATT contracting parties to reach agreement on an acceptable 'Protocol' and then China's rapid attainment of contracting party status."

China, very excited about this promise to help it enter GATT, publicized that membership was likely in 1993. Throughout China, the government sponsored seminars on the implications of GATT membership. Membership as early as 1993 was undoubtedly too ambitious a goal. But then the Clinton administration took a tougher line toward China, and China realized that the cost in terms of destruction of its state enterprises would be higher than expected. It began to back off on key issues. In March 1993, the official in charge of such things in Washington, Donald Newkirk, said that he would be retiring in seven years and doubted that China would fulfill the requirements by then.

GATT membership is just one of the issues that will arise as China moves rapidly toward a market economy. U.S. law

treats market economies differently from non-market economies. When China becomes a certified market economy, the
immigration requirements of Jackson-Vanik—originally designed to force the Soviet Union to allow free emigration of
Soviet Jews—will no longer apply. On the other side of the
coin, the trade requirements are much higher for products in a
market economy; there is already a major legal case arguing
that Chinese-exported ceiling fans are produced in a market
environment and therefore must satisfy the higher requirements. Unless the U.S. administration delineates a clear
boundary, the transition could become a political football and
a legal nightmare.

Despite the two major agreements of 1992, there are still
areas in which the United States will quite reasonably press
China for reforms. China's services sector remains heavily
protected. Foreign investors are normally required to promise
to export the majority of their production—although for the
time being these promises are largely unenforced. In many
situations, such as the pricing of raw materials, foreign investors are treated unfavorably compared with domestic investors. Enforcement of prior commitments will take time.

The economic situation is extremely complex. The estimated 1992 U.S. trade deficit with China of $19 billion is
clearly unsustainable.[9] Many of China's trade practices do not
yet conform with the practices of the Western capitalist system. On the other hand, the rate of progress in negotiating fair
rules of trade is far beyond anything that has been achieved in
recent years with other countries. China's global surplus was
declining sharply because a large deficit in early 1993. What
tends to get lost in the vociferous differences over trade policy
is that exports have been the prime area of growth in the U.S.

[9]This estimate is from the U.S. Embassy in Beijing, "Draft 1993 Trade Act
Report," November 1992.

economy in recent years, and that they are its greatest hope for substantial growth in the foreseeable future. U.S. exports to China are large, have seen the most impressive growth of any region, and now support many tens of thousands of American jobs.[10] If Washington throws away the principal export opportunity of the 1990s, it also throws away its principal opportunity to generate new high-tech jobs and to enhance U.S. market share of the leading industries.

HUMAN RIGHTS ISSUES

Since 1989, the organizing principle of U.S.-Chinese relations has been the image of the tanks crushing demonstrators in and around Tiananmen Square. By themselves, the strategic and economic issues would be difficult but manageable. But Tiananmen Square put human rights at the core of the relationship. As a result, U.S. thought on any Chinese-American issue, from arms sales to proper royalties for the image of Donald Duck, has taken on a righteous fervor.

The importance of the principles that were abused in Tiananmen Square has led to a search for a policy tool powerful enough to express the feelings that arose on June 4, 1989, and to strike a decisive blow in favor of those principles. Most of the available tools seem inadequate to the task. Refusal to sell weapons, a policy that already has been implemented, is appropriate but minor. Any limited economic measures seem

[10]According to Siemens, China's need for power plants in the 1990s is equal to total world capacity to build them. According to AT&T, China will add 11–15 million telephone lines per year in the 1990s whereas the United States will add only 4–5 million. And China has placed more orders for aircraft than any other country in the 1990s.

similarly inadequate. Military threats are dangerous and inappropriate. Most political measures, such as denunciations and expansion of Voice of America broadcasts, are perceived as mere words. There is just one measure that seems to Congress powerful enough without carrying the risks of military threats: that one measure is depriving China of its most-favored-nation status.

Most-favored-nation status is simply the provision of normal trade status to another country. It confers basic membership in the international trading system by providing an assurance that the country will not be discriminated against by giving special advantages to other countries. In practice, what it means for U.S. trading partners is that the country's exports will be charged tariffs at normal rates rather than at the ruinous Smoot-Hawley rates which destroyed world trade earlier in the century and which were one of the prime causes of the Great Depression. At the end of 1992, out of more than 160 countries, only six outlaw countries were deprived of MFN status: Cambodia, Cuba, Laos, North Korea, Romania, and Vietnam. The United States does not consider depriving Japan of MFN status even for very large trade deficits and many unfair practices. It does not eject Thailand, Malaysia, or Indonesia for much more extensive violations of intellectual property rights and (in Indonesia's case) fair market access than China's. Nor has it deprived many African countries of MFN for far more serious violations of human rights than China's. Without MFN, the tariffs on the most important categories of toys rise from 6.8 to 70 percent; most clothing tariffs rise to 90 percent.

For all these reasons, depriving a country of MFN status is no ordinary sanction. Most sanctions take for granted that a country is a member of the world economic and political system and, in that context, send a message that Washington will impose specific penalties for not obeying specific rules. In contrast, depriving MFN status expels the country from the system. It doesn't say, We're going to charge you more to deal with us. It says, We don't want to deal with you at all.

What would be the specific impact of taking MFN status away from China? The biggest blow would fall on Hong Kong and adjacent areas. Since Hong Kong has moved almost all of its industry across the border, Hong Kong industry is completely dependent on its ability to export from China. That industry disproportionately serves the U.S. market. The Hong Kong government estimates that the lost trade would amount to about $2,000 for each of its residents. Tens of thousands of jobs would be lost in this one city. Taiwan would also be hit hard; for instance, almost all of Taiwan's shoe industry uses the Chinese coast as a manufacturing platform. Coastal Guangdong and Fujian would be particularly devastated. These are the areas which are export-dependent; not coincidentally, they are the most liberal areas of China. Their people are the ones who watch the most foreign television, deal with foreigners on a daily basis, and work for private and foreign-owned companies rather than state enterprises. The politicians who have succeeded in these regions are the ones who have pushed reform the fastest and been the most open to foreign practices. In short, life in these areas is the freest in China, and the leaders who have succeeded have been the ones who pushed the hardest to make it that way.

As I was finishing this chapter, I spent three days traveling around southern Guangdong once again. Mile after mile in all directions, one just sees construction. People and companies have torn down their old buildings and leveraged themselves to the hilt in confidence that the continuing reforms will enlarge their trading opportunities. If their market collapses, they will collapse; the domino consequences might well make the Great Depression look like a picnic. The people would never forget who did it to them—super-reformist politicians and Americans.

From Beijing, the consequences would look very different. The trade cutoff would be painful but hardly unbearable. Most of China's growth is domestic, not trade-oriented. The area around Beijing is not dependent on exports to the United States. Since other countries would still trade, the national consequence would be a painful wound rather than a fatal blow. And for bureaucratic socialist leaders, there could be political pleasure within the economic pain. It would discredit the super-reformers once and for all. From the viewpoint of Beijing's conservatives, it would demonstrate decisively the dangers of opening the country too much to foreign influence, of making oneself too vulnerable to foreign powers. It would convince many Chinese that the Americans will use the economic opening to attempt to destroy China's progress rather than to welcome it into the world community. Destroying the super-reformers, and bolstering the nationalist credentials of the conservatives, would be one of the greatest imaginable political windfall for those in Beijing who advocate the slowest approach to economic reform and the most repressive political policies.

Depriving China of MFN status would isolate the United States. Not one other country in the world would support the policy. Most Asian leaders have spoken out actively against it.[11] The progress of Chinese reform has granted all Asian countries not just economic benefits but more importantly the

---

[11]See, among many others, Michael Richardson, "Asian Leaders Question Clinton Tactics on Rights," *International Herald Tribune,* January 21, 1993, and "Lee Warns US on Human Rights," [referring to Singapore's former Prime Minister Lee Kwan Yew], *South China Morning Post,* January 29, 1993.

benefit of a China which has shifted from disruptive revolutionary influence to constructive support. In addition, since MFN is reciprocal, the collapse of U.S. exports to China would cost well over 100,000 American jobs.

Thus MFN deprivation is a peculiar new type of weapon: Aimed at China, it devastates all one's friends and aids one's adversaries. This awareness has drained away much of the enthusiasm for actually removing MFN status. So the theory became: don't actually take it away, just use it as a lever to extract huge concessions. But it is very dangerous to make threats that one is not willing to implement. It is especially dangerous in the context of U.S. relations with China, where there are so many intense conflicts and so many U.S. pressures on the structure of the Chinese system that there is a very real risk of complete breakdown. In particular, when strong voices in Washington are calling for the partial dismemberment of China and committing the United States to changing China's form of government, there is some point at which Beijing's leaders will decide that sovereignty is at stake and they can go no further. Economic growth is their core strategy, but the purpose of that strategy is the recovery of national pride and sovereignty. A breakdown of MFN status would cast China out of the international system and reverse many of the benefits of its having joined in the first place.

An analogy to South Korea clarifies the political dynamics of the "big lever" theory behind this debate. In 1976, much of America's political leadership expressed the same kind of anger at the Park Chung Hee regime that it expresses against China now. Congressional leaders, especially liberal Democrats, called for the United States to repudiate power politics and stand up for American values. Leading newspapers focused anger on South Korea, portraying student demonstrations in front-page stories and stating that the regime was doomed to collapse because it was undemocratic and abused human rights. Therefore, they argued, America should withdraw its troops before South Korea became another South Vietnam. These reports made the most negligible mention of South Korea's extraordinary economic growth. People looked for the most powerful lever to express their disdain for Park's abuses of human rights and their determination to stand up for American values. There was only one really powerful lever available: Pulling out the American troops that protected South Korea against the huge army of North Korea. The early advisers of Jimmy Carter convinced him to make the pullout of troops the central symbol of how his foreign policy would differ from that of his predecessors.[12]

As it happened, my own research on South Korea showed that the economic takeoff was generating broad support for the regime. The South Korean economy was extremely egalitarian, particularly in keeping rural incomes fairly comparable to urban incomes—a unique accomplishment that not even Taiwan had been able to duplicate. Most important, the South Korean regime had developed institutions (the army, the government ministries, the competitive business system) that were world-class in leadership, technical competence, and effective organization. Confronted with evidence that the theory of South Korea being another Vietnam was simply not true, advocates of the "big lever" theory did a complete reversal—not of the policy advice, but of the justification for it. They argued that South Korea was now so strong that it no longer needed U.S. troops. This argument they supported with statistics showing that South Korea had about as many planes, tanks, and so forth as North Korea, or that South

[12]I served as one of the nineteen members of the Foreign Policy Task Force in the 1976 Carter campaign for president and chaired the Asia Policy Group. Carter's public commitment to withdraw the troops predated the formation of the task force and was invulnerable to challenge.

Korea's smaller numbers of these things were compensated by the better quality of its arms. They conveniently ignored the fact that North Korea was configured for surprise attack against a South Korean capital that was just on the other side of the border.

Publicly, no clear distinction was ever drawn between the theory of withdrawing the troops because South Korea was repressive and therefore weak, and the theory of withdrawing them because South Korea was now so strong. These utterly contradictory theories were espoused simultaneously. In the leading media and the most prominent universities, the argument that South Korea was experiencing rapid and egalitarian growth, and that this was stabilizing, became anathema. Above all, it was politically incorrect to argue that rapid economic growth was creating the preconditions for freedom and democracy. A middle class was emerging; workers were becoming educated; the number of industrial workers had gone from a few tens of thousands in 1950 to millions. Society was becoming more differentiated and more difficult to control—people were less afraid, both of starvation and of North Korea. The economy was becoming too complex to control from the president's office, so the government would lose control over people's jobs. A tame opposition had been legitimized, and there were signs that it would become less tame. All this would gradually enlarge the sphere of individual freedom and eventually produce overwhelming pressure for democratization. This argument produced indignant accusations that one was just rationalizing a callous disregard for human rights.

When Carter took office, he moved swiftly to begin the troop withdrawal. But every U.S. ally in Asia opposed the policy, and even the Chinese—formally very close allies of North Korea—privately expressed their dismay at the potential destabilization of the region.

While much of the emotional drive behind Carter's policy came from the desire of human rights advocates to punish Park Chung Hee for his (very real) abuses of human rights, South Korean human rights activists despised the policy. I interviewed all the major dissident leaders, and not one supported the troop withdrawal. Kim Dae Jung, the leading dissident, said: "That Carter. He doesn't give a damn about human rights. If he did, he would know that I am a refugee from North Korea and he is making me vulnerable to Kim Il Sung. More important, why does he think I am able to stay alive in South Korea? Only because of the leverage the U.S. Embassy has because of the American troops here!" Never in the history of the United States had relations with so many Asian countries deteriorated so quickly as in 1977. The withdrawal policy defeated every one of its nominal objectives, especially human rights and arms control. It even cost more money to move the troops back to the United States than to keep them in Korea.

In 1978, new intelligence estimates showed decisively that North Korean forces were much stronger than previously believed. Carter quietly shelved his withdrawal policy. By that time, the estimates were primarily an excuse for abandoning a disastrous idea. Domestically, the emotional fire had burned out, and it seemed more important to make concrete progress on real problems than to strike political postures. In Asia, despite some major achievements such as the normalization with China in 1979, Carter never recovered his credibility.

By 1993, South Korea's strength had grown enormously and North Korea was foundering. (The number of U.S. troops in South Korea was basically irrelevant to the nuclear controversy under way with North Korea.) But all the people who had advocated pulling the troops out in 1977, on the grounds that South Korea was strong enough to take care of itself, were convinced of the importance of retaining U.S. troops in

South Korea in 1993.[13] What happened was that powerful emotions searched for the big lever and did not reflect very much about the consequences of pulling it. Symbol (standing up for human rights) had become more important than substance (actually helping human rights). Domestic political exploitation of the policy outweighed the consequences.

The debate over most-favored-nation status for China has been a precise rerun of the Korean troop withdrawal fiasco. The debate concentrates on MFN because it is the big lever, not because it is a useful lever. The emotional energy created by Tiananmen Square mirrors the emotional energy created by Vietnam. The symbol of doing something decisive takes precedence over the reality of defeating one's own goals. Posturing for domestic political reasons (China was seen in the 1992 campaign as Bush's only foreign policy vulnerability) takes precedence over the danger of a major international conflict.[14] As in 1977, all the Asian countries oppose the policy of threatening to withdraw MFN status.[15] Indeed, not one country in the entire world supports it.

[13]See for instance the appointment testimony of Secretary of State designate Warren Christopher. Christopher served as Deputy Secretary under Carter. Anthony Lake, who reputedly sold the Korean withdrawal to Carter, was Clinton's national security adviser when the Clinton administration emphasized the importance of keeping the troops in Korea.

[14]One particularly honest congressman has made this explicit, arguing that with a Democratic president in office it is time to change the congressional tune on MFN. See Lee H. Hamilton, Chairman, Committee on Foreign Affairs, U.S. House of Representatives, "A New U.S. Policy for China," mimeo., April 1, 1993, p. 4.

[15]In early 1993 top Asian political leaders endorsed the Bangkok Declaration, which criticized the Clinton/congressional approach to human rights policy. Top diplomats took a similar line in the report of the "Commission for a New Asia" organized by Malaysia. In June a large group of Japanese scholars endorsed such criticism. All this mirrored the 1977 Asian reaction to Carter's Korean policy.

There are several conditions in which this kind of expulsion from the system represented by MFN would be justified. If the adversary were a small country that could be brought to its knees and turned into a democracy—for instance, a highly developed version of Panama or Grenada—then this sort of sanction would do much good and virtually no harm. If the adversary were a genocidal monster such as Pol Pot's Cambodia or Hitler's Germany, then maximum isolation would be the minimum appropriate sanction. It would be particularly appropriate against a country like Burma, where a vicious regime is not just abusing the human rights of its people but also destroying their livelihoods through insane economic policies. China fits none of these criteria. The complexity of China's situation renders dangerous the simplicity of pulling the one big lever. America needs to press China on human rights, but also to celebrate its progress; to demand restraint on military sales, but also to welcome the constructive thrust of China's overall policy.

How, then, does one promote freedom and democracy in China? The most important part of the answer is: Spur economic development. Educated people will demand more freedom than uneducated people. Employees of private and foreign enterprises will act more freely than employees of state enterprises. People who can move around are freer than people confined to their hometowns. People who travel to foreign countries will have a broader range of ideas and experience, and a wider range of freedom, than people who must stay at home. People who do not fear starvation will have more confidence and act more freely than hungry people. Skilled workers in large modern factories will form unions more easily than dispersed peasants. People in a complex, highly differentiated modern economy will have more freedom than in a peasant economy because the government will have more difficulty controlling them. That is what human rights policy must encourage. Chinese policy since 1978 has consisted of ideological backpedaling in order to justify choices that have become clearly necessary to sustain the drive for wealth and power. The last thing that will work in favor of Chinese freedom is economic sanctions that slow the social differentiation of China and hamper its opening to the outside world.

Above all, politicians wrongly devalue the importance of *political* levers in promoting democracy. The impact on the Chinese people of being able to watch Clinton criticize Bush, and to watch Bush gracefully accept defeat in a peaceful election, is simply overwhelming. When the people of coastal China watch events in Tiananmen Square on Hong Kong television while government leaders deny that it is happening, the basis of Chinese politics shifts overnight. When the families of dissidents are visited month after month by foreign admirers, the morale and courage of movements for freedom and democracy experience a great leap forward. These influences are far more potent than economic sanctions. Washington can follow up with public pressure to resolve the most serious abuses, constantly pushing back the margin of abuse, as it did during more sober times in South Korea. The lesson of Taiwan and South Korea is that such policies work if given time.

PITFALLS IN U.S.-CHINA RELATIONS

Quirky Perceptions

American relations with Asia have always been bedeviled by quirky perceptions and misperceptions of Japan and China, because Americans know less about Asia than they do about Canada and Europe. During the horrors of Cultural Revolution in the 1970s, the most popular American writers on

China presented Mao's bloody legions as slightly overzealous social reformers; rich New Yorkers developed a passion for chinoiserie and ordinary Americans an extraordinary fascination with panda bears. In the early 1980s, as things began to improve slightly, liberal journalists started writing very negative books about China, and Ronald Reagan threatened to upgrade ties with Taiwan.

Now that life is startlingly better, many of the same writers who whitewashed the Cultural Revolution (among many others, Ross Terrill) are presenting China as a demon and themselves as great exponents of human rights. Americans must learn to beware foreign policy "experts" who once rationalized the Cultural Revolution, now demonize the great takeoff, and in between explained that the real problem with the Soviet Union was just an arms race in which both sides reacted to each other. Most of today's misperceptions derive from two sources. First, faulty analogies with the former Soviet Union, which lead people to assume that China must be on the verge of collapse or must be aggressive. Second, the dramatic image of Tiananmen Square and the absence of high-impact images of the equally important positive developments in China.

Time Scale

The process of creating a modern economy or a modern polity is not measured in years but in decades. This book has constantly referred to processes that take a generation or two. (I take a generation to be about twenty-five years.) Western societies find it extremely difficult to make very long term plans and to grasp things that may take years to occur. Members of Congress accuse businessmen of having very short term perspectives; they are absolutely right. But most politicians cannot think in terms of policies that have payoffs more than two or four years in the future, and this is just too short for policies designed to enhance human rights or democracy in most Third World countries.

It is axiomatic that successful democracy requires a society dominated by an educated middle class. This understanding dates all the way back to Aristotle. Any college student who has studied the subject could explain why. A country dominated by a rural society of semi-literate people earning under $100 a month is not ready for democracy. This axiom has been put to the test. Virtually every Third World country has tried a premature leap to democracy and failed. None has sustained it except a handful that fulfilled the requirement of an educated middle class—unless one counts India as a successful society.

Just as economic development has its sequences, so too does political development. As we saw in Chapter II, the sequence starts, in the case of Taiwan and China, with political controls that seek to control the life and thought of each individual in society in great detail. It progresses to a situation where the government represses all dissident actions but does not try to control daily life and thought in detail. Then comes the situation in China today, where the laws are still repressive but people feel able to speak rather freely and have access to diverse ideas. Then gradually, and initially in response to business necessity, the rule of law begins to replace the rule of political whim; the concept that the state can be sued by a private business for malpractice cannot be separated in any society from the concept that the state can be sued by a private citizen for infringing his legal rights. Eventually enough dissident groups make enough fuss, and full suppression becomes so troublesome, that the regime comes to tolerate organized opposition, first without legalizing it and later by making legal arrangements. In short, the three ingredients of democracy gradually emerge: genuine choice; the rule of law; and the requisite freedoms to make the choices meaningful. The final step is some kind of formal democratization. All of this takes time.

China is already taking small, hesitant steps along these lines. Like its economic policy, its political policy is gradualist. In almost a third of recent low-level elections, voters have chosen someone other than the Communist Party's designated nominee. Open policy disagreement is now common. Dissenting votes are multiplying in both policy and leadership elections. More non-communists are succeeding to senior jobs. The majority of political positions are now filled by the "excess candidates system," whereby three candidates are nominated for two jobs, thereby giving the electorate some choice. In March 1993, a new vice president of China, Rong Yiren, who is a non-communist businessman, was appointed. In the same month's National People's Congress vote for prime minister, Li Peng won overwhelmingly (2,573 votes), but was humbled by an unprecedented 210 no votes and 120 abstentions. One delegate actually voted for Zhao Ziyang, the liberal former prime minister who was detained at the time of Tiananmen Square; not so long ago, that vote would have meant a lifetime in prison. Does this make China a democracy? No. The party is still supreme and unchallengeable. Will progress at this rate make China a democracy in ten years? No. Are these tremendous changes that raise expectations and make backsliding difficult? Yes. Will China ever become a democracy exactly like ours? Probably not, but we should welcome the expansion of human freedom and political choice even in variations different from our own.

The emergence of the preconditions for democracy took twenty-six years in South Korea, if one reckons from Park Chung Hee's military revolution in 1961 to the democratic election of 1987—and six years longer to the election of civilian president Kim Young Sam in 1993. South Korean democracy appears as stable and prosperous as any other in the Third World. (Earlier elections were sometimes free, but the democracy had no chance of stability.) Park Chung Hee, so hated by American human rights advocates, is universally regarded as the father of his country and the one who installed the prerequisites of democracy. All public opinion polls in today's democratic Korea show him to be the most respected leader the country has had.

China is a lot bigger and more complex than South Korea and the process will take longer. China's leaders think in decades: Note Deng Xiaoping reflecting publicly on whether a hundred years would be a more appropriate time frame for Hong Kong to have a separate system rather than the mere fifty years currently provided. If they are serious about promoting democracy, American leaders must learn to think along the same lines.

Elite vs. Mass Perspectives

Political leaders tend to see global politics as a game between politicians. When members of Congress weigh the appropriateness of sanctions on China as a response to Tiananmen Square, they are thinking about punishing Li Peng and Deng Xiaoping for their brutal decisions. The whole focus is on finding a stick big enough to beat the leaders. But the primary effects of many economic policies may not fall on the leaders. They may—and, in the case of MFN deprivation, do—fall primarily on the little people. If one considers the little people, one comes to very different conclusions. To a member of Congress determined to punish Li Peng, and seeing no lever other than MFN that looks big enough, the opponent of this policy appears as a callous person who does not care enough about human rights to use the only powerful tool available. To the ordinary American who spends a good deal of time among the people of Guangdong and Hong Kong, the delivery of a devastating economic blow to these millions of people who are just climbing out of hunger seems like a massive version of the Vietnam War tactic of "burning down the village in order to save it."

Proper policies have to take both aspects into consideration. What is the effect on the leaders, and what is the effect on the people? If one can use a sharp economic blow to knock out Nicaragua's Sandinistas at the cost of short-term pain for the population but long-term improvement in their lives, then sanctions seem like a very good idea indeed. If, on the other hand, one is likely to impoverish huge numbers of people for long periods of time with negligible or regrettable impact on the leaders, then advocates of the policy need to do some very serious soul-searching to ask whether they really care about people.

Self-Fulfilling Predictions

There are serious differences of opinion between those who believe that China is an inherently aggressive power that is just biding its time until it builds up strength and those who argue that it does not have the former Soviet Union's aggressive history and that it has learned that wealth and power are best acquired through a policy of peace. This book has argued that China has set out on a course of peaceful development. It has argued that the image of an aggressive China derives largely from false analogies to the behavior of the former Soviet Union. But there is no way to be sure about the future. Today's peaceful giant could become tomorrow's aggressive superpower. What the United States must ensure is that it does not create a self-fulfilling prediction. If it treats China as an aggressive power, and adopts an attitude of hostility, then China will surely react against all U.S. interests and seize every strategic position that would enable it to fight successfully. If on the other hand the United States maintains its strength but adopts a posture of welcoming China into the world community, then it risks virtually nothing. While China will eventually become strong, it cannot challenge the United States' fundamental interests in the near future. China's entire military budget, including generous estimates of all the things that are not in the official statistics, amounts to less than $30 billion. The United States' is just under $300 billion. There is time to wait and see.

If the United States extends the hand of friendship, and if China still becomes aggressive, then Washington will face any conflict with a united people behind it. But if the United States treats as an enemy a China that has greatly reduced its defense budgets and made peace with all its neighbors, then it could prove difficult to persuade the American public and foreign allies to support a sustained conflict. The lesson of two generations of confrontation with the former Soviet Union is that it is difficult to sustain support even against a blatantly aggressive, totally militarized power. If there is to be a long-term conflict, the U.S. leaders would serve their country well to ensure that the onus of conflict is unmistakably on the other side.

PRINCIPAL RISKS

U.S. foreign policy toward China needs to address several major risks: the Bismarckian Germany risk, the prewar Japan risk, the vacuum risk, and the ideological confrontation risk.

The Bismarck risk results from a scenario where China's takeoff triggers Asian fears and those fears in turn cause an escalating arms race and danger of conflict. So long as there is an overarching U.S. security umbrella, as there has been for the entire postwar era, this scenario will not get out of control. With the umbrella, countries like Japan and Thailand will feel protected. Local political strains will not create such tension that problems like the reunification of Korea become un-resolvable. But without the umbrella, local big power struggles over the future of Korea and other problems are likely to escalate once again into confrontations with global consequences. Those consequences will be more global than ever because the capabilities of Asian countries will be so much greater than ever before. China and Japan can quickly become major conventional powers—with an extensive overseas reach. China is already a serious nuclear power, and Japan, South Korea, and Taiwan could attain that status quickly. So could India and Pakistan.

This argues for the United States to maintain its umbrella, which, as we saw earlier, in return requires maintenance of a major military presence. This will not provoke China or anyone else, because the U.S. security role is universally accepted in the region, except by North Korea, as a benign one. But the need for a continuing U.S. security presence creates a dilemma because U.S. economic performance is simply too weak to sustain its relative role in the face of Asian dynamism. In order to resolve this dilemma, the United States needs to maintain its current presence but accept that Asian countries' growth will gradually reduce U.S. relative weight in the region. Washington must focus all its incremental energy on improving domestic economic performance. To do this, it must avoid all gratuitous conflicts that could damage its global economic position. It must, in short, refrain from costly engagement in worthy but expensive causes all over the globe, and it must particularly eschew the temptation to cut off its economic arm in quixotic ideological confrontations with China and other Asian countries.

If the United States cannot do this, it must quickly try put in place a regional security arrangement and withdraw militarily from the region. As long as the United States remains militarily engaged in the Western Pacific, politicians will orate and vote under the illusion that the hegemonic U.S. position of the Cold War years remains; they will attempt to manage both relationships among Asian countries and the domestic political arrangements of newly powerful Asian countries. This will lead to the worst of all possible worlds for the United States and for Asia: an assertive foreign policy combined with a regional presence inadequate to back it up.

The second risk is a China where the military shakes off civilian reins and embarks on an expansionist policy, as happened in prewar Japan. This is least likely to occur in a situation where the civilian leadership looks successful, where there are minimal foreign conflicts to justify military preeminence inside China, and where the risks of a very assertive policy seem unacceptable. Washington can contribute in each of these areas. It should facilitate the civilian leadership's economic drive, because that is the criterion by which the success or failure of the civilian leadership is being judged. It should avoid conflict except where it is unavoidable, and it should fight over carefully defined economic, military, and other issues rather than launching broad, undifferentiated attacks on China and its system; this is the opposite of the present congressional instinct. And it should quietly maintain its regional military presence to make clear the high cost of a change from the present benign Chinese foreign policy.

The vacuum risk derives from the fragmentation of the former Soviet Union and the likely collapse of North Korea. The resulting vacuums in Central Asia and Korea create huge threats to the peace of the world. To manage these, Washington, Beijing, and Tokyo must maintain a working relationship and a constant dialogue. They do not have to agree on everything. They do not have to create a tricondominium to manage the situations in detail, but they must understand one another's positions sympathetically and must share a high degree of restraint. In the present environment, such understanding and mutual restraint are not terribly difficult to achieve. But if the parties are at each other's throats, then these situations will become unmanageable. Again, this requires that conflicts be handled in a highly differentiated fashion. It does not mean abandoning important national interests; it does mean not going for the other fellow's jugular, in the manner advocated by much of the U.S. Congress and some foreign policy advisers in the executive branch.

There is also a risk of broad ideological conflict between the United States and Asia. This is completely unnecessary, because the differences are not primarily in values but rather in strategies for attaining broadly shared values. Most Asian countries have moved faster than any other part of the Third World in the direction of stable freedom and representative government. (Most of Latin America is on a cycle; most of Africa respects neither democracy nor human rights; and most of Eastern Europe's new democracies lack viability.) But they find themselves bitterly criticized by both the right and the left in Washington for not making instant transitions to full Western-style systems. The Asian point is that such instant transitions never lead to stability and prosperity, just rapid collapse into worse poverty and worse dictatorship.

One of the classic dilemmas of democratic theory is the balancing of popular rule with competence. One device for marrying the two is representation: the people may not be capable of voting directly on budget details, but in theory they can choose representatives who can vote with competence. Another device is to remove certain things from the voting arena; in one classic formula, nobody thinks that airplane passengers should vote on the maneuvering of the plane in a storm. The creation of an independent central bank and the delegation of most of the details of policy making to large professional bureaucracies are variants of the airplane-in-a-storm approach. During wartime, democracies give more weight to expertise: they elect more competent leaders (Roosevelt, Churchill) at the expense of interest group considerations, centralize more power in those leaders, and give those leaders far more leeway to install competent subordinates at the expense of patronage and seniority considerations.

The conflict between Washington and—in 1993—all Asian capitals is about this balance between populism and technocracy in poor countries. The Clinton/Carter policy assumes that one can start from the end of the developmental process, that one can install the full panoply of interest group politics without spending decades assuring that competent institutions can withstand the onslaught of divisive, inflationary, and corrupting pressures. It assumes that one can provide the whole range of individual freedom at a time when budding police and judicial systems face gigantic challenges from criminal triads, terrorism, subversion, and insurgency. It assumes that a deeply impoverished society, fully exposed to modern consumerism, will tolerate indefinitely the slow growth that is an inevitable consequence of a system dominated by patronage and interest group considerations.

Most Asians, including a large majority of those profoundly devoted to democratic values, believe the opposite. Their experience is that democracy cannot survive without a modicum of order and that, until powerful modern institutions are created, the enemies of freedom can exploit the ponderous machinery of Western judicial systems to create disorder. They believe that the poverty of their societies is the analogue of wartime imperatives for Washington, and they have discovered that, if they relieve their citizens' poverty, their people will support them just as Americans supported

Franklin D. Roosevelt. They have discovered that successful economic growth and successful institution building have consistently led to greater freedom and greater democratization in contemporary Asia. They believe in a strategy of creating competence at any cost and then liberalizing gradually to whatever degree is consistent with competence. In contrast, Washington frequently demands that they install a fully liberalized system first and then create competence to the extent that it is consistent with interest group dominance. Most Asians believe that imposition of such a system on China would lead to catastrophe and destabilization of China could destabilize the region.

> "Would the West be as tough on the regime in Beijing," asks Deputy Foreign Minister Kishore Mabhubani of Singapore, "if China were located, say, where Mexico is? Would the West be as sanguine about the prospects of millions of boat people sailing from China if the regime broke down and chaos prevailed?"[16]

So long as there are no examples of sustained rapid growth and stable democratization along the lines of the Washington ideologues' strategy, and so long as there are numerous examples of success according to the Asian strategy, Washington is going to have a hard time convincing the Third World of its case. So long as Washington takes an extreme line on this, it will gradually mobilize all of Asia against it, and lose its leverage over China as well as the rest of the region. The way to promote human rights is to create a world environment conducive to democracy and freedom (a job at which Washington has succeeded magnificently), to keep proclaiming the ideals of freedom and democracy, and to keep nudging the process

---

[16]*International Herald Tribune,* October 20, 1992, p. 8.

along incrementally in various Asian countries. Constant pressure helps, because Asian leaders too easily get comfortable with tough controls even when their societies have moved beyond the need for them. Creating great confrontations just mobilizes the whole region in opposition.

COLD WAR II OR CONFLICTED COOPERATION?

The greatest risk of all, a new and unnecessary cold war with China, is very severe. The most sensitive spots are Taiwan, Hong Kong, and Tibet. The Bush administration in 1992 made the decision to reverse a decade-old policy and sell high-performance fighter aircraft to Taiwan, just prior to an election that brought advocates of Taiwan independence closer to power than they have ever been—and closer than virtually any observers thought likely. Washington backed Patten's push for democracy in ambiguous words that stopped just short of backing a British decision to repudiate fundamental aspects of the agreement about how Hong Kong will be governed as it reverts to Chinese rule. President Clinton's Secretary of State adopted the language of congressional advocates of Tibetan independence by referring to Tibetans as if they were not citizens of China:[17]

> The general approach that [Assistant Secretary of State-designate] Winston Lord is recommending is the one that we'll be following—that is to try to use MFN to encourage better

[17]Unofficial transcript of Warren Christopher's testimony before U.S. Senate Appropriations Subcommittee on Foreign Operations, March 30, 1993. Winston Lord's subsequent testimony was much more careful.

performance, better conduct in China on the many areas where we're disappointed, as far as their attitude on proliferation, as far as their abuses of trade, and as far as their human rights abuses, *both with respect to their own citizens and with respect to people living in Tibet.* (Emphases added.)

Draft congressional legislation has taken a much stronger line than that, referring to Tibet as occupied territory. As we saw in the epigraph to this chapter, the U.S. Secretary of State has declared that it is the policy of his government to change China's form of government—albeit peacefully—into a democracy. (As all diplomats know, the phrase "peaceful evolution" is currently the most dangerous expression in the Chinese leadership's vocabulary, a code phrase for foreign subversion of their system.) The Congress has voted several times to use the most powerful weapon of economic war at its disposal—removal of most-favored-nation status—in order to achieve political change in China, and this strikes at the heart of China's strategy for national rejuvenation.

In other words, the leaders in Beijing see Washington coming to the verge of launching multiple challenges to China's territorial integrity, declaring that it is U.S. policy to change the nature of China's government, and striking at the core of China's national strategy of economic rejuvenation. This is the stuff that wars, cold and hot, are made of.

Of course, nobody in Washington intends a war with China; they are just expressing American values. They would be horrified to think that those words could lead to a vast increase in China's military spending, to curtailment of all Chinese cooperation in the UN Security Council, to broad reduction of economic intercourse, to an escalating conflict that could last for many generations, and to isolation from all of today's Asian allies. Frequently, the target of the rhetoric is not so much China as domestic constituents. But the nuances of intention tend to fade away as they are translated across the

Pacific. They do so when Washington perceives Beijing, and it is not surprising that they do so when Beijing perceives Washington.

The above set of demands does not add up to a normal peaceful relationship between major nations, even between major nations which have serious conflicts of interest. Ronald Reagan would never even have considered mounting such a challenge to the Soviet Union in, say, 1982. Had he done so, the Warsaw Pact denouement might have exploded in war. If Beijing were demanding independence for Alaska, sending emissaries to impose immediate changes in the governance of New York, and giving advanced weaponry to independence fighters in Puerto Rico, while voting in favor of economic war and having its foreign minister declare the transformation of the United States into a communist state a primary objective of Chinese foreign policy, Washington would be concerned.

Moreover, these criticisms from Washington were preceded by a preemptive flurry of Chinese trade concessions, freeing of many political prisoners, modest political liberalizations, and expressions of desire for good Chinese-American relations. There is a risk that Beijing will draw the lesson that concessions just attract more intense demands.

Conversely, Beijing would be well advised not to overreact to the rhetorical hubris of newly elected officials in Washington. The CIA will not be landing subversive forces in Tibet. President Clinton wants to concentrate on domestic policy. The American people believe strongly in human rights, fair trade, and efforts to prevent nuclear proliferation, and they will support firm efforts by their elected government to attain those objectives. But they will never support a Cold War-scale confrontation of the kind seemingly implied by the words of Warren Christopher quoted above unless they believe the other side started it. If rhetoric and actions escalate quickly and confusingly, then each side's people will indeed believe that the other side started it. Chinese diplomacy should beware this risk. Beijing too often indulges in excessive rhetoric—even more often than Washington—that hurts its nation even when it has a good case. This certainly happened in Hong Kong. So China would be well served by a policy that emphasizes a willingness to negotiate, conspicuous concessions wherever those are appropriate, careful explanations, considerable patience, and a moderation of rhetoric. None of this compromises Chinese sovereignty.

Chinese leaders should understand that the best antidote to the American fixation with Tiananmen Square is to show as many Americans as possible the good face of China. Just as American interests in freedom are served by encouraging extensive foreign contact with the Chinese people, Chinese interests in creating a more balanced image of China are best served by encouraging a lot of Americans to come and see for themselves. Almost all Americans saw Tiananmen Square on television: Chinese leaders have to understand the profound effect that had on the American people. Yet each year hundreds of thousands of Americans are visiting China and seeing the other side. The balance will come, but it will take time. Nobody can visit China today without experiencing the joy of revival of the Chinese people.

Many psychologists define maturity as the ability to handle contradictory aspects of a situation. The United States and China need a mature relationship. Washington needs to learn to deal with both faces of Beijing. An American president needs to look at Deng Xiaoping and be able to say: This man bears heavy responsibility for Tiananmen Square; this man is a Communist; this man has approved nuclear and missile sales to dangerous nations. And at the same to say: This man has done more to alleviate world poverty than any other man in world history; this man has made China a more peaceful nation than we would ever have believed possible; this man's decisions have helped America attain all of its post–World War II objectives in Asia; this man will probably occupy a more esteemed place in Chinese history than Park Chung Hee in South Korea. American leaders need to show that they can simultaneously defend their interests and join the Chinese people in celebration of their extraordinary success.

Chinese leaders need to see that American leaders have a missionary zeal to change other countries, even when they don't know much about those countries. They will sell out their nation's most solemn promises for a few votes. Around election time, U.S. foreign policy is driven more by television images than by balanced analysis. At the same time, despite being the most powerful country in world history, the United States has no ambition to conquer other countries; this makes it a force for peace. Americans have hearts big enough to celebrate the successes of the Chinese people even as they compete with them. In the long run, free debate and freedom of information lead to rational behavior. And over the long span of history, U.S. policies reflect the goodwill of the American people.

This is the moment of triumph for history's most powerful democracy and the moment of rejuvenation for history's most populous nation. China has been the pinnacle of civilization for much of world history. The United States has been the decisive power in the global balance for most of the twentieth century. Both nations have preferred throughout most of their history to focus their ambitions on development at home rather than expansion abroad; both are run by leaders who say that they wish to continue that preference. Nonetheless, these two great civilizations must now engage one another— for better or worse—to a degree that has never before occurred. Much of the future of humanity will hinge on whether both sides can approach this engagement with the appropriate gravity, humility, and earnest effort to understand one another's real motives.

AUTHOR'S NOTE

The book is part of an odyssey. I have long been trying to understand the Asian takeoff, trying to pierce the veils of ideology, and trying to do what little I can to improve the lives of some struggling people.

As an undergraduate at Harvard I studied China, with the strong support of Ezra Vogel. I immersed myself in the sociological literature that proved to the satisfaction of, among many others, Aristotle, Marx, and Weber that peasants cannot form a coherent political force, together with a study of how Mao Zedong had managed to do just that. Then I went to the Philippines to study, with the help of military leaders and above all of jailed Philippine communist leader Luis Taruc and his colleagues, why the same techniques failed in the Philippines.

The mid-1960s provided a vivid introduction to the surreal world of faddish Western perceptions of China. As a student during the early Cultural Revolution I had to abandon my preferred specialty (Developing Nations) in Harvard's Social Studies Department because it was dominated by an avowed Maoist with limited tolerance for anyone who didn't admire Mao; such left-leaning was quite common, but there was no risk anywhere in the university of being equally browbeaten by a conservative. This highly politicized environment dominated much intellectual life despite the fact that most of the senior scholars (Fairbank, Vogel, Reischauer, Pelzel, Schwartz) retained their balance. As part of a summer job in 1968, I compiled for the Pentagon extensive documentation on the Cultural Revolution, and in the process documented extreme savagery from transcripts of Chinese radio broadcasts that were available to all scholars in every major university library. The facts were indisputable. They came from the Chinese themselves. Even so, this view went against the trend. At the last meeting of my department before graduation, each of us spoke of our career plans. I said that before graduate school I was going to document the horrors of the Cultural Revolution; everyone hissed. It was politically correct to apologize for the Cultural Revolution and treat it as an uplifting of the human spirit.

I was always a political activist as well as a scholar. In my high school years, I became a devotee of Martin Luther King, Jr., and even incurred punishment from my high school for participating during school vacation in a peaceful March on Washington for civil rights. After I returned from the Philippines in 1964, I was disappointed to find that the anti-Vietnam War movement had swept aside the civil rights movement. I took the conservative side and organized a more scholarly, more conservative student group which proved largely ineffective. But I did manage to lead the Harvard China Conference, a national-level gathering of scholars and students interested in hearing the most distinguished representatives of all viewpoints on China.

Notwithstanding my conservative views on the Vietnam War, I absorbed much of the liberal thinking of the day, including a view of South Korea and Taiwan as pitiless and irredeemable authoritarian regimes. When I left Yale Graduate School to work at Hudson Institute, this view of those regimes put me at odds with Herman Kahn. Herman hired people to argue with him, and we argued relentlessly. For two years, he introduced me to distinguished visitors by saying, "This is Bill Overholt. He spent seven years at Harvard and Yale and it nearly ruined him, but we're trying to rehabilitate him." Herman told me he was going to rub my nose in the reality of South Korea, and eventually he did. Other people would not have been so moved by what I found in South Korea, but I had lived in the peasant world of the Philippines and I instantly recognized the tremendous progress the country was making under Park Chung Hee. I became fascinated, and travelled all over South Korea, heading up into the mountains to check that the progress was not just along the coasts or the main roads. It wasn't. The contrast with the stagnation and decline of the Philippines shook me.

My first professional consulting paper at Hudson was an urgent task for the National Security Council staff under Kissinger shortly before Nixon's trip to China. Somebody there wanted to know, if we make a deal with China over Taiwan, will Beijing honor it? What evidence can we bring to bear on this? I assembled all available data on a wide variety of deals China had made. Given my view of Cultural Revolution China, it was a shock to find that China's record in honoring its promises was at least as good as America's. This was not what Herman Kahn expected to hear, nor was it what these particular NSC staff members expected. Kahn questioned me intensely, and subjected my findings to the withering fire of the most conservative members of Hudson's staff, then backed the report. This was unusual in the policy world. In fact, Hudson's and Kahn's ideological unpredictability kept the Institute on thin financial ice. People in government largely contracted for support for preconceived views. The findings of that study twenty-two years ago, now generally accepted among scholars, and my observations of China's policy in the intervening two decades, inform many of the conclusions of this book's chapters on Hong Kong.

Among my first two major Pentagon consulting projects was an assignment to find ways to use political regionalism in Southeast Asia to defeat regional communism. Washington had backed several such efforts, notably MAPHILINDO, ASPAC, and ASEAN. I quickly concluded that these were useful ideas but wouldn't defeat communism anywhere. But, building on ideas from Kahn's book *The Emerging Japanese Superstate,* we articulated the concept that the rapid economic growth of the smaller countries would, if protected and nurtured, save Asia from communism and change the world. This thesis encountered considerable ridicule, just as Kahn's argument that rapid economic growth would make Japan an important country again had done. (*The New York Times* had responded to his Japan thesis with the comment, "This is a silly book.") When I got permission to publish a summary of the thesis openly, in July 1974, under the title "The Rise of the Pacific Basin," much commiseration came forth: I had wrecked my reputation, said most people, because everyone knew that the oil price rise, which had occurred between submission and publication, would bankrupt all these oil-dependent countries such as Japan, South Korea, Taiwan, Hong Kong, Singapore, and Thailand.

During the 1970s, sound academic opinion held these small countries in contempt. They were authoritarian, corrupt, abusive of human rights, and therefore unstable and unreliable. I attempted every year to present the unarguable thesis of the Pacific Asian economic takeoff, and its stabilizing and liberalizing consequences, to academic conferences. But to little avail. By the 1980s, much had changed. The Pacific Asian takeoff, like the Japanese takeoff before it, had transformed itself from politically incorrect to conventional wisdom. This book argues that China is the latest phase in the Pacific Asian takeoff. Most of the arguments to the contrary mirror precisely the arguments of the mid-1970s as to why South Korea and Thailand could never succeed.

In 1976, during a partial leave of absence from the Hudson Institute in which Zbigniew Brzezinski and I founded a journal, *Global Political Assessment,* I joined Jimmy Carter's campaign as one of nineteen members of his Foreign Policy Task Force and head of the Asia Policy Group. Quickly I discovered that I would have the same problem with some of Carter's advisers that Herman Kahn had had with me. The leading newspapers spent 1976 whipping up a feverish campaign against the alliance with South Korea, which they portrayed as nothing more than a vicious dictatorship that would soon prove to be another South Vietnam. Two of Carter's younger confidantes (never Brzezinski, who wisely stood aside on this issue) from the beginning persuaded the President to catch this emotional wave by making withdrawal of U.S. troops from South Korea the defining symbol of his foreign policy, the symbol that, allegedly unlike Kissinger and Nixon, a Carter administration would give proper priority to human rights and would steer America away from another Vietnam. My work on South Korea convinced me that such an analysis of that country was wrong and the policy consequences potentially catastrophic. For me, this was a loss of political virginity, a bitter exposure to the contradiction between what worked in electing a president and what was good for the country.

For the first issue of *Global Political Assessment* (November 1976), I condensed a long paper I had written at Hudson called "The Coming Crisis of Soviet Communism." This argued that numerous domestic and international trends were forcing the Soviet Union into a period of historical decline. Brzezinski accepted most of this argument but was wary of the thesis—too radical to be politcally acceptable. Once ensconced in the White House, however, Brzezinski invited me there to present the argument to the full National Security Council staff in May 1977 when the issue appeared. He wisely sat quiet while the Soviet specialists in the White House delivered a memorable hammering to these crazy ideas.

Almost a decade later, when Gorbachev attained power, I had often in issues of *Global Political Assessment* criticized the Gorbachev strategy as disastrous for his country. For each issue, my consultant on the Soviet Union wrote a superb account of what Gorbachev was doing and why, then praised the strategy. Based on the Asian experience, I removed the praise and substituted a scholarly form of ridicule. In an adjacent section of each issue, we chronicled the extrordinary success of China's reforms.

Since, 1980, I have worked for Bankers Trust in various research and executive capacities, the last eight years in Hong Kong. While in Hong Kong, I've been deeply involved in several movements for human rights and democracy. Most notably, I played a central but quiet role in the Philippine Revolution of 1986 and a major supporting role in failed efforts to convince President Aquino to support an Asian-style economic reform. And I supplemented business trips to Bangkok with journeys to Manerplaw, the jungle headquarters of Burma's democratic guerrilla movement, to advise leaders of Democratic Alliance of Burma in their struggle against the military regime. After Tiananmen Square, and now more familiar with China, I wrote an article saying that, although this looked very bad for China, in the end Deng Xiaoping would come out a hero and Gorbachev, then at the height of his popularity, would be seen as a fool and lose his job. No major newspaper or magazine in the world would publish it, so I put it out in January 1990 as a Bankers Trust brokerage piece. In June 1990, shortly after the anniversary of Tiananmen Square, the *International Herald Tribune,* which had rejected the article five months earlier, agreed to publish it. Photocopied all over the world, that article became the most widely distributed essay I have ever written. It led to innumerable speaking engagements and through these to an approach by an American company, Chinavest, for a consultant paper on the prospects of the Chinese economy. When I showed that paper to Ezra Vogel for criticism, he responded with a formal request for permission to make it part of the Harvard core curriculum in East Asian studies; that and his direct encouragement for further research provided a vital boost to the project. Another response to some of my speeches was an offer by business friends, mostly associated with the Young Presidents Organization, to support the research by subsidizing a partial leave of absence from Bankers Trust.

I do not expect the views presented here to gain early or wide assent. Events may well help the critics because it would not be a surprise if the book's publication coincides with unpleasant reactions to China's latest cycle of inflation—and possibly as well with the succession to Deng Xiaoping, which will of course be followed by a power struggle. I shall remain unrepentant because the other Asian takeoffs have overcome such episodes. I hope that some readers will weigh the unpopular ideas expressed here with some of the same open mind that I had when Herman Kahn told me he was going to rub my nose in the reality of South Korea.

Page references in italics represent charts or maps.